Introduction to FOOD AND BEVERAGE SERVICE

GRAHAM BROWN
KARON HEPNER
ALAN DEEGAN

PEARSON
Longman

Harlow, England • London • New York • Boston • San Francisco • Toronto
Sydney • Tokyo • Singapore • Hong Kong • Seoul • Taipei • New Delhi
Cape Town • Madrid • Mexico City • Amsterdam • Munich • Paris • Milan

Pearson Education Limited
Edinburgh Gate
Harlow
Essex CM20 2JE
England

and Associated Companies throughout the world

Visit us on the World Wide Web at:
www.pearsoned.co.uk

First published in Australia by Hospitality Press under the title of The Waiter's Handbook
Published in 1994 by Blackwell Scientific Publications

ISBN 978-0582-35775-4

British Library Cataloguing-in-Publication Data
A catalogue record for this book is
available from the British Library.

Library of Congress Cataloging-in-Publication Data
A catalog entry for this title is
available from the Library of Congress.

19
12

Printed in the UK by Ashford Colour Press Ltd, Gosport, Hampshire

Introduction to Food and Beverage Service

Contents

Introduction

Introduction to Food and Beverage Service has been designed as a basic training aid for waiters involved in the service of food and beverage.

Regardless of the styles of the establishments where waiters are employed, the skills of the industry do not differ in their basic application, but only in their interpretation. Good professional service is as important in the café as in the fine dining-room.

The term 'waiter' indicates a professional waiting person regardless of their sex or place of employment. The term 'professional' relates to a waiter who demonstrates both a positive hospitable attitude and the application of technical ability.

The book contains all the knowledge you need for NVQ/SVQ levels 1 and 2 in Food and Beverage Service, including both the practical skills and the underpinning knowledge. It gives you a broad introduction to industry and how the waiter fits into it, making clear the key objectives of professional food and beverage service and the essential techniques involved in their application. With the test-yourself questions at the end of each chapter, and the extensive glossary at the end of the book, it also makes an ideal revision and reference tool.

At the foundation of good service is a knowledge and appreciation of the rules and laws governing hygiene and health and safety. After the introduction to the industry, this is where the book starts. The main text introduces the reader to all the equipment a waiter is likely to use and its application. There is also a chapter on beverage product knowledge. Food product knowledge, menu terminology and industry jargon are all covered in the extensive glossary. The glossary covers the terms and items most commonly found in today's menus which draw on so many different culinary traditions, as well as explaining the long-established terms of classical French cuisine.

Techniques used throughout the book are described for a right-handed waiter. A left-handed waiter should reverse the techniques, except that all beverages are placed to the guest's right and both left- and right-handed waiters work anti-clockwise around the table.

The book recommends that both food and beverage service should take place anti-clockwise round the table, starting with the guest on the right of the host, and finishing with the host. For various reasons some establishments choose to serve in the opposite (clockwise) direction. This fails to allow for the custom of placing the principal guest immediately to the host's right. However, in this and in many other points of detail, there is room for differences of practice; the important thing is that there should be consistency within each operation.

Whatever the style of establishment and whatever the style of service, the waiter's job is to give customers satisfaction when they go out to eat or drink. This book shows you how to do your job professionally!

ACKNOWLEDGEMENTS

Cartoons by Dee Büman.
Figs 2.1 and 2.2 are reproduced with the kind permission of Chris Hudson, Ettington Park Hotel.

1 . Hospitality and The Waiter

Why should waiters who work in cafés or who serve counter meals in pubs feel any less professional in their role than waiters who offer silver service?

Guests have a right to professional service no matter how much they are spending.

1.1 Waiting staff are employed in a huge variety of establishments in the hospitality industry, but, no matter what type of restaurant or other venue they work in, the waiter's basic role does not differ.

The number of food and beverage service staff, and their positions in an establishment's hierarchy, depend on the size of the operation and the services it offers, but the function of the waiting staff, large or small, remains the same. So does the need for the waiters to be professional in what they do.

In any establishment, large or small, formal or informal, the industry demands that the waiting staff should have a professional attitude to their jobs.

When you have read this chapter you will have a basic understanding of:

- Different types of food and beverage operations
- The role of the waiter
- The classification of food and beverage service employees
- The organization of food and beverage service staff
- The need for high standards of personal presentation and hygiene
- The need to keep the working environment hygienic and safe.

1.2 DIFFERENT TYPES OF FOOD AND BEVERAGE OUTLETS

The hospitality industry offers employment to people of differing personalities, backgrounds and skills through a wide diversity of the types of outlets serving food and beverages.

Hospitality may be defined as meeting the needs of guests in a variety of establishments including all the following at which food and beverage service staff might be employed:

- *Cafés* offer teas, coffees, soft drinks, snacks and often light meals usually from breakfast to early suppers. They require fast service to ensure a fast turnover of customers.
- *Cafeterias* are often attached to institutions such as museums or educational establishments or maybe recreational facilities such as swimming baths. They offer light refreshments, teas,

coffees and soft drinks, and snacks. Some department stores have more elaborate cafetérias serving full meals.

- *Food halls/food courts* are becoming popular, especially in shopping centres. Food outlets serving a wide variety of different types of fast food surround a common central dining area. The guests buy their choice of food at the relevant counter, and service staff are responsible for clearing the eating areas.

- *Public houses* are one of the fastest growing types of food outlet. The meals available range from simple bar snacks bought over the counter to informal restaurant-style service of three-course meals.

- *Casual dining restaurants (bistros).* Here appearance and atmosphere provide an environment for casual dining but table service is offered. Service staff must be capable of friendly informality in their dealings with guests while remaining professionally efficient.

- *Ethnic restaurants.* In these popular establishments the style of the service may be as much a part of the cultural experience offered to guests as the food itself.

- *Functions (receptions/banquets/conventions).* The number of guests and the style of function can vary enormously so functions demand extreme flexibility from both management and service staff.

- *Fine dining restaurants* usually have a suitably comfortable or impressive ambience for the fine cuisine on offer. Service staff are expected not only to be discreetly professional in what they do but also to be highly skilled, and knowledgeable.

1.3 THE ROLE OF THE WAITER

The term waiter includes food and beverage service personnel of either sex.

It is the role of the professional waiter to ensure that guests enjoy a satisfactory total dining experience; the job involves much more than simply serving food or beverages.

To fulfil this role adequately a waiter needs a range of qualities and attributes, including a pleasant personality, honesty, efficiency and punctuality. Also a waiter must always be fastidious about self-presentation and personal hygiene.

A professional waiter will also have a good knowledge of the products being served, what they consist of and how they are presented. Good waiters will also understand the organization of the establishment in which they are working, and how other members of the team contribute to the dining experience of the guests.

1.4 *Duties of the waiter*

The work of the waiter includes:

- Preparation and maintenance of the work area

- Maintaining good customer and staff relations
- Making recommendations and assisting guests in making selections
- Order taking and recording
- Service and clearing of food and beverages.

1.5 CAREERS IN FOOD AND BEVERAGE SERVICE

Figure 1.1 shows all the different levels of jobs through which waiters can progress during their careers. While you are studying for your basic qualifications you are most likely to be an apprentice or an assistant waiter, but from there you can gradually work your way up to managing your own restaurant or bar,

Classification	Definition of duties	Typical job title
Apprentice	Clears side board, fetches and carries.	Commis debarrasseur Bus boy (US)
Assistant Waiter	May be involved in some service: serving vegetables, etc.; placing plates; serving from trolley hors d'oeuvres or sweets.	Commis de rang
Junior Station Waiter	Similar to the Station Waiter but with a smaller station.	Demi chef de rang
Station Waiter	In charge of a number of tables. Taking orders and serving in the correct sequence.	Chef de rang
Station Head Waiter	Responsible for a part of the restaurant containing a certain number of tables. Duties similar to those of the Head Waiter.	Maître d'hôtel de carré
Head Waiter	In direct charge of restaurant and service. May take orders and pass them to the Station Waiter.	Maître d'hôtel
Restaurant Manager	Responsible for restaurant personnel and service.	Directeur du restaurant
Floor Waiter	Responsible for complete service to rooms or suites; all meals and beverages.	Chef d'étage
Lounge Waiter	Responsible for service of food and beverages in the lounge.	Chef de salle
Wine Butler Wine Waiter }	Responsible for the service of all drinks during the meal.	Sommelier

Fig. 1.1 Traditional job classifications in restaurants.

perhaps, or running a large hotel. Your career depends on the extent of your ability, commitment and ambition, but however far you want to go, you must start with the right training.

1.6 NATIONAL VOCATIONAL QUALIFICATIONS (NVQs)

In 1986 the Government set up the National Council for Vocational Qualifications (NCVQ) to review vocational qualifications in all industries and simplify them. As a result of this National Vocational Qualifications (NVQs) have been set up which are recognized by employers throughout the UK. In Scotland the same standards are used but the qualifications are called Scottish Vocational Qualifications (SVQs).

There are four levels of NVQs and SVQs. The first two levels are for people working as operatives. Level 1 covers simple tasks. Tasks in level 2 are more complex and involve more responsibility. Level 3 is for supervisors and level 4 is for managers.

NVQs and SVQs are divided into individual units, each covering a task or skill that people need at work. You can do only the units you need in order to do your job well or you can work towards a range of units that make up the full NVQ. In the hotel, catering and hospitality industries you have to achieve the units on health and safety and on hygiene plus a range of optional additional units in order to obtain a full NVQ. If you do not complete the full NVQ, you can still use the record of those units you have completed as evidence for an employer of the skills you possess.

NVQs are assessed unit by unit in your place of work or a realistic work environment. You need to demonstrate that you can perform the task well and that you have the underpinning knowledge necessary to show you understand the task and the reasons for it.

There are many colleges running courses leading to NVQs. You can find out about them by contacting your local Careers Office or the Hotel and Catering Training Company, International House, High Street, Ealing, London W5 5DB, Tel: 081 579 2400.

1.7 THE ORGANIZATION OF FOOD AND BEVERAGE SERVICE STAFF

Whilst most jobs advertized will refer to the classifications given in Fig. 1.1, the details of the duties of individual jobs will vary widely from establishment to establishment, according to its size, the nature of its business and the traditions of the organization. Figure 1.2 shows a typical restaurant brigade (staff structure). Positions commonly found include:

■ Food and Beverage Manager
    In larger operations a Food and Beverage Manager is usually

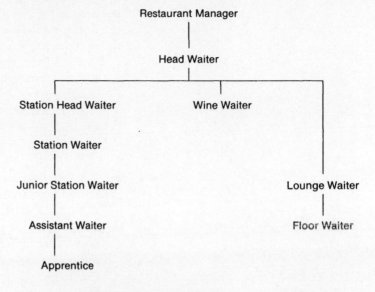

Fig. 1.2 Typical staff structure in a large restaurant.

responsible for the success of the food and beverage operations from a business point of view. He or she will be responsible for such matters as compiling the menus (in consultation with the kitchen staff) to make sure that the required profit margins are achieved, purchasing food and beverage items and deciding portion sizes, and staff recruitment and training.

■ Restaurant Manager

In operations where there are several bars and restaurants, such as large hotels, each restaurant may have its own manager responsible to the Food and Beverage Manager. He or she will be responsible for the work of the staff within that restaurant and for seeing that the policies of the Food and Beverage Manager are carried out. Either the Restaurant Manager or the Head Waiter will be responsible for staff duty rosters.

■ Head Waiter

The Head Waiter is responsible for all the service staff in the restaurant and for seeing that all the preparation, service and clearing work is efficiently carried out. In smaller establishments he or she may also be responsible for taking reservations and for greeting and seating guests. In larger establishments there may be a special Reception Head Waiter with these duties.

■ Station Head Waiter

The Station Head Waiter is responsible for the service of a **station** or group of tables. He or she takes the orders and carries out the service at the tables of the station, assisted in larger establishments by less experienced and knowledgeable staff. Each station may have its own workstation or sideboard. (This sideboard is also called the waiter's 'station'.)

- Waiter

  If the stations are looked after by a service team, less experienced waiters are responsible to the Station Head Waiter. They perform duties such as plate service of dishes and the services of sauces, sometimes assisted in the simplest tasks by a trainee.

  A trainee waiter is sometimes called a **commis** (pronounced *commee*) waiter, who should not be confused with a commis cook, that is a cook in training, working under the chef.

- Wine Waiter

  The wine waiter is a specialist, responsible for the service of all alcoholic drinks to the tables. He or she must, of course, have a thorough knowledge of the wines on the establishment's wine list, and be able to recommend wines suitable to accompany the various menu items. And, of course, know how to serve them correctly.

  A **sommelier** (pronounced *som-may-lee-ay*) is another word for a specialist wine waiter.

1.8   PRESENTATION AND HYGIENE

One all-important aspect of the professionalism of waiting staff is the attention they give to personal hygiene and presentation. A waiter when at work, in or out of uniform, must invariably be absolutely clean and tidy in all respects. This is the first and most obvious sign that waiters are professional in their approach to their work.

The first (visual) impression of waiting staff received by guests comes from the waiters' appearance. First impressions are extremely important for the commercial success of an establishment.

Good grooming and meticulous attention to personal hygiene not only express a positive attitude to guests but also build self-confidence in the individual waiter.

High standards of personal hygiene are also essential for all workers involved in the service of food and beverages for health reasons.

High standards of hygiene in the waiting staff are also essential if guests are to enjoy their dining experience. Their enjoyment will be considerably lessened if their food or drinks are served by a waiter with bad breath or dirty finger nails.

Waiters must select their footwear with care and pay attention to good posture when standing and moving. It is almost impossible for a waiter with sore feet or an aching back to maintain a pleasant and helpful attitude to the guests.

Waiters' hairstyles should be suitable to the establishment in which they are working. In general they should be in tune with current fashions, but hair must be tidy and should be swept away from the face. This projects an air of self-confidence and is also more hygienic.

Unobtrusive jewellery, make-up and perfume may all be used, but with discretion. They must not be over-done.

Whether the waiter's uniform is provided by the establishment or not, it is the waiter's responsibility to make sure that the uniform is kept clean and well-presented at all times.

When uniforms are being selected it is important that their size and design make adequate allowance for the extensive body movement a waiter's work demands. Natural fibres are preferable to man-made ones because they allow the body to breathe and they are safer in case of burns.

1.9 *Hygiene checklist*

In law, hygiene is your personal responsibility. You could be prosecuted if a customer suffers through your failure to maintain good standards of hygiene.

- Keep your uniform clean and well-pressed.
- Wear comfortable shoes and keep them clean.
- Never let any hair fall into food. Wear a style that is easy to keep tidy and keep your hair off your face.
- Have a bath or shower every day and wear a deodorant to eliminate body odour.
- Jewellery and perfume should only be worn in accordance with establishment rules.
- Wash your hands thoroughly every time you go to the toilet.
- Do not smoke anywhere near food. If you do smoke, wash your hands afterwards.
- Keep your hands away from your face, especially your mouth and nose.
- Any cuts or burns should be covered to avoid the risk of contaminating food.
- Any illness or infection should be reported to your supervisor.
- All food service personnel must have the essential food hygiene certificate (as required by The Food Act 1990).

1.10 FIRE SAFETY

One of the first things to learn when you start a new job is the establishment's safety code for the staff and guests. You should always follow the rules of your establishment, but there are a few universal rules that must be followed everywhere:

- Raise the alarm immediately you discover a fire and warn people around you to move away.
- Don't panic. The premises should be evacuated in a quiet and orderly manner.
- Never put yourself or others in danger by staying near a fire you cannot control.
- Any fire-fighting equipment should only be used in accordance with establishment rules.

- Any safety and emergency procedures should be followed.
- Never return to the scene of a fire until given the all clear.
- You should assemble at the stated fire point.

1.11 ACCIDENTS (STAFF OR GUESTS)

Remember that you will be held responsible in law for any accident that occurs because of your negligence. Health and safety legislation has been laid down to prevent and deal with accidents.

The Health and Safety at Work Act 1974 is concerned with protecting the health and safety of employees and the public. It is a legal obligation to ensure as far as reasonably practicable, the safety and health and welfare of employees. Supervision and training must be given to all staff. It is the responsibility of the employee to ensure that their acts or omissions do not affect others adversely.

In the event of an accident:

- A First Aider should be notified immediately. Comfort and reassure the injured person.
- Any emergency services should be contacted, following establishment procedures.
- Any accident must be recorded in accordance with the establishment's method of documentation.

1.12 *The legal obligation to maintain a safe working environment*

Any hazards or potential hazards which threaten the safety of staff or client should be identified and preventive action taken, following establishment procedures which should have already been drawn up in accordance with health and safety regulations. These hazards or potential hazards should be reported as soon as possible to lessen the risk of staff and clients.

Quick preventive action could prevent injury to staff or clientele and damage to equipment and buildings.

By doing this you are complying with the law.

1.13 SECURITY

It is the duty of all staff to help maintain security in the following areas:

- Work areas
- Staff facilities
- Client facilities
- Public areas
- Store rooms
- Cellars
- Refrigerators
- Freezers.

Keys, property and the above areas should be secured against unauthorized access at any time. This will help guard against damage and pilferage.

Any property which goes missing, whether it belongs to staff or to customers, should be reported to a supervisor at once and any appropriate action taken.

Any suspicious persons should be challenged politely or reported to security.

Any lost property should be documented and kept secure until claimed.

1.14 *Suspicious items or packages*

A suspicious item or package may be any bag, package or parcel which has been left unattended without any apparent reason. In current circumstances it is essential that any such item is reported immediately to a supervisor in case it is a bomb. Do not investigate the package yourself in case you set it off.

Safety and security rules must be followed in a calm and orderly manner. Act reasonably and don't panic! *Establishments have their own safety and security procedures; all staff must be aware of them and follow them explicitly.*

1.15 QUESTIONS

(1) Name eight different sorts of establishments where food and beverage service are required?

(2) Describe four attributes of a professional waiter.

(3) What are five important duties carried out by a waiter?

(4) What are NVQs?

(5) Who is a commis waiter?

(6) Who is responsible for personal hygiene?

(7) There are eleven points on the hygiene checklist. What are they?

(8) Name two things you should never do at the scene of a fire.

(9) How can you help to keep the work environment safe?

(10) What should you do if you see an unattended package?

2 . The Menu

Why bother to provide a menu if the descriptions of the menu items are not true to the items served?

2.1 The words 'the menu' have at least three meanings for the waiter. The menu means:
- the range of food items served in an establishment, including their organization into a number of courses
- the arrangement by which the items are offered (the type of menu, as in 'set menu', 'à la carte menu', etc.), and
- the physical object on which the list of these items (and courses) is written for guests to choose from.

This chapter is concerned with the menu in the first two of these senses. The handling of the menu as a physical object and its presentation to guests is dealt with in a later chapter (see 6.2–6.4).

When you have completed this chapter you will have a basic understanding of:
- The framework of the modern menu
- The sequence of the courses
- Food items which are not part of the framework of courses
- The different types or classes of menu.

2.2 THE STRUCTURE OF THE MENU

There is necessarily a menu of some kind or other for any meal, however simple. For example, cornflakes followed by toast and marmalade is a popular breakfast menu. However the menu this chapter is concerned with is the menu for a main meal of the day, luncheon or dinner.

The classical French menu or 'classic menu' (see Glossary) had more than twelve courses. It offered the diner a wide variety of items served in a well-understood traditional sequence. Modern menus have fewer courses but they may cause confusion as to the appropriate sequence of service.

Menus are laid out so that the different courses appear in the order in which they would normally be served. They are usually presented in a framework of five courses, as follows:
- Appetizers
- Potages (soups)
- Entrées

- Main courses
- Desserts.

Appetizers are such items as hors d'oeuvres, p̂âtés, or oysters, which are designed to stimulate rather than to satisfy the appetite.

Potages may be thick (*crème dubarry*) or thin (*consommé*). The less common French word *soupe* (with an *e*), often used as *soupe du jour* (soup of the day), can mean either a thick or thin soup. Soups are usually hot, but some soups are served chilled, for example, vichyssoise or gazpacho.

In the classical French menu the *entrée* was a course served after the fish and before the main meat course with a sorbet served after it to refresh the palate. The entrée will come between the fish and the grills on an à la carte menu and between the fish and the relevé on a classic banquet menu. In the modern menu the term is used to cover such items as small helpings of pasta dishes, seafood crêpes, elaborate salads, miniature sausages, or fish (if not chosen as the main course). The entrée is a course which certainly does more than stimulate the appetite but which is not so substantial as to make the main course unwelcome.

Many British establishments list all the first three of these courses under the general heading of 'starters', or sometimes 'hors d'oeuvre'.

The term 'entrée' can cause even more confusion because it is often, especially in the USA, used to mean the main course itself although the word literally means 'entrance', or 'way in', i.e. a starter.

There is, fortunately, no possible confusion about what the main course is. It is the most substantial course of the meal. Guests usually choose the main course first and then select other courses to suit it. Similarly, when chefs design menus, they usually start with the principal or main course and then plan the other courses to complement it.

Dessert is another term which can cause confusion. In the modern menu it is used to mean the sweet course at the end of a meal, although the term is occasionally reserved for fruit and nuts, etc., served after the sweet dish or pudding has been cleared.

2.3 *Sequence of courses*

In most formal circumstances the courses are served in the order assumed in the standard modern menu, but this structure may not readily apply to the menus actually offered in many less formal or non-traditional establishments. When this is so it is the responsibility of the waiter to determine in what order the guests wish their courses to be served.

2.4 ITEMS OUTSIDE THE MENU STRUCTURE

Not all the food items served with a meal are included in the formal structure of the menu.

2.5 *Pre-dinner food items*

Items served before the first course may include:

- Canapés
- Crudités
- Hors d'oeuvre chauds or entrées volantes.

2.6 *Sauces and accompaniments*

Now that our eating habits draw on so many different cultural traditions, the range of different sauces and accompaniments available is huge. It is appropriate for some of these items to be placed on the table for the guests to help themselves; others should be offered to the diners by the waiter (see 8.6).

It is the waiters' responsibility to make sure that their stations' mise-en-place includes the necessary sauce and accompaniment items, such as different kinds of mustard, coarse-ground black pepper, chutneys, ketchups, etc. appropriate to the menu of the establishment. (For a table of accompaniments (and covers) see 6.15.)

2.7 *Cheese*

Cheese may be ordered prior to dessert (as is the usual custom in France, for example), in place of dessert, or after dessert, depending on the guest's preference.

The correct procedure for serving cheese and the appropriate accompaniments depends on the types of cheese being served. Fashions change in what accompaniments are considered 'appropriate', and different establishments have different practices. There is no one correct procedure applying to all establishments.

2.8 *Accompaniments to coffee*

Like pre-dinner food items, accompaniments to coffee are not included in the menu framework, but are an addition to it.

The range of items that may be offered with coffee is limited only by one's imagination. The service of after-dinner mints is standard practice, but many establishments now treat their coffee accompaniments as their personal signature. These items may be petits fours, personalized chocolates, biscuits or glacé fruits, for example.

2.9 TYPES OF MENU

The different types of classes of menu are distinguished by the variations in the selections offered and by their pricing structure.

2.10 *A la carte menu*

An à la carte menu is a menu which offers choices in each course and in which each item is individually priced and charged for. Menu items when selected by the guests are cooked to order. The literal meaning of the French words *à la carte* is 'from the card'. Examples of à la carte menus are shown in Fig. 2.1.

A la Carte

*Sliced warm Breast of Duck marinated in Honey,
Ginger and Bacon with Pistachio Nuts on a Winter Salad
£10.50*

*Grilled breadcrumbed Scallops set on buttered Leeks and
ribboned by an Orange and Saffron Sauce
£12.75*

*Puff pastry parcel of Wild Mushrooms, nesting on
Root Vegetables, cordoned with a Pink Peppercorn Sauce
£6.95*

*Chicken filled with a Herb Creamed Cheese, roasted
and sliced, with a Lentil Sauce
£8.75*

★ ★ ★

*Noisettes of Lamb, set on individual fondant potatoes,
garnished with a Filo Pastry tartlet of pureed Spinach,
served with a Red Wine Truffle Sauce
£18.75*

*Pan fried Calves Liver with Foie Gras, served on nests of
Red Cabbage and Celeriac surrounded by cloves of roast Garlic
in a rich Madeira Sauce
£19.75*

*Steamed fillet of Sea Bass topped with a Salmon Mousse
wrapped in Lettuce leaves and ribboned with a Butter Sauce of
Chives and Shallots
£19.50*

*Rosette of Scotch Beef Fillet accompanied by braised Fennel,
a Tomato filled with Morrel Mushrooms and a
Dijon Mustard Sauce
£21.00*

★ ★ ★

*Layers of Dark Chocolate sandwiched with Milk and White
Chocolate Mousses
£6.75*

*A duo of Pancakes, filled with Passion Fruit Souffle,
complimented by a Raspberry Coulis
£7.50*

*Apple and Almond Flan served with a Brandy and Prune Icecream
on a Vanilla Sauce
£6.50*

*Deep fried Seasonal Fruits served in a Tuille cage
served on an Apricot Coulis
£7.25*

★ ★ ★

*Freshly Brewed Coffee and Handmade Sweetmeats
£2.75*

Fig. 2.1 A la carte.

Table d'Hote Dinner

Thinly sliced Oak Smoked Scottish Salmon served with Crabmeat bound in a Marie Rose Sauce

Leek, Potato and Onion Soup served with a Cheese Croute

Deep Fried Poached Egg, laid on a tossed Winter Leaf salad in a Walnut Oil dressing, surrounded by Seasonal Vegetables

Warm Breast of Pigeon with a slice of Black Pudding served in a Wild Mushroom and Shallot Sauce

★ ★ ★

Scotch Sirloin Steak served with Traditional Garnish

Pan fried Breast of Chicken with strips of Root Vegetables and draped with a Sauce of Tomato and Tarragon

Noisettes of Pork fillet set on a bed of Peppers and cordoned with a Kummel Sauce

Poached Escalope of Salmon complimented by a light Horseradish and Mint Cream

Fresh Market Vegetables and Potato

★ ★ ★

Seasonal Fruits and Berries coated and glazed with a Champagne Sabayon

French Lemon Tart complimented by a Strawberry Coulis

Chocolate Shortbread biscuits filled with a Drambuie Cream accompanied by an Orange Compote

A selection of English and French Farmhouse Cheeses with homemade Banana Bread

★ ★ ★

Freshly Brewed Coffee and Handmade Sweetmeats

£28.00

Fig. 2.2 Table d'hôte.

The term à la carte when applied to a restaurant is often misinterpreted. The term does not relate to a particular type of establishment nor to its pricing or to the services it offers; the term refers solely to the type of menu, and to the fact that the food is cooked to order.

2.11 Table d'hôte

A table d'hôte menu is a menu which offers some (usually limited) choice and is charged at a fixed price per person for the whole menu. *Table d'hôte* is, literally, French for 'the proprietor's (mine host's) table'. Examples of table d'hôte menus are shown in Fig. 2.2.

A modestly-priced 'business lunch', in which three or four items only are offered in each course and the guest pays a fixed price for the whole meal, would be a typical use of the table d'hôte menu.

More exclusive restaurants also often make use of the table d'hôte menu as its limited number of menu items allows the chef to select fresh ingredients of the best quality and to treat each dish with maximum attention. Because a more limited range of choice has to be catered for than in a typical à la carte menu there is less wastage.

Table d'hôte menus are also popular for festive occasions, for example Christmas Day or Mother's Day.

2.12 Fixed price menu (prix fixe)

A fixed price menu is one which offers set items (one for each course) pre-arranged by the host. Set menus are used predominantly for functions, for example, weddings and banquets.

2.13 Carte du jour

Carte du jour literally means 'card of the day'. It offers choices available for a particular day only. It allows the chef to offer a list of 'specials' or variations in addition to a pre-printed à la carte menu, or it can be used as a table d'hôte menu prepared for use on the one day only.

2.14 Cycle menu

A cycle menu is a group of menus which are rotated on a set cycle. Cycle menus are usually used in the institutional sector of the industry, for example in hospitals, prisons, on airlines and in employee food-service operations (works canteens, etc.).

The cycle menu is used to avoid boredom for both customers and staff, and also to ensure that the diet of the people eating in the institution is sufficiently varied to be healthy. In a hospital, for example, the cycle might be set to fit the average length of stay of the patients.

Menus should not be designed to a seven-day cycle as this results in the same items always being served on the same day of the week, producing a boring predictability.

2.15 QUESTIONS

(1) What are the five courses most commonly found on a modern menu?

(2) Why are hors d'oeuvre always small items?

(3) What is the French name for a thin soup?

(4) Which course on a menu do guests usually choose first?

(5) What items are provided outside the structure of the menu?

(6) Describe an à la carte menu.

(7) What is a typical use of a table d'hôte menu?

(8) What sort of menu is most commonly used for large functions?

(9) What does *carte du jour* mean in English?

(10) What are the advantages of using a cycle menu in an institution?

3 . Food Service Equipment

Why should a guest be embarrassed by having to use inappropriate equipment for a particular dish?

3.1 There is a huge variety of cutlery and tableware in use in hospitality establishments today. Not only does the basic cutlery come in a variety of styles, but the range of specialist equipment is almost endless. This chapter does not attempt the almost impossible task of describing every piece of equipment a waiter may encounter; what it does is to introduce all the equipment commonly found in modern establishments. Remember though that there is a great variety of possible styles so that the illustrations are only representative of examples of particular pieces of equipment; other styles may be equally common and valid.

When you have read this chapter you should be familiar with:
- The appearance and use of the various types of cutlery used for the eating and service of food
- The various types of crockery and tableware used for the eating and service of food
- The various pieces of equipment required for the preparation of food in the dining-room.

Glassware and beverage-service equipment are dealt with later, in chapter 13 (see 13.2, 13.3, 13.4, and 13.7).

3.2 CUTLERY

Basic cutlery (silverware)

Large fork (table fork)
Used as
- Main fork or joint fork
- Serving fork (see 8.2)

Large knife (table knife)
Used as
- Main knife or joint knife

Small fork (dessert fork)
Used as
- Entrée fork
- Pasta fork
- Salad fork
- Dessert (or pudding) fork
- Fruit fork

Small knife
Used as
- Side knife (for buttering bread or spreading pâté)
- Entrée knife
- Cheese knife
- Fruit knife

Steak knife
(Note the serrated edge)

Fish knife
Used for
- Fish
- Serving delicate or large items (see 8.3 and 8.7)

Fish fork (webbed fork)
Used for
- Fish

Service spoon (tablespoon)
Used for serving (see 8.2)

Pudding/dessert spoon
Used for
- Desserts (see 4.13 and 6.13)
- Pasta

Soup spoon

Teaspoon
Used for
- Tea
- Cocktails (e.g. prawn or fruit cocktails)
- Ice creams
- Dessert coupes
- Sugar spoon

Coffee spoon

3.3 *Other cutlery items sometimes placed on the table*

Parfait or sundae spoon
Used for
- Desserts
- Ice cream

Grapefruit spoon

Pastry fork

Oyster fork

Snail (escargot) **fork**

Snail (escargot) **tongs**

Lobster picks

Lobster cracker

Butter knife
Used for serving butter

Cheese knife
Used for serving cheese

Tea-strainer

Sugar tongs

3.4 *Cutlery items used for serving*

Carving knife

Bread knife

Gâteau (cake) slice

Soup ladle

Nutcracker

Grape scissors

3.5 **TABLEWARE**

Common items of tableware (also called crockery or china) include:

Cover plate
Used as a presentation or showplate in the setting. Can be a simple large plate also used as a service plate or an underplate for service.

Large plate (dinner plate)
Used for the main course. Oval plates are sometimes used instead of round ones.

Fish plate
Used for fish, and sweets and desserts.

Small (side) **plate**
Used for bread and bread rolls, also cake.

Soup bowl
Used for cream soups, also as an oatmeal (porridge) bowl, for breakfast cereals, and as a pasta bowl.

Consommé tasse (consommé cup and saucer)
Used for clear soups. Note that the consommé bowl is always served on a matching saucer.

Large soup tureen (with lid)
Often used for service from a guéridon rather than on the table (see 10.4).

Coupe
A stemmed vessel, made of glass, silver, or stainless steel. Used for cocktails (seafood or fruit), desserts, ice cream.

Ravière
Oval or rectangular dish, used primarily for pasta or for presenting hors d'oeuvres.

Ramekin
Comes in various sizes. Used for baked eggs, custards and soufflés.

Tea or **coffee cup** and **saucer**
Sizes vary considerably. Some establishments use a smaller size for coffee than for tea.

Demitasse and **saucer/small coffee cup** and **saucer**.
Used for coffee. (*Demi-tasse* is French for 'half-cup'.)

Coffee pots
Various styles including:

Long spout

Vacuum infusion pot or Cona pot
(Cona is a trade name)

Plunger cafetière

Tea pot

Hot water pot

Sugar bowl

Milk or **cream jug**

Salad bowl (individual)

Salad bowl (for table service)

Saladier or salad plate
Crescent-shaped, used for salads or sometimes vegetables

Snail (escargot) **plate**

Sauce-boat (saucière)

Serving flats, platters
Varying sizes

Salt and pepper set
Often called the cruet, a term which can include a mustard pot also. The salt pot has a single hole so that salt can be poured neatly at the side of the plate. The pepper pot has three or more holes so that the pepper can be shaken evenly over the dish.

Pepper-mill (grinder) and **salt mill**

Sugar shaker (caster) (also called a dredger or sifter)

Plate cover (cloche)
There are two styles:

Flat plate cover

Dome

Butter dishes

Bud vase

3.6 LARGE EQUIPMENT

Warming racks (guéridon service)

Guéridon trolley

Flambé trolley

Carving trolley (dome) (see 12.17)

Chafing dish/Flambé pan (see 12.13)

Réchaud (cooking lamp or warmer) (see 12.12)

1. Gas cylinder burner

2. Spirit lamp

3.7 **QUESTIONS**

(1) What are the uses of a small fork?
(2) What sort of edge does a steak knife have?
(3) What can a teaspoon be used for apart from stirring tea?
(4) What do snail tongs and fork look like?
(5) What is a cover plate used for?
(6) What is a fish plate used for apart from serving fish?
(7) What is a ravière?
(8) Describe two sorts of coffee pots.
(9) What two sorts of plate cover are there?
(10) What is a réchaud?

4 . Food Service Preparation

Who suffers when guests call you over and complain that their glass is chipped, or that there is lipstick on the edge of the glass, or that there is no salt in the shaker?

Guests are inconvenienced and their dining experience may be spoiled, but it's the waiter who suffers!

4.1 A guest's first impression can make or break the total dining experience. Careful and thorough preparation of the dining area before guests arrive is therefore essential. While standards are set by management, it is the responsibility of all employees to maintain those standards by demonstrating individual professionalism in their work.

On completion of this chapter you should have a basic understanding of the following:

- Taking reservations
- The use of floor plans
- The need for an appropriate atmosphere
- Clothing tables
- Preparation of service stations
- The laying of covers
- A variety of napkin folds.

4.2 TAKING RESERVATIONS

Before you take a booking make sure you know the answers to the types of questions you are likely to be asked, for example:

- What kind of cuisine do you offer? (French, Italian, Cantonese, etc.)
- What style of menu do you offer? (A la carte or table d'hôte?)
- Do you accept cheques? Or credit cards? Which cards?
- Are you licensed?
- When are you open? For both lunch and dinner?
- Are children welcome?
- Can you cater for disabled people in wheelchairs?
- Are you air conditioned?
- Is there a no-smoking area?
- Do you have car-parking facilities?
- Do you cater for functions?
- How do I find your establishment?

Most reservations are taken over the telephone. A friendly and helpful telephone manner is essential however busy you are because potential customers are easily put off at this early stage and they may never call again:

- Always answer the telephone promptly when it rings.
- Have a pen and paper or the reservations book to hand.
- State clearly the name of the establishment.
- Offer the caller your assistance (e.g. 'Good morning, may I help you?').
- Answer any questions clearly and politely. If you do not know the answer, find someone who does or offer to call back.

Before beginning to take the booking make sure you have the reservations book in view. The first things to be clarified are *when* the table is required and *how many* people there are in the party. Only when you have established that a suitable table is available when one is wanted, continue taking the reservation, asking for the following additional details:

- The host's name. (Have it spelt out if you are not sure.)
- The time of arrival.
- A contact telephone number.
- Any special requirements (such as a table in a quiet corner).

Confirm all the details by repeating the name, the date, the time of arrival, the number in the party and the contact phone number. Make sure all the details have been clearly written into the reservations book.

Complete the conversation with a show of hospitality – 'Thank you Mr Bryans. We look forward to seeing you on Thursday evening'.

4.3 FLOOR PLANS

The floor plans for a restaurant or a function are dictated by the number of covers and the style of the service to be offered. When these have been established a floor plan is prepared by the dining-room supervisor as a guide for the set-up of the dining area and to assist in the seating of guests.

Key points to consider when preparing a floor plan are:

- To position the tables so as to allow for sufficient movement by guests and service staff.
- To consider the placement of covers to avoid guests complaining of inappropriate placement, for example near doorways, kitchens, toilets, behind pillars or in draughty areas.
- To accommodate guests' specific needs, for example, a business meeting, handicapped guests, honeymoon couples, family groups, etc.

4.4 SETTING THE MOOD

The total dining experience is much affected by the atmosphere created by management for the guests. The mood of the dining environment should reflect the time of day, the location, and an atmosphere that is consistent with the desired character of the establishment.

Key points to be considered by management or staff in setting the dining atmosphere are:

- *Lighting:* daylight or bright lighting is preferred for daytime meal services.

   Subdued light is more appropriate for evening dining.

   Candlelight can enhance the mood for evening dining but should not be usually used for daytime events.
- *Views:* tables should be set to take best advantage of the views from the dining-room (subject to the limitations of space).
- *Music:* background music can be appropriate to set the mood. (In dining-rooms where music is played special consideration must be given to the placement of tables.)
- *Decor:* the decor should be consistent to create a harmonious atmosphere.

   Colour selection plays an important part in the dining experience. Some colours are warm, others cold; some are romantic, others business-like, and so on.

   While individual waiters may have no control over the colour and general decor of the dining-room, they are often responsible for the details. Live plants and fresh flowers, for example, make a major contribution to the overall presentation and to the mood a room encourages. They must be carefully placed, well-presented and well-maintained.

Fig. 4.1 Clothing a table before service.

4.5 HOW TO CLOTH A TABLE

There are many different sizes and styles of table and tablecloths used in the industry, and there are different ways of folding tablecloths adopted by different laundries. There can therefore be no one correct technique of clothing tables. The tablecloth fold used in the following procedure (shown in Fig. 4.1) for clothing a table is called a concertina fold. It is one of the more commonly-used folds. The procedure as described assumes that the table has four legs at the corners of the table.

4.6 *Clothing procedure*

- Check the table for steadiness: and position it for ease of access for service. Should the table be unstable it must be stabilized.
- Stand centrally between two legs of the table.
- Position the folded cloth on the table with the two woven edges towards you and the two folds of the concertina facing away from you.
- Position the vertical centre crease in the centre of the table, holding the concertina fold.
- Lean across the table and release the bottom layer of the cloth to hang over the far edge of the table.
- Re-position the horizontal crease of the cloth in the centre of the table.

■ Release the hold on the centre fold and draw the top fold towards you.

■ Having centred the cloth both vertically and horizontally, the cloth should now be positioned with an equal drop all round, with the folds of the cloth covering the legs.

4.7 *Changing a cloth during service (Fig. 4.2)*

Cloths often have to be changed during food service, when guests are present at other tables and new covers are to be laid, or when there has been a serious spillage. In these circumstances cloths must be changed with a minimum of fuss, and, most importantly, without at any time exposing the bare tops of the tables to view. The procedure is as follows:

■ Remove any articles remaining on the table to the sideboard.

■ Stand centrally between the two legs of the table.

■ Holding the concertina fold, position the vertical centre crease of the clean cloth in the centre of the table.

■ Lean across the table and allow the bottom layer of the clean cloth to hang over the far edge of the soiled cloth.

■ Take the soiled cloth in both hands, holding it between the little and ring (fourth) fingers.

■ Concertina the soiled cloth towards you while opening the clean cloth above it.

■ Fold the soiled cloth and remove it discreetly.

4.8 STATION MISE-EN-PLACE

Mise-en-place (French for 'put in place') can be defined as the equipment and food that is prepared ready for service before service begins. Station mise-en-place is the preparation of a waiter's workstation in a food-service area, housing all the equipment required for service.

A waiter's station, whether it is simply a clothed table or a special sideboard equipped with shelves, drawers and, sometimes, a hot box (plate/food warmer), should carry the following:

■ All the necessary cutlery, for example, side knives, soup spoons, main (table) knives and forks, sweet spoons and forks, tea and coffee spoons

■ Service utensils (tablespoons and forks)

■ Crumbing down equipment

■ Service plates

■ Tea/coffee service equipment (milk jugs, sugar bowls, cups and saucers, teaspoons, etc.)

■ Glassware (tumblers, wine glasses – white and red)

■ Underliners (an underplate lined with a doily or napkin)

■ Bread service equipment (and butter – see 4.9)

■ Napkins

■ Service trays

■ Toothpicks

■ Menus

Fig. 4.2 Changing a cloth during service.

- Wine lists
- Spare docket books and pens (a docket and pen will be carried by the waiter)
- Waiter's friend (usually carried by the waiter – see 13.4)
- Condiments (sauces, pepper-mill, etc.)
- Clean table linen
- Additional items to meet the specialist requirements of the establishment.

If the sideboard is equipped with a plate/food warmer, it must be turned on approximately 15 minutes before service begins.

Items from the service station used during service should be replaced or replenished during or at the end of the waiter's shift, or at the beginning of the next shift, as decided by the supervisor.

4.9   PREPARING BUTTER

Butter is prepared before the guests arrive. Chill individual portions of butter, whether they are curled, sliced, or moulded, by placing them separately in iced water. This prevents the pieces of butter from sticking together. After they have been chilled place the portions of butter on butter plates and keep them in the refrigerator until they are required for service. Take the butter plate to the table when you are serving the bread (see 5.7).

4.10   HOW TO LAY A COVER

A 'cover' may be defined as:
- A place setting at a table for one guest, laid to suit the type of menu offered.
- The number of guests to attend a function – 'There will be 75 covers at the Rotary dinner', or to indicate the seating capacity of a dining area – 'The Lawson Room seats 50 covers'.

There are two principal types of cover – à la carte/basic cover, and set menu cover. The difference will be explained below. But whatever the type of cover to be laid, the following rules apply:
- All cutlery and glassware should be cleaned and polished before they are placed on the table.
- The main knife and fork should be positioned 1cm from the edge of the table and 25–29cm apart (depending on the size of the establishment's dinner plates).
- Sideplates are always positioned to the guests' left.
- Side knives are placed on the sideplate, to its right-hand side and parallel with the main knife and fork so that a bread roll can be placed on the plate.
- The blades of all knives on the cover should face left.
- The first or only wine glass is positioned 2.5cm from the tip of the main knife. Additional glassware is positioned at a 45° angle to the left of the first glass. (See 4.14.)
- A folded napkin is placed in the centre of the cover. (See 4.15.)

4.11 ## TYPES OF COVER

A la carte/basic cover (Fig. 4.3)

Fig. 4.3 A la carte cover/basic cover.

An à la carte menu features a variety of dishes individually priced. The guests then select the dishes they would like, usually up to and including the main course.

The basic à la carte cover is the cover usually set when the guests have a wide choice. It provides a 'show place' and the basic equipment needed for the meal. After the guests have ordered, this basic cover is then corrected to suit the customers' actual orders (see 6.17).

An à la carte cover includes:
- Fish knife and fork
- Fish plate
- Sideplate
- Side knife
- Wine goblet
- Napkin.

Other items on the table might include a centrepiece, such as a bud vase or candle, a tent card advertising the chef's speciality, a cruet and an ashtray in the smoking area.

4.12 ### Table d'hôte cover (Fig. 4.4)

Fig. 4.4 Table d'hôte cover.

A table d'hôte menu features pre-arranged items at a fixed price for the whole meal. Because it is known within a narrow range what will be served to the guests, the cutlery and glasses for the whole meal are laid in advance. The cover illustrated is for a table d'hôte offering a plated appetizer, soup, a fish entrée, a main course and a dessert.

The cutlery required for this menu is:
- Small knife and fork
- Soup spoon
- Fish knife and fork
- Main knife and fork
- Sideplate
- Side knife
- Dessert spoon and fork
- Glassware
- Napkin.

Note that the various items of cutlery are set so that the cutlery used for the first course is outermost, and the remaining cutlery is set in the order in which it will be used, working inwards from the outside.

4.13 ## DESSERT CUTLERY (Figs 4.5 and 4.6)

Fig. 4.5 Table d'hôte cover, with dessert cutlery.

As an alternative to laying the dessert spoon and fork prior to the meal, we suggest that dessert cutlery should be taken to the table on a service plate and laid only when needed for the sweet course. This will allow additional room on the table and ensure that the

Fig. 4.6   Table d'hôte cover, with small spoon.

cutlery will be absolutely clean when the time comes for it to be used.

Note that not all desserts require a spoon and fork; some may require a fruit knife and fork, or a small spoon.

4.14   GLASSWARE

The wine glasses, like the cutlery, are also set in the order in which they will be used. They are set in at an angle of 45° from the first glass to be used, which (as already noted) is placed about 2.5cm from the tip of the main knife.

Should the table not have sufficient room for the glassware to be set in a row (Fig. 4.7), it may be set in a triangle (Fig. 4.8).

Fig. 4.7   Wine glasses: standard setting.

Fig. 4.8   Wine glasses: triangle setting.

4.15   NAPKIN FOLDS

A folded table-napkin is placed on the table for the guests' use and to contribute to the appearance of the cover and the whole dining environment. The way in which the napkin is presented depends on the type of establishment and the type of service.

It is an advantage if napkin folds are kept simple as less handling is involved. Less handling makes for more hygienic napkins (as well as being less time-consuming). However, some establishments require more elaborate folds for aesthetic reasons.

Detailed in Figs. 4.9–4.17 are examples of some commonly used professional napkin folds. Either starched linen or paper napkins can be used for folding.

A professionally folded napkin will stand by itself without the aid of cutlery or glassware.

Fig. 4.9 Napkin folds.

Fig. 4.10   Sail.

Fig. 4.11   Cone.

Fig. 4.12 Pocket

Fig. 4.13 Bishop's hat (mitre).

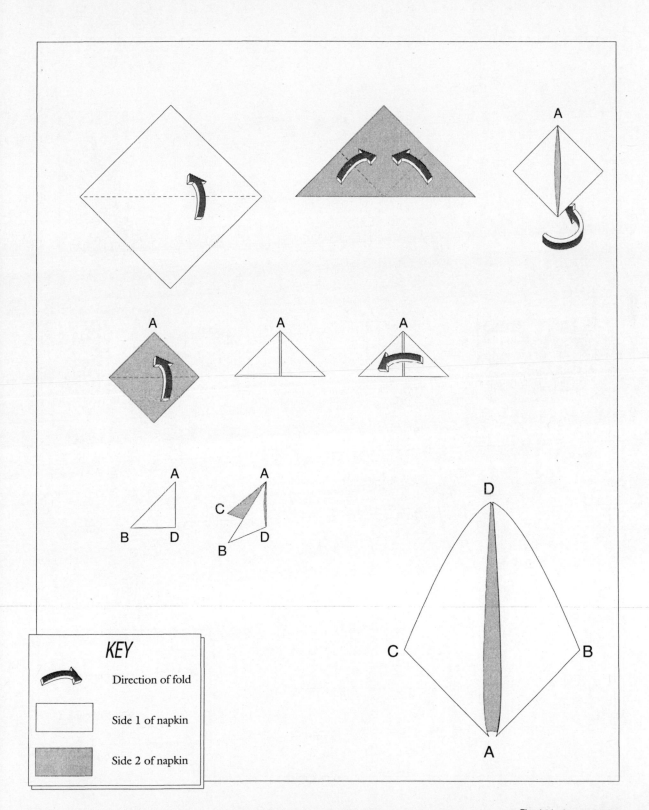

KEY

Direction of fold

Side 1 of napkin

Side 2 of napkin

Fig. 4.14 Inverted sails.

Fig. 4.15   Envelope.

Fig. 4.16 Fan.

Not to scale

Fold and unfold to crease

KEY

Direction of fold

Side 1 of napkin

Side 2 of napkin

Fig. 4.17   Star.

(stretched view)

Fig. 4.17 Star *continued*.

4.16 QUESTIONS

(1) Why are high standards of presentation essential?

(2) What are the two first questions you need to ask before you take a reservation?

(3) What additional details are needed to complete the reservation?

(4) What are three important points to take into consideration when preparing a floor plan?

(5) What are four key points in creating the right atmosphere?

(6) How can you change a soiled tablecloth without exposing the table top to the guests?

(7) Waiters should always check their stations before service starts. What items should they check for?

(8) How is an à la carte cover set?

(9) How is a table d'hôte cover set?

(10) What are two alternative ways of positioning wine glasses?

(11) Can you do all the napkin folds in section 4.15 without looking at the diagrams?

5 . Food Service Procedures: The Preliminaries

The objective of food service is to meet the needs of guests and to ensure that their dining experiences are both pleasurable and memorable. Why then should a guest be inconvenienced by the service? A guest who has to duck and dive throughout a meal to make way for the service will only remember that the service was not pleasurable.

5.1 Food service procedures vary considerably throughout the industry. Whether an establishment offers traditional services, modern service, or its own particular variation, is of little importance; what matters is that the establishment is consistent in the services it offers.

Because of the great variety of food service procedures in use today, many people entering the industry for the first time become confused about what are the 'correct' practices. The answer is, of course, that no one set of techniques is correct in all circumstances. What we have tried to do in this and the following chapters is to present common-sense solutions to the various problems and challenges of service which will be applicable in most circumstances, but the reader must always be aware that in some establishments other techniques and practices may be required.

On completion of this chapter you should have a good understanding of the following:

- The order of service
- Greeting and seating guests
- Opening napkins
- Service of water
- Service of bread
- Taking orders for pre-dinner drinks
- Serving pre-dinner drinks.

5.2 THE ORDER OF SERVICE

The 'order of service' is a sequential check-list of services from the arrival to the departure of the guest. It will differ in detail depending on the style of the establishment and the services it offers.

The sequence of service will take into account the particular tasks required to achieve a smooth flow of service that suits the special needs of each guest.

Many points must be considered when an order of service is defined, for example whether iced water will automatically be offered, whether hot or cold towels will be provided, and how the food and beverage services are to be co-ordinated. (There may be a specialist wine waiter.)

If several groups of guests arrive simultaneously at tables which are the responsibility of a single waiter then it is necessary to read the differing needs of the various groups and adjust the order of service to ensure that the tasks can be performed without overloading the station.

5.3 CHECK-LIST OF SERVICE

A written check-list of service ensures the consistency of the services offered and acts as a guideline to part-time and new waiting staff. What follows is an *example* of such an order of service from the time the guests are taken to their table.

- Greet and seat the guests.
- Open the napkins.
- Offer iced water.
- Take orders for apéritifs
- Serve the bread and butter.
- Offer the menu and suggest specials and inform the guests of variations to the menu.
- Allow time for the guests to make their choices.
- Take the food order up to and including the main course.
- Offer the wine list.
- Transfer the food order to the kitchen and cashier dockets and place the order with the kitchen.
- Take the wine order.
- Serve the wine.
- Correct the covers, up to and including the main course.
- Serve the first course.
- Clear the first course.
- Top up wines, and open fresh bottles as ordered.
- Serve additional starter courses.
- Clear the course preceding the main course.
- Call away the main course.
- Serve the salad.
- Serve the main course.
- Enquire (after the guests have had the opportunity to taste the food) whether the meals are satisfactory.
- Clear the main course.
- Clear the sideplates, salad plates and butter dishes.
- Check and, if necessary, change ashtrays. (If ashtrays are being used they should be changed regularly throughout the meal, especially just before food is served – see 11.6 and 11.7).
- Brush/crumb down.
- Offer hot (or cold) towels.
- Offer the wine list for the selection of dessert wines (or, if the guests prefer it, continue to serve the wine selected earlier).
- Offer the menu for dessert, suggesting specials and inform the guests of variations to the menu.

- Take dessert or cheese order.
- Transfer the dessert order to the kitchen and cashier dockets and place the order with the kitchen.
- Correct the covers.
- Serve the dessert wines or other beverages selected.
- Serve the dessert or cheese course.
- Take the order for coffee/tea. (The coffee/tea may be served with the dessert/cheese course if requested by the guest or as a separate service.)
- Transfer the coffee/tea order to the cashier docket.
- Take the after-dinner drinks order.
- Correct the cover.
- Serve the after-dinner drinks.
- Serve the coffee/tea.
- Serve the petits fours.
- Prepare the bill.
- Offer additional coffee/tea.
- Present the bill when it is requested.
- Accept payment and tender change.
- Offer additional coffee/tea.
- See the guests out of the restaurant.

5.4 GREETING AND SEATING GUESTS

First impressions are extremely important. Guests arriving at a restaurant gain their first impression of the establishment substantially from the willingness of the staff to acknowledge their presence and the greeting they receive. If the greeting is both warm and efficient guests will immediately feel that they can expect the rest of their experience to be pleasurable, and they will feel confident that they will be in the hands of reliable professionals.

The waiting service begins with the greeting and seating of the guests (Fig. 5.1).

In larger establishments guests may be received by a head waiter or supervisor and taken to the table (after checking reservations, etc.) where they are introduced to their table waiter, who takes over responsibility for their service. In smaller restaurants a single waiter will be responsible for the whole operation. In either case the procedure is as follows:

- Acknowledge new guests as soon as they arrive.
- Approach the guests with an appropriate welcome, for example, 'Good evening'.
- If the guests have come to eat, enquire whether they have a reservation. Check the reservation. If no table has been booked, check that one is available.
- When checking the reservation, note the host's name – the table will usually have been reserved in the name of the host. It is important to establish who the host is. (The host may, of course, be female or male.)

Fig. 5.1 Offer the guest a chair.

- Show the guests to their table.
- Offer the guests a chair to encourage them to be seated.

5.5 OPENING NAPKINS (Fig. 5.2)

Opening the napkin for your guests ensures that the napkin is out of the way when drinks and food are to be served. Some guests

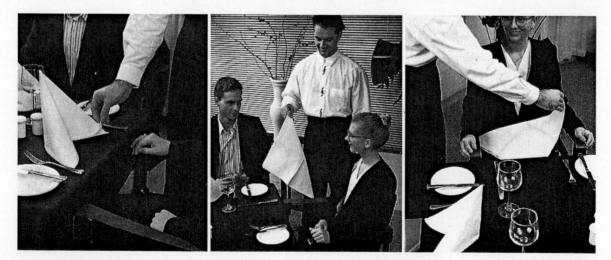

Fig. 5.2 Opening a napkin.

will open their own napkins as soon as they sit down, others will wait for you to open theirs for them. The technique is:

■ Standing to the right of the guest, pick up the napkin with your right hand.
■ Shake the napkin from its fold into a triangle.
■ Place it across the guest's lap with the longest side of the triangle closest to the guest.
■ Move anti-clockwise around the table opening the napkins, opening the host's last.

5.6 WATER SERVICE (Fig. 5.3)

Iced water may be offered to the guests after the greeting/seating procedures. The purpose of serving iced water is to refresh the guests' palates, and allow them time to select a pre-dinner drink.

Iced water is a valuable addition to the meal experience, and is appreciated by guests. It should always be available, although in some establishments it may not be the practice to serve it unless it is asked for. (Some countries, including the USA and Japan, require fresh water to be made available, and visitors from those countries will expect iced water to be available without their having to ask for it.) The procedure for serving water is:

■ The water glass is positioned to the right of the wine glass above the table knife.
■ Water is poured from the guest's right.
■ Move anti-clockwise round the table pouring the water, serving the host last.
■ Continue to offer water throughout the meal, as required.

In some establishments jugs of iced water may be left on the table for the guests to help themselves. Mineral water (see also section 14.21) is becoming an increasingly popular alternative to tap water. It is popular with guests because they prefer the taste, and it has the advantage for the establishment that guests are willing to pay for it whereas tap water is usually served free of charge. Mineral water can be served either in bottles or by the glass.

Fig. 5.3 Serving iced water.

5.7 BREAD SERVICE

Bread, in some form or other, is usually served as soon as the guests are seated. It may be placed in a basket on the table, or served individually (silver service). The advantage of the individual service of bread is that it leaves more room on the table. The silver service technique is:

■ Carry the bread basket and butter plate in the left hand, using the two-plate method (see 7.5).
■ Place the butter plate in the centre of the table.
■ Transfer the bread basket to the flat of the left hand.
■ Serve from the guest's left.
■ Hold the left hand (with the bread basket) down over the edge of the sideplate.

- Transfer the bread from the basket to the sideplate, using service cutlery (see 8.4).
- Move anti-clockwise around the table, serving the host last.

5.8   APERITIFS

Fig. 5.4   Carry the drinks to the table on the tray.

Apéritif (pre-dinner drink) orders should be taken as soon as possible after guests have been seated. The waiter should encourage the guests to try something a little adventurous or different by suggesting speciality cocktails or beverages, allowing guests time to consider their preferences.

- Offer the drinks/cocktail list, or suggest a variety of the beverages available.
- Assist the guests in making their selections by explaining what is in the various cocktails and what they are like (see section 14.2).
- Many guests will not want alcoholic drinks at this stage, especially if they are driving, so be prepared to suggest non-

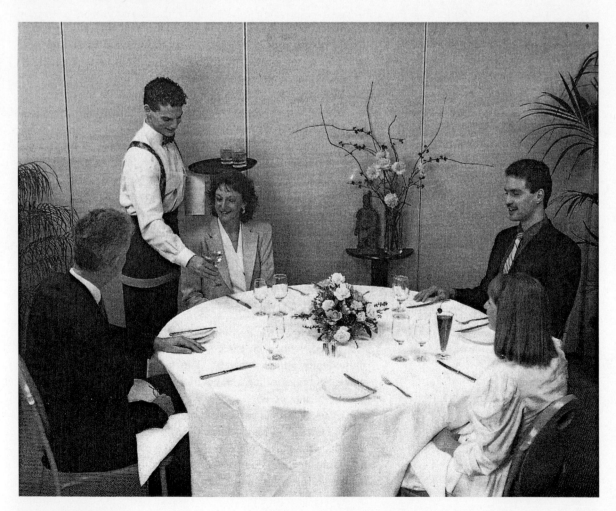

Fig. 5.5   Serving aperitifs.

alcoholic alternatives – a Longboat, for instance, made with lime cordial, and ginger beer.

- Record the orders in sequence round the table, anti-clockwise.
- Note any special requirements (no ice, etc.).
- Record the sales following the house control system.
- Place the order with the bar.

5.9 *Serving apéritifs*

- Arrange the drinks in sequence of (anti-clockwise) service on a drinks tray.
- Carry the drinks to the table on the drinks tray (Fig. 5.4).
- Hold the tray on the left hand away from the table (see 15.13).
- Serve the drinks in sequence around the table anti-clockwise, serving the host last (Fig. 5.5).
- Place each drink to the right of the guest's wine glass.

Your guests should now be comfortably settled and ready to turn their attention to the menu.

5.10 QUESTIONS

(1) What is the purpose of the 'order of service?'
(2) Why is it important to establish who is the host?
(3) Describe the procedure for opening napkins.
(4) Why serve iced water?
(5) When and how is bread served?
(6) How can guests be encouraged to order apéritifs?
(7) In what order should apéritifs be served?

6 . Taking Orders and Correcting the Covers

GUEST: What would you recommend today?

WAITER: Everything is good!

Well, that was a big help, wasn't it?

6.1 Once the guests are comfortably settled, and have been provided with their apéritifs and bread, they are ready to turn their attention to the menu and to selecting what they want to eat. The menu is offered, the order is taken, and the cover is corrected.

When you have completed this chapter you should have a thorough understanding of the following:

- Presenting the menu
- Food sales and sales techniques
- Taking food orders
- Use of a service plate
- Correcting the covers.

6.2 PRESENTING THE MENU

A waiter should not simply take orders and serve what is ordered. The waiter's job is more pro-active – waiters should make things happen. They are salespeople as well as service people.

Presenting the menu is a time for suggestive selling. The waiter has the opportunity actively to sell items on the menu, and 'specials' and side dishes which may not be on it. At no other time does the waiter have so much of the guests' attention, and it is an opportunity not to be missed.

Before presenting the menu you must understand all the items on it and be able to describe how they are cooked and served. (You may find the Glossary helpful for this.) You must also know the details of the daily specials.

Menus should be offered in such a way as to encourage the guests to select their meals reasonably quickly, without appearing to put any pressure on them to do so.

6.3 *Different forms of menus*

Menus come in different forms. In traditional restaurants the menu is usually presented in a cover, but in less formal establishments it can be written on a blackboard, or a card, or a souvenir place-mat, or almost anything else.

Particular venues may well have devised their own methods to

Fig. 6.1 Presenting the menu.

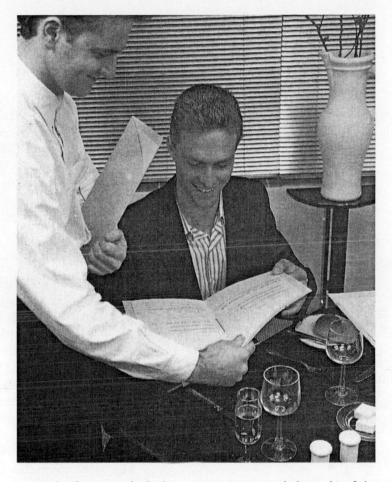

suit the form in which their menus appear and the style of the operation. Of course, these special 'house rules' must be followed by the waiting staff.

6.4 *The technique of presenting a menu*

If the menu is in a cover, it should be opened before it is presented (Fig. 6.1) to encourage the guests to read it and make their selections.

- Carry the menu on the flat of the left arm.
- Open the menu from the top with the right hand.
- Present the menu to the guest's right.
- When all the guests have received a copy of the menu, suggest items which do not appear in the menu or any variations to the menu items.

6.5 DESCRIBING AND RECOMMENDING DISHES

You are now likely to be asked questions about the specials, and about the items on the menu. You must be able to describe the dishes, and how they are cooked and served, concisely, accurately, and attractively.

You may also be asked to make recommendations. Be prepared

to assist the guests in making their selections. To say 'Everything is good!' is not helpful. Establish what sort of dish the guest may want – fish or meat, hot or cold – and then direct the guest to those dishes which seem most appropriate.

6.6 *The waiter as salesperson*

This is the time when the waiter's skill as a salesperson comes into play. 'Hard sell' techniques are seldom effective. Sales are made by suggesting items which the guests might well have ordered had they known of them. What you are providing is better service – making the guests' experience more complete and enjoyable, rather than a series of sales pitches. You might helpfully say, for example, that the fish of the day is fresh from the market, or that medallions of venison are a new menu item and have proved very popular.

It is a basic sales technique not to invite negative answers. Instead of saying, 'Would you like a starter?' which invites the answer 'No', rather ask 'What would you like to start with?'

Some establishments (in particular American-based chain restaurants) give detailed instruction to their waiting staff in sales techniques; in others the whole emphasis is on helpful service without any mention of the word sales – 'sales' might almost be thought of as a dirty word – but the effect of good service should be the same in either case: contented guests and profitable food sales for the establishment.

To be an extremely effective salesperson the waiter need only be sincerely helpful, friendly, attentive and enthusiastic, and have a thorough knowledge of the menu and be able to describe and recommend suitable items.

6.7 CHILDREN

Unruly bored young children are the waiter's (and their parents') nightmare. Give them something to eat or do as soon as possible: paper, pens, crayons if you can manage it, at the very least some bread and butter to eat. They must be kept waiting for their food as little as possible. It could be a good idea, for example, to serve their main course when the adults are served their starters.

6.8 TAKING AND PLACING FOOD ORDERS

Food orders are taken as soon as the guests have made their selections. You must be alert to the signs that the guests are ready to order so that they are not kept waiting. They may, for example, close their menus and place them on the table.

6.9 *Order-taking techniques*

To ensure prompt service and fulfilment of the guests' orders, the waiter must record all the necessary information, so that there is no doubt which guest ordered what.

Orders can be taken in various forms, depending on how many guests there are at the table, and the procedures of the establishment. Some establishments have pre-printed forms which simply have to be ticked. Often the waiter will have to use a blank docket.

The way the order is taken must serve three functions. It must be clear to the kitchen what dishes are to be prepared (and whether there are any special requirements). The waiter must be able to see which dish is to be served to which customer. And when the bill is prepared it must be clear what has been ordered and consumed. The essential is *clarity*.

The great enemy of clarity is the use of personally-devised abbreviations. If abbreviations are used they must be consistent and in a style agreed by *both* the waiting and kitchen staff. Avoid letter abbreviations; use at least part of the name of the dishes ordered – according to the agreed style.

6.10 *Procedure for order-taking*

- Ensure the guests are ready to order.
- Take the order of the guest on the right of the host first, and work anti-clockwise round the table, finishing with the host's order.
- Take the order, up to and including the main course.
- Note any special requirements (for example, a special dietary requirement, such as no milk to be used in the preparation of the dish, or a service requirement, such as meals required very quickly because the guests are going on to a show).
- Repeat the order to the guests to make sure that the order is correct.
- Transfer the order to the kitchen docket (using either a manual or a computer system), including the special instructions.
- Record the sale, for billing purposes, following the house control system.
- Place the order with the kitchen.

6.11 CHECKING SYSTEMS

Control or checking systems are used to:
- Provide the cashier with the information to make up the bills,
- Keep a record of all food and drink used,
- Keep a check on stores so that wastage can be minimized and pilferage discovered,
- Store information so that the cost of each menu item can be calculated accurately and the profit made on it worked out,
- Provide a breakdown of sales and financial statistics.

There are four main types of checking systems in use in catering establishments:
- Triplicate checking system – a traditional system used in medium and large-sized hotels and restaurants (see Fig. 6.2).

- Duplicate checking system – usually used in small restaurants and fast food restaurants (see Fig. 6.3).
- Electronic billing machines – used in some establishments where the waiter rather than the cashier prepares the bill.
- Computerized systems – used in large establishments and chain restaurants (see Fig. 6.4).

6.12 *Triplicate checking system*

The check must be clearly written in the same language as the menu to avoid misunderstandings. Only agreed abbreviations should be used. The check must contain:

- Table number
- Number of covers
- Date
- Waiter's signature.

Fig. 6.2(a) Triplicate checking system.

Any cancellation of a check must be authorized by the head waiter. This is also required if any alterations are made to the check.

Often more than one check is needed for a meal: for instance, the sweet course often requires a second check to be written. In these cases the check should be headed 'Suivant', which means 'following' in French, to show that it is the second check for a particular table. Three copies of this check are needed as with the original check.

TABLE No. 2 Covers 4 ← — Top Kitchen

SUIVANT

2 Crêpe suzettes
2 Fromage

Date 1-8-93
Signed R. Miles

TABLE No. 2 Covers 4

SUIVANT

2 Crêpe suzettes
Fromage

Date 1-8-93
Signed R. Miles — Flimsy Waiter

TABLE No. 2 Covers 4

SUIVANT

2 Crêpe suzettes
2 Fromage

Date 1-8-93
Signed R. Miles — Copy Cashier

Fig. 6.2(b)   Second check for the same table.

If an extra portion of food is required because not enough portions were sent from the kitchen a check must be issued headed 'Supplement'. This check should be signed by the head waiter. There is usually no charge for such orders.

If there is an accident with a dish and a check is written for a repeat order it should be headed 'Accident'. This check should also be signed by the head waiter and no charge should be made. The same procedure is followed with the three copies.

If the wrong dish is sent from the kitchen it should be returned with a check headed 'Retour' or 'Return' and the name of the correct dish and the returned dish should be written on the check.

6.13 Duplicate checking system

This system uses only two copies of a check. It is usually used in establishments offering a limited menu and may be pre-printed. It can also make use of perforated strips – each one for a different course. The waiter tears off the strip and sends it to the kitchen as required. The check should contain the following information:

- Serial number of check pad
- Waiter's code number
- Table number
- Date.

The duplicate copy is also used as the bill.

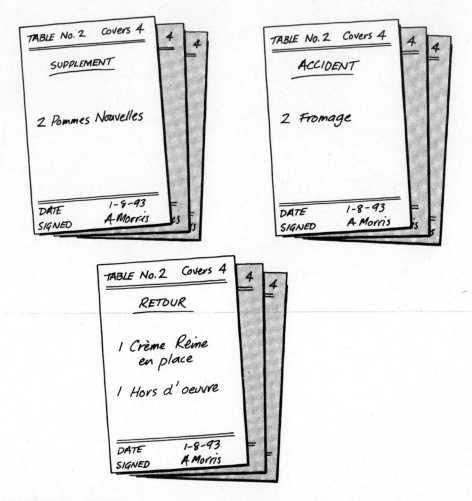

Fig. 6.2(c) Extra checks for the same table.

SERIAL No. 1993			WAITER No. 10	
1993	4 cuts 2 Crème Reine 2 Hors d'oeuvre	10	6·00 8·50	
1993	4 cuts 2 Tournedos Rossini 2 Entrecote grillée	10	20·00 14·00	
1993	4 cuts 2 Crêpes Suzettes 2 Fromage	10	15·00 8·00	
1993	4 cuts 4 café	10	6·00	
1993	4 cuts 4 petite fours	10	4·00	
TABLE No. 4 DATE 1-8-93				
		TOTAL	£81·50	

Fig. 6.3 Duplicate checking system.

The waiter must ensure that all items are entered on the bill. If the waiter presents the bill and the guests pay the cashier, an analysis of the waiter's takings will be drawn up by the cashier.

6.14 *Electronic billing machines*

Accuracy and speed are the biggest advantages of this system. Bills may be prepared by the waiter, thus cutting out the need for a cashier.

Each waiter will have a key with his or her own letter on it, a stationery folder, food order pads and bills with consecutive numbers, a paying in slip and a float.

When taking the order each course will be written on the order slip and placed in the billing machine before being taken to the kitchen. The correct keys must be pushed to price the order accurately. To use the machine the waiter must insert his or her key into the appropriate position.

How to use an electronic billing machine

(1) Place the waiter's key into correct locking position.
(2) Place the check into machine.
(3) Press buttons to price the dishes concerned.
(4) Press food/beverage button to show what the money was received for.
(5) Press identity key.
(6) The check will now print out.

6.15 *Computerized checking systems*

A system of computer links between hotels is now quite common and provides up-to-the-minute information on reservations and other bookings. Computerized checking systems are widely used in restaurants in the UK.

When this type of system is used the waiter takes the order and then enters it on the restaurant or floor service key pad. All the waiters will have their own unique, individual number for security. The order will be printed out at whichever dispensing point is required: kitchen, cellar, bar or stillroom. This saves a great deal of time and effort for the waiter who will have to make only one trip to collect the order.

A bill will be opened for the particular table as soon as the order is keyed into the computer. Itemized bills will be printed out for presentation to the customer.

Computerized systems are ideal for analysing sales and takings and performance in sales for individual staff. Some large restaurant groups have a direct computer link by telephone to head office which will speed up any sales information required.

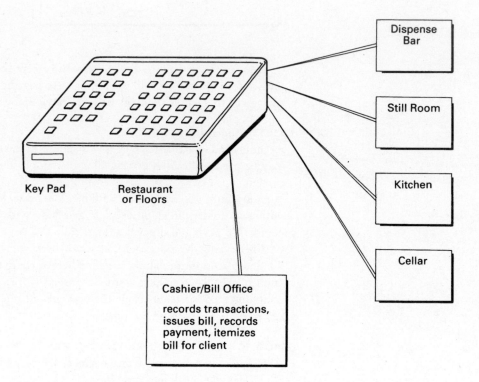

Fig. 6.4 Computerized checking system.

6.16 USE OF THE SERVICE PLATE

A service plate (Fig. 6.5) is a dinner plate, covered with a folded napkin to reduce noise. It is used to carry all small items used in food service to and from the table – cutlery, cruets, etc.

Service plates should be readily available at all service points. At no time should waiters carry cutlery in their hands because the

Fig. 6.5 The service plate.

more the utensils are touched, the greater the possibility that bacteria will contaminate them.

- Carry the service plate on the flat of the left hand.
- Use the right hand to lift the items from the service plate and place them on the table.

6.17 CORRECTING THE COVERS

To correct a cover (Fig. 6.6) is to adjust the cutlery originally laid to meet a guest's specific order.

Covers are corrected after the orders have been taken and placed with the kitchen. They are corrected up to and including the main course.

Guests use the outer cutlery for their first courses and move inwards for each succeeding course.

Cutlery for the dessert and the cheese is corrected after those orders have been taken later in the meal.

- Prepare the cutlery for each guest, up to and including the main course, on a service plate.
- Starting with the guest on the right of the host, move anti-clockwise, correcting the covers.

Fig. 6.6   Correcting the covers.

- Correct the knife section of the first guest and the fork section of the next guest by standing between them.
- To adjust the cutlery, lift the item not required and replace it with the correct item. Place the items required in sequence of use, that is with the first-course items on the outside and the items for the later courses inside and nearer the plate in the order in which they will be used.
- Pick up the cutlery holding it between the thumb and the index finger at the neck or join between the handle and the top. This will ensure that no fingerprints can be seen on the cutlery after it has been placed and that the cutlery remains clean.
- All cutlery used when adjusting the covers is placed parallel to the main place setting. This applies to dessert spoons and forks when the covers are adjusted for the dessert and cheese orders as well as to the cutlery used for the earlier courses.

6.18   Dessert cutlery

As we have already noted (see 4.13), dessert cutlery is usually corrected after the main course has been cleared, just before the dessert course is served. This means that the dessert cutlery must be brought to the table and placed. The procedure is:

- Arrange the required dessert cutlery for the whole table on a service plate and take it to the table.
- Correct the cover by standing between each pair of guests and placing a spoon to the right of the guest on your left and a fork to the left of the guest on your right.
- Move anti-clockwise round the table, repeating the procedure.
- If the dessert cutlery required is only a small spoon and not a full-size dessert spoon and fork, the small spoon is placed to the right of the cover.

If the dessert cutlery was already on the table across the top of the cover as part of the cover for a set menu it must be moved down before the dessert course is served. Stand between two guests and move the spoon of the guest to your left and the fork of the guest to your right, repeating the procedure round the table as you would have done had you brought the dessert cutlery to the table on a service tray.

6.19 Table of accompaniments and covers

Dish	Accompaniment	Cover
Hors d'oeuvre variés	Oil and vinegar	Fish plate, fish knife and fork
Grapefruit	Caster sugar	Coupe, doily, side plate, grapefruit spoon
Tomato juice	Worcestershire sauce	Glass, doily, side plate, tea spoon
Oysters	Oyster cruet, Tabasco sauce, chilli vinegar, lemon, cayenne pepper, pepper mill, brown bread and butter	Oyster dish, oyster fork, finger bowl
Potted shrimps	Lemon, breakfast toast, peppermill, cayenne pepper	Fish plate, fish knife and fork
Snails	Brown bread and butter	Tongs, snail fork, snail dish
Smoked eel Smoked trout Smoked mackerel	Horseradish sauce, cayenne pepper, pepper mill, lemon, brown bread and butter	Fish plate, fish knife and fork
Smoked salmon	As above but without the horseradish sauce	As above
Caviar	Lemon, breakfast toast, sieved egg white, sieved egg yolk, chopped shallot, or blinis	Caviar knife or fish knife, fish plate
Chilled melon	Caster sugar and ground ginger	Dessert spoon and fork, fish plate
Asparagus Globe artichoke	*Hot:* hollandaise, beurre fondue *Cold:* vinaigrette	Finger bowl, joint fork (asparagus tongs and rack)

Dish	Accompaniment	Cover
Soups		
Minestrone	Parmesan cheese, toasted flutes	Soup spoon
Soupe à l'oignons à la française	Croûte with Gruyère cheese	Soup spoon
Purée soups	Croûtons	Soup spoon
Cream of tomato soup	The only cream soup to be accompanied by croûtons	Soup spoon
Turtle soup	Cheese straws, lemon, brown bread and butter, measure of sherry	Consommé cup, dessert spoon
Bortsch	Sour cream, beetroot juice, duck patties	Soup plate, dessert spoon
Farinaceous dishes		
Spaghetti	Grated parmesan cheese	Soup plate, joint fork, dessert spoon
Gnocchi Romaine Parisienne Piedmontaise	} Grated parmesan cheese	} Fish plate, dessert spoon, and fork
Fish		
Grilled herring	Mustard sauce	Fish knife and fork, fish plate
Deep fried fish coated in bread crumbs à l'anglaise	Tartare sauce	Fish knife and fork, fish plate
Deep fried fish coated in batter à l'orly	Tomato sauce	Fish knife and fork, fish plate
Poached fish *hot*	Hollandaise sauce or beurre fondue	
Poached fish *cold*	Mayonnaise or sauce vert	
Meats		
Roast beef	Horseradish sauce, roast gravy, yorkshire pudding, mustard	Joint plate, joint knife and fork
Roast pork	Apple sauce, roast gravy, sage and onion stuffing	" "

Dish	Accompaniment	Cover
Roast lamb	Mint sauce, roast gravy	Joint plate, joint knife and fork
Roast mutton	Red currant jelly, roast gravy	" "
Boiled mutton	Caper sauce	" "
Boiled ham	Parsley sauce or onion sauce	" "
Curry	Poppadums, bombay duck, chutney, chopped apple, sultanas, banana, coconut	Joint knife and fork, dessert spoon, soup plate
Irish stew	Pickled red cabbage, Worcestershire sauce	As above
Poultry		
Roast chicken	Bread sauce, roast gravy, bacon rolls, game chips, stuffing, watercress	Joint knife and fork, joint plate
Roast turkey	Cranberry sauce, roast gravy, chestnut stuffing, chipolatas, game chips, watercress	" "
Roast duck or goose	Apple sauce, roast gravy, sage and onion stuffing, watercress	" "
Game		
Wild duck	Orange salad with acidulated cream dressing, roast gravy	Joint knife and fork, joint plate
Partridge, grouse, pheasant	Bread sauce, roast gravy, game chips, fried bread crumbs, *hot* liver pâte on a croûte, watercress	" "
Hare	Red currant jelly, force meat balls	" "
Venison	Red currant jelly and cumberland sauce	" "

Dish	Accompaniment	Cover
Savouries Welsh rarebit, canapé, Ivanhoe, croûte baron	Cruet, cayenne pepper, pepper mill. Worcestershire sauce should be offered with meat items.	Small knife and dessert fork, fish plate
Cheese	A variety of biscuits, cruet, celery, radishes, caster sugar with cream cheese	Side plate, side knife, possibly a small fork
Desserts	Salt, caster sugar	Fruit knife and fork, fruit plate, finger bowl, grape scissors, nut crackers and a spare side plate for debris

6.20   QUESTIONS

(1) How should a menu be presented?
(2) What is suggestive selling?
(3) What qualities are needed to be a successful salesperson?
(4) What are two good ways to keep children occupied while they are waiting for their food?
(5) What are the three essential points to make clear on an order?
(6) What are the four types of checking systems in use in catering establishments?
(7) Why should a service plate be used for carrying cutlery?
(8) What is the procedure for correcting the covers?
(9) When should the dessert cutlery be corrected?
(10) Which way should you travel round the table when correcting covers?

7 . Styles of Service: Plate Service

Why should guests have to experience delays in the service of food to their table caused by a waiter's inadequate skills?

7.1 The manager of a food-service establishment has the choice of a number of different styles of service. Management should select a style of service to complement the type of food being served, and to accommodate effectively both the guests' and the establishment's needs.

An operator who understands the various service styles can utilize a particular service, or combine two or more different styles of service, to achieve greater productivity (and profitability) and enhance guest satisfaction.

The two most commonly used food-service styles are plate service and silver service.

The various styles of service and the techniques required by them are all explained in detail in this or later chapters. They are:

- Plate service (this chapter)
- Silver service (chapter 8)
- Guéridon service (10.5–10.6)
- Family service (10.7–10.8)
- Buffet service (10.9)
- Cafeteria service (10.10).

These styles of service can be used in new and interesting ways to encourage custom. Cafeteria service, for example, is used in modern food halls, while guéridon service is used imaginatively for salads and desserts in some bistros and restaurant chains. Silver service is commonly used instead of the usual plate service at large tables at banquets.

In plate service the food is plated in the kitchen or at a service point and served to the guest on the plate. In silver service the food is presented on serving dishes and is transferred from a serving dish to the plate in front of the guest with the use of a spoon and fork.

There are of course variations on these two basic techniques. For example, the main food item, perhaps the meat, can be placed on the plate in the kitchen and served using the plate service technique, and then the vegetables can be served at the table using the silver service technique. This constitutes a combination of the two service techniques, not a new technique.

This chapter deals with plate service techniques and procedures. Silver service technique is explained in the next chapter.

When you have completed this chapter you should have a thorough understanding of:

- Plate service procedures
- The use of service cloths for carrying hot plates
- Two-plate carrying technique
- Three-plate carrying technique
- The use of underliners.

7.2 PLATE SERVICE SKILLS AND TECHNIQUES

Plate service is a basic and commonly-used form of service. It demands that the waiter should be skilled in carrying plates without disturbing the food arranged on them. The methods used to carry the plates depend on the number of plates to be carried.

In professional plate service no more than four plates are carried at a time. It is possible to carry more than four plates but, as this relies on balance, it is not usually considered professional service.

The two professional methods most used in the industry are the two-and three-plate carrying techniques. These involve carrying either two or three plates in the left hand, leaving the right hand free. The right hand can be used to carry another plate, thus allowing three or four plates to be carried at once.

When plates are cleared the same plate-carrying techniques should be used (see chapter 9).

All professional waiters must be proficient in plate carrying and clearing techniques.

Fig. 7.1   In modern plate service plates are placed from the guest's right.

7.3 PLATE SERVICE PROCEDURE

Traditional plate service required food to be served to the left of the guest, and that the empty plates should be cleared from the right. In modern plate service, however, plates are both placed and cleared from the guest's right as this causes the least disturbance to the guest.

Modern plate service practice has come about because dining space is now more intensively utilized than in the past, and there is less room for movement between guests. The plate-service waiter can unobtrusively place a plate of food in front of a guest from the right (Fig. 7.1), while holding other plates in the left hand safely behind the guest's head. (Left-handed waiters reverse the technique and serve and clear from the left.)

Modern plate service does not interfere with beverage service as food and beverage service do not take place at the same time.

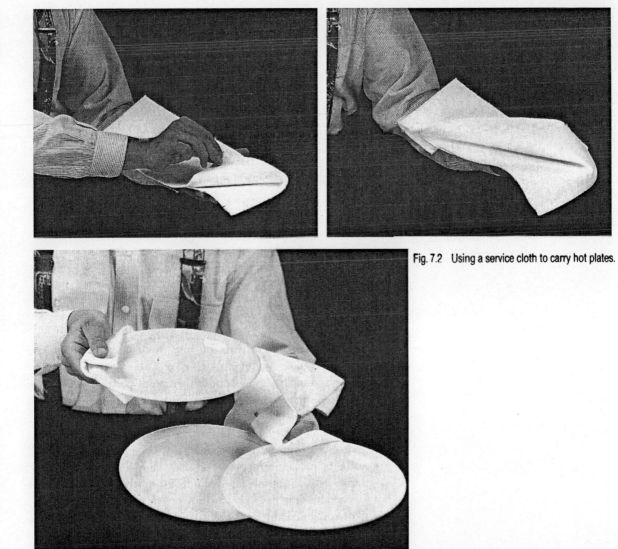

Fig. 7.2   Using a service cloth to carry hot plates.

Unless otherwise instructed serve the guest immediately to the right of the host first and then move anti-clockwise round the table serving each guest in turn, regardless of sex. The host should be served last. Note, though, that in some establishments you may be required to serve ladies before gentlemen, or this may be requested by the guests.

7.4 THE SERVICE CLOTH

Clean service cloths should be used to protect the hands and wrists from burning when you are carrying hot plates (Fig. 7.2).

- Place the cloth along your left hand and forearm, with the open section of the cloth inwards; the cloth should not protrude beyond the tips of the fingers.
- Fan the end of the cloth open to protect the hand: this allows both the two-plate and three-plate carrying methods to be used (see 7.5 and 7.6).
- A second folded service cloth should be held in the right hand to protect it, when holding plates or transferring them from the left hand to the table.

7.5 TWO-PLATE CARRYING TECHNIQUE (Fig. 7.3)

- Plates are picked up so that when they are placed the main item will be on the side of the plate facing the guest. Remember that the first plate to be picked up in the left hand will be the last to be placed on the table.
- Hold the first plate between your thumb, index finger and the middle finger of your left hand. If the plate is hot use a service cloth. (See 7.4).
- Then place the second plate on a platform above the first plate, supporting it by your ring (or fourth) finger, your little finger and the base of your thumb and lower forearm.
- You may carry a third plate in your right hand (Fig. 7.4), also in a service cloth if necessary.
- Carry the plates to the table holding them away from your body, with the shoulders held back, so that the plates are not resting against the front of your body.
- Bring the plates in front of your body only when limited access to the table requires it.
- To place the plates in front of the guests, position yourself at the back right-hand corner of a guest's chair, holding your left hand (and its plates) out of the way behind the guest's head.
- Leaning forward, place the plate in your right hand in front of the guest from the guest's right.
- The plate should be placed so that the main item (the meat, fish, etc.) is immediately in front of the guest, and the vegetables further away at the 'top' of the plate.
- Move behind the next guest to your right and transfer the second plate to your right hand and place it in front of the guest from the guest's right.

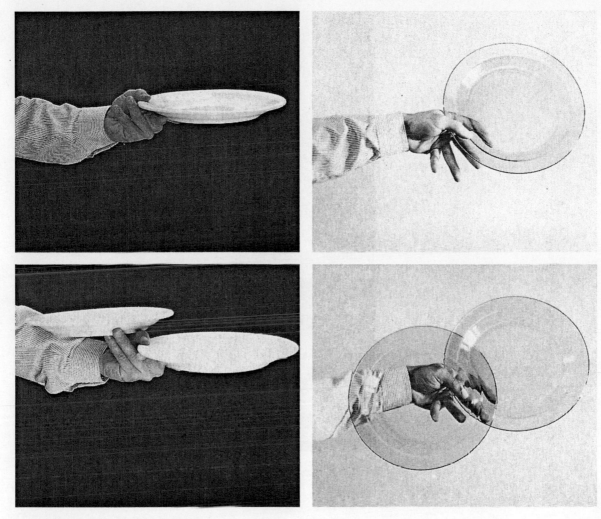

Fig. 7.3 Two-plate carrying technique (courtesy Graham Brown and Karon Hepner).

■ Continue anti-clockwise round the table repeating the procedure.

7.6 THREE-PLATE CARRYING TECHNIQUE (Fig. 7.5)

If four plates must be taken to the table at the same time, three plates should be carried in the left hand using the three-plate carrying method.

■ Hold the first plate between your thumb, index and middle fingers of the left hand (as in the two-plate technique). If the plates are hot use a service cloth (see 7.4).

■ Place the second plate into the crease of the palm of your left hand under the edge of the first plate, supporting it by your ring and little fingers.

■ Plate the third plate so that it sits on the flat of your forearm and the rim of the second plate.

Fig. 7.4 Carrying three plates to the table.

- Carry the fourth plate in your right hand (Fig. 7.6).
- Carry the plates to the table, holding them away from your body, with your shoulders held back, so that the plates are not resting against the front of your body.
- The plates should only be carried in front of your body when limited access to the table requires it.
- To place the plates in front of the guests, position yourself at the back right-hand corner of the guest's chair, holding your left hand and its plates out of the way behind the guest's head.
- Leaning forward, place the plate in your right hand in front of the guest from the guest's right, using your right hand.
- Move behind the next guest to your right and transfer the third plate to your right hand and plate it in front of the guest from the guest's right.
- Continue anti-clockwise round the table repeating the procedure.

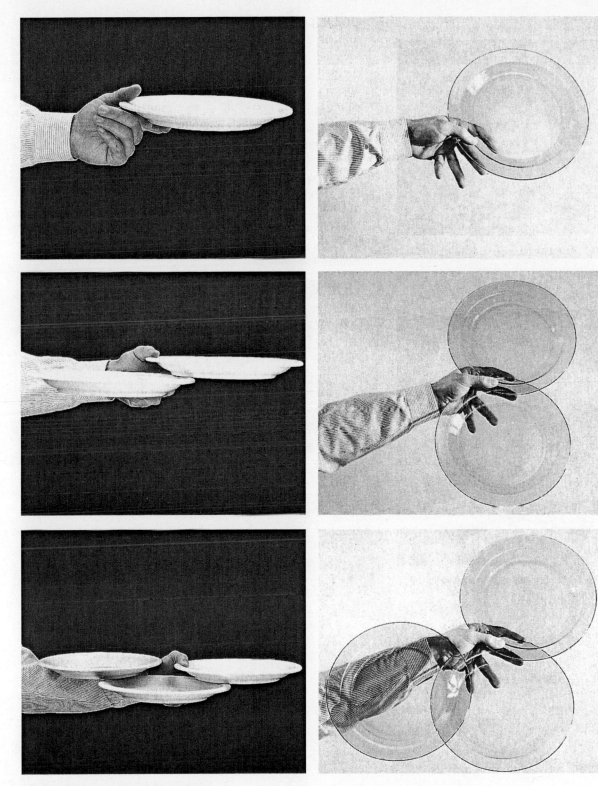

Fig. 7.5 Three-plate carrying technique (courtesy
Graham Brown and Karon Hepner).

Fig. 7.6 Carrying four plates to the table.

7.7 UNDERLINERS

An underliner or underplate is a plate placed under the service equipment (the vessel containing the food) when it is served to guests. Underliners are not primarily intended to enhance the appearance of the food being served; their purpose is to make it easier to carry and clear service equipment that is difficult to handle, and to provide something for guests to place their used cutlery on when the service equipment itself is not suitable for that purpose.

It is usual for a doily or napkin to be placed on the underliner to prevent the service equipment from sliding.

Underliners should only be used for a specific purpose. They are often used when serving items in soup bowls and coupes (Fig. 7.7). They should also be used when serving oysters on ice to prevent condensation.

7.8 QUESTIONS

(1) Which are the most commonly used food-service styles?
(2) What is the maximum number of plates that professionals carry to the table at once?
(3) On which side of the guest does the waiter stand in modern plate service?
(4) What is the use of the service cloth?
(5) Describe the two-plate carrying technique.
(6) Where should the plates be held when carrying them to the table?
(7) Which way round should plates be placed in front of the guests?
(8) Describe the three-plate carrying technique.
(9) What are underliners used for?
(10) How can you stop the plates sliding around on their underliners?

Fig. 7.7 Underliners used for soup bowls and coupes.

8 . Silver Service

Obviously this 'waiter' hasn't mastered the basic silver-service skills – he's using kitchen tongs instead of a spoon and fork!

8.1 Silver service is the technique of transferring food from a service dish to the guest's plate from the left (Fig. 8.1) with the use of service cutlery. This usually means a serving spoon and fork, but occasionally it consists of knives, especially fish knives. Silver service requires the waiter to be able to use the cutlery to serve the food with one hand.

Professional silver service depends on mastering the technique of using service cutlery held in one hand to transfer items to the guest's plate from a service dish held in the other hand.

When you have completed this chapter you will understand:
- The technique of using a serving spoon and fork
- The technique of using knives for service
- Silver service of bread rolls
- Silver service procedures for the main meal
- Silver service of sauces
- Silver service of delicate or large items.

Fig. 8.1 Silver service takes place from the left of the guest.

Fig. 8.2 Holding the service cutlery.

Fig. 8.3 For large round items turn the fork.

8.2 USE OF A SPOON AND FORK

■ Place a fork over a spoon in your right hand, both facing up (Fig. 8.2). They should rest across your middle, ring, and little fingers with their bases resting in line with the bottom of the little finger, leaving the index finger and thumb free to move the cutlery. The handles should not protrude beyond your little finger.

■ Slide your index finger between the fork and the spoon, and hold the fork between the tip of your index finger and the tip of your thumb so that you can lift the fork with your index finger and thumb.

■ Holding the fork between the tips of your index finger and your thumb, raise the fork from the bowl of the spoon, keeping the ends of the handles of the fork and the spoon together with your little finger.

■ At no time allow the index finger and thumb to slide more than half-way up the handles of the cutlery.

■ You can now lift food items with the spoon and hold them firmly in place with the fork while you transfer them to the guest's plate.

■ Pick the food up from the side, drawing the cutlery towards you as you lift it.

■ If the item to be moved is small or very thin, you can remove your index finger. This enables the fork to be pressed more tightly against the spoon, holding the item firmly. To release the item insert the tip of your index finger to separate the cutlery.

■ For large round items, such as bread rolls, you may turn the fork, enclosing the item (Fig. 8.3).

■ The tops of some items, broccoli hollandaise for example, must not be touched when they are served. In those cases turn your hand so that you can pick up the item from its sides.

Some waiters thread the fork through their fingers when using the cutlery for silver service. To the novice this may seem an easier and safer technique, but it has its limitations and is not recommended for professional service. It is much too slow, for example when several different items requiring different service cutlery have to be served quickly one after the other. Also it is difficult to apply when two knives are being used to serve (see 8.3, 8.7).

8.3 USE OF KNIVES FOR SERVICE

Two knives, preferably fish knives, are sometimes used for the service of soft or large items, for instance, a folded omelette, that requires more support than can be given by a service spoon and fork (Fig. 8.4).

■ Hold the two knives in the same fashion as a spoon and fork.

Fig. 8.4   Using fish knives for silver service.

- Fan out the knives to give greater support to the item you will be moving.
- Place the knives under the food item, supporting it while you transfer it to the guest's plate.

8.4   SILVER SERVICE OF BREAD ROLLS

- Hold the bread basket on the flat of your left hand.
- Silver service takes place from the left of the guest.
- Place your left hand low above the edge of the guest's sideplate (no more than 5cm above the plate).
- Pick up the bread roll with the service cutlery, and transfer it to the sideplate.
- Move anti-clockwise round the table, offering a bread roll to each guest.

8.5   SILVER SERVICE PROCEDURE – THE MAIN MEAL

- Place clean hot plates in front of the guests from the right from a stock carried in the left hand (Fig. 8.5).
- Hold the serving dish on a service cloth on the flat of your left hand, with your hand under the centre of the service dish.
- Calculate the size of the portion allowed for each guest, and decide how it should be presented, considering the other items to be served. (For example, two green vegetables may be separated by a white item, giving satisfactory visual balance.)
- As before noted, silver service takes place from the left of the guest. (From the right the service plate would present a barrier between the guest's plate and the waiter's right hand used for transferring the food items.)
- Hold the serving dish over the guest's plate, no more than 5cm above it.

Fig. 8.5   Place clean hot plates in front of each guest.

Fig. 8.6   When a food item is picked up from the serving dish the service cutlery is moving towards you.

Fig. 8.7   When the item is released on the guest's plate the service cutlery is moving away from you.

- Place the main item of the course to the front of the guest's plate.
- Place the vegetables around and behind the main item away from the guest in the pattern already decided for plate presentation.
- Note that no items are placed on the rim of the plate.
- Garnishes are placed to enhance the presentation.
- If you are serving small items such as Brussels sprouts, transfer a small number at a time. You can then position them carefully on the plate.
- Pick up food items on the side of the serving spoon closest to you (its left side) and release them from the same side of the spoon. When a food item is being picked up from the serving dish, the service cutlery is moving towards you (Fig. 8.6); when the item is released on the guest's plate the service cutlery is moving away from you (Fig. 8.7).
- Plate presentation should be consistent: the different food items in a dish should always be presented in the same pattern to all guests who have selected that dish.
- Move anti-clockwise round the table serving each guest in turn, with the host last.

8.6   SILVER SERVICE OF SAUCES

In silver service, accompanying sauces should not be carried on the same serving dish as the food. They are offered and served separately, using a sauce-boat (*saucière*) and a serving spoon or special ladle (Fig. 8.8). Sauces are never poured direct from the sauce-boat. A spoon (or ladle) is always used to serve them.

- Carry the sauce-boat on an underplate on the flat of your left hand, with the lip of the sauce-boat facing to the right.

Fig. 8.8 Silver service of sauces.

Fig. 8.9 Draw the spoon across the sauce-boat towards you to collect the sauce.

- Serve the sauce from the left of the guest.
- Lower the underplate over the guest's plate, so that it is not more than 5cm above it.
- Hold the serving spoon (or ladle) in your right hand with the handle of the spoon above the lip of the sauce-boat.
- Draw the spoon across the sauce-boat towards you to collect the sauce (Fig. 8.9).
- Carry the spoon away from you to sauce the appropriate item. Note that the sauce should only cover one third of the item.
- Other accompaniment items, such as mustard or apple sauce, are placed to the left of the main item.
- Move anti-clockwise round the table offering the sauce or accompaniment to each guest in turn, with the host last.

8.7 SILVER SERVICE OF DELICATE OR LARGE ITEMS

Two knives, preferably fish knives, are used to serve delicate or large items such as fillets of fish which are difficult to handle with a service spoon and fork.

- Two (fish) knives take the place of the service spoon and fork.
- Hold the knives in your right hand in the same way as a service spoon and fork, and fan them out (Fig. 8.10).
- Transfer the food item to the guest's plate with the fanned knives.
- Remove the knives when the food touches the plate.
- In addition to the knives, carry a set of ordinary service cutlery (a serving spoon and fork) on the serving dish to serve the vegetables and garnishes.

Fig. 8.10 Hold the knives in your right hand and fan them out.

8.8 QUESTIONS

(1) What is silver service?

(2) Which side of the guest do you stand for silver service?

(3) What is the professional way to hold the spoon and fork?

(4) How do you pick up small items of food?

(5) What sort of things are served with two fish knives instead of the usual service cutlery?

(6) Which way round the table do you move during silver service?

(7) In which direction should the cutlery be moving as you pick up food from the service plate?

(8) How would you plan the presentation of the food on the plate?

(9) How and when are sauces served in silver service?

(10) Where are other accompaniments placed?

9 . Clearing the Table

'Is this the same waiter who has been so helpful and knowledgeable?'

9.1 The same clearing techniques are used for both plate service and silver service. They rely on similar plate-carrying techniques; the two-plate and three-plate techniques already described (7.5 and 7.6).

On completing this chapter you should understand and have mastered:

- Clearing procedures
- Two-plate clearing technique
- Three-plate clearing technique
- Clearing sideplates
- Clearing soup bowls and oddly-shaped dishes.

9.2 CLEARING PROCEDURES

When the plates are cleared after a course it is usual for the whole table to be cleared at once when all the guests have finished. Guests usually indicate that they have finished by placing their cutlery together on the plate (Fig. 9.1). As they don't always do

Fig. 9.1 Clearing the table. These guests have indicated that they have finished by placing their knives and forks together on their plates.

this you must be alert to other signs from the table that everyone has finished, and if necessary you must ask guests about whom you are doubtful whether they have finished or not.

Once you have established that all the guests have finished the course, clear the plates using one of the following techniques.

9.3 TWO-PLATE CLEARING TECHNIQUE (Fig. 9.2)

- Start with the person to the right of the host.
- Standing at the back right-hand corner of the guest's chair, lean forward and pick up the used plate and cutlery with your right hand.
- Transfer the plate to your left hand, holding it between the thumb and index finger. Place your thumb over the end of the fork handle. Use the knife to move the left-overs to the front of the plate.
- Place the knife under the handle of the fork at right angles to it.
- Moving anti-clockwise round the table, place yourself behind the next guest. Holding your left hand (and the first guest's empty plate) behind the guest, lean forward and pick up the second used plate and its cutlery.
- Transfer the second plate to your left hand. Position it on a platform above the first plate, supporting it with your ring finger, your little finger and the base of your thumb and lower forearm.
- Place the fork alongside the other fork on the first plate, and, using the knife, push the left-overs down off the second plate onto the front of the first plate to join the scraps already there.
- Place the knife alongside the knife on the first plate.
- Moving anti-clockwise round the table, collect the remaining plates and cutlery. Stack the plates on the second plate and arrange the cutlery on the first plate, following the same procedure as for the second plate.
- The number of plates which can be collected in this way will depend on the waiter's skill and experience. When you have collected as many plates as you can confidently carry, take the plates and cutlery to the station (side-board) and place them on a tray for removal, or take them directly to the dish-washing area, according to the practice of the establishment.

Fig. 9.2 Two-plate clearing technique.

9.4 THREE-PLATE CLEARING TECHNIQUE (Fig. 9.3)

The three-plate clearing method is similar to the two-plate method, with the added advantage that the left-over food items and the used cutlery are carried on separate plates.

- Start with the person to the right of the host.
- Standing at the back right-hand corner of the guest's chair,

Fig. 9.3 Three-plate clearing technique.

Fig. 9.4 Clearing sideplates with dinner plates: two-plate technique.

lean forward and pick up the used plate and cutlery with your right hand.

■ Transfer the plate to your left hand, holding it between the thumb and index finger. Place your thumb over the end of the fork handle. Use the knife to move the left-overs to the front of the plate.

■ Place the knife under the handle of the fork at right angles to it.

■ Moving anti-clockwise round the table, place yourself behind the next guest. Holding your left hand (and the first guest's empty plate) behind the guest, lean forward and pick up the second used plate and its cutlery. (Up to this point the technique has been exactly the same as for the two-plate method.)

■ Place the second plate in the crease of the palm of your left hand under the edge of the first plate, supporting it by your ring and little fingers. Place the fork alongside the fork on the first plate, and using the knife, move the left-overs from the first plate down onto the second plate. Place the knife alongside the knife on the first plate.

■ Moving anti-clockwise round the table, pick up the next guest's used plate.

■ Place the third plate so that it sits on the flat of your forearm and the rim of the second plate. Place the fork alongside the forks on the first plate and use the knife to move the scraps onto the second plate. Place the knife alongside the other knives on the first plate.

■ Continue anti-clockwise, collecting the plates, stacking the additional plates on the third plate, transferring the scraps onto the second plate and placing the knives and forks neatly on the first plate.

■ When you have collected as many plates as you can confidently manage, take them to the station (or the dish-washing area).

9.5 CLEARING SIDEPLATES

Clearing sideplates at the same time as dinner plates
If there are only three or four guests at the table, the sideplates may be collected at the same time as the used dinner plates, using the two-plate or the three-plate technique. Continue anti-clockwise round the table a second time, collecting the sideplates and knives. If using the two-plate technique (Fig. 9.4) the procedure is:

■ Collect the sideplates and knives from the guests' left using your right hand.

■ Transfer the sideplate to the pile of empty plates supported by your left hand and arm, holding your left hand well away from the table.

Fig. 9.5 Clearing sideplates with dinner plates: three-plate technique.

Fig. 9.6 Clearing sideplates separately from dinner plates.

- Use the knife to move left-overs to the front of the first dinner plate.
- Place the knife on the first plate beside the other knives.
- Continue until all the sideplates have been collected and stacked on dinner plates.

If the three-plate clearing technique is used (Fig. 9.5) collect the knives and forks on the first plate and the scraps on the second plate, piling the sideplates on the cleared main course plates which are stacked on the third plate position.

9.6 *Clearing sideplates separately from dinner plates*

If there are more than four guests at the table, you will not be able to collect the sideplates at the same time as the dinner plates, but will have to collect them separately, using the two-plate method (Fig. 9.6).

- Take a dinner plate to the table. It will provide you with a conveniently larger working surface than a sideplate.
- Treat this plate as if it were the first dinner plate collected, and use it as the receptacle for scraps and the side knives.
- Proceed round the table anti-clockwise, collecting the sideplates and knives from the guests' left, as described above.

9.7 **SOUP BOWLS, COUPES, AND ODD-SHAPED SERVING DISHES (Fig. 9.7)**

Unusual and relatively difficult plates to carry, such as soup bowls, coupes, oval pasta dishes etc. will usually have been served on an underliner (see 7.7). As clean underliners are usually re-used they need not be stacked with the dirty dishes. They should therefore not be stacked but held separately from the used dishes, using the two-plate or three-plate carrying methods (9.3 and 9.4).

9.8 **QUESTIONS**

(1) How can you tell when all the guests have finished a course?
(2) Describe the two-plate clearing technique.
(3) Where should the dirty plates be held?
(4) How is the cutlery prevented from falling off the plate as it piles up?
(5) Describe the three-plate clearing technique.
(6) What is the advantage of the three-plate clearing technique?
(7) How many plates should you collect at once?
(8) What technique is used to collect sideplates at the same time as dinner plates?
(9) When should sideplates be collected separately from dinner plates?
(10) How should unusually shaped plates be collected?

Fig. 9.7 Clearing unusually shaped plates.

10 . Other Forms of Service

10.1 Apart from the basic table-service procedures – plate service and silver service – a waiter may encounter and be expected to be proficient in other specialist forms of service. Some of these are described in this chapter.

On completion of this chapter you will have a basic understanding of the techniques and procedures of:

- Soup service from a tureen or individual soup cup
- Guéridon service
- Family service
- Buffet service
- Cafeteria service.

No wonder the guests get confused at a buffet when the staff can't understand what they should be offering.

10.2 SOUP SERVICE FROM A SOUP CUP OR TUREEN

A tureen is a deep bowl with a lid to keep the contents warm. Individual soup cups or, for a number of people, one large tureen may be used as an alternative to the plate service of (pre-filled) soup bowls. Individual soup cups (occasionally with covers) may be offered in a silver service procedure, while service from a large tureen is best performed at a guéridon.

The use of a tureen ensures that the soup stays hot until it is served at table.

10.3 *Individual soup cups (Fig. 10.1)*
- Plate a hot empty soup bowl on an underliner for each guest from the guest's right.
- Carry a full individual soup cup on a service plate held on the flat of your left hand to the guest.
- Pour the soup from the cup into the guest's soup bowl, pouring away from the guest.
- If the soup contains items which cannot easily be poured, for example vegetables or noodles, carry a dessert spoon on the service plate and use it to spoon them into the soup.

Fig. 10.1 Silver service of soup from individual soup cups.

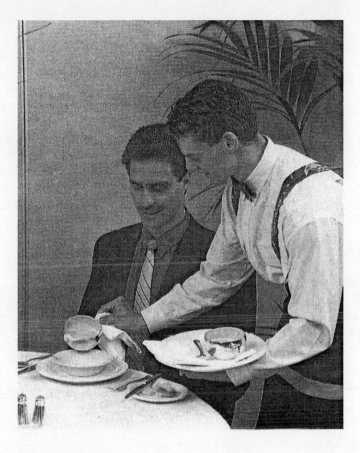

10.4 *Large tureens*

- Set a guéridon with hot soup bowls, underliners and a soup ladle, and place it near the table (see 10.5).
- Take the lid off the tureen and present the soup to the host.
- When the soup has been approved, place the open tureen on the guéridon.
- Hold a soup bowl on an underliner in the left hand, and use the right hand to ladle soup from the tureen into the bowl.
- Scoop the soup from the bottom of the tureen to ensure an even consistency.
- Place the soup bowls in front of the guests from each guest's right, using the usual plate service procedure.
- If the soup requires extra garnishing, serve the garnish from the left of the guest, using silver service procedure.

10.5 GUERIDON SERVICE

The term *guéridon* means a trolley (or side table) used for the service or preparation of foods in the dining environment.

Guéridon *service* specifically refers to the transfer of food from a serving dish to the plate on a guéridon. Guéridon *preparation* is the preparing or finishing of foods on the guéridon, for example table-cooking or the tossing of salads.

This section is concerned with guéridon service only. Guéridon preparation is dealt with in chapter 12.

10.6 *Guéridon service technique*

■ Set the guéridon with the appropriate mise-en-place for the service or preparation to be performed. It is essential that the mise-en-place is complete with all items before service begins. You should not leave the guéridon during service.

■ Place clean hot plates on the guéridon.

■ Present serving dishes containing the food prepared in the kitchen to the guests, and then place them on the guéridon.

■ At the guéridon use both hands to manage the service cutlery, holding the serving spoon in your right hand and the fork in your left.

■ Hold the spoon below the fork as you collect the food (Fig. 10.2).

■ Position the main item to the front of the plate, with the vegetables around and behind it, allowing some space between the different food items, as in silver service (see 8.5).

■ Sauces may be served at the guéridon or may be served at table, using the silver service technique.

■ Place the plated meals in front of the guests from their right, using the usual plate-service technique.

Fig. 10.2   Hold the spoon below the fork as you collect the food.

10.7 FAMILY SERVICE

Family service is a simple method of service in which serving dishes are placed on the dining table, allowing the guests to select and serve themselves. This style of service enables the guests to select only what they require and in appropriate portions.

Family service is often offered in addition to plate service. For example, the main item may be plate-served, and the guests left to help themselves to vegetables or salad.

10.8 *Family service technique*

■ Before serving plates are placed on the table you must make room on the table for them.

■ Using a service cloth, place clean hot plates from a stack in front of the guests from the guests' right.

■ Place the serving dishes on the table, each with a set of serving cutlery resting on the sides of the dishes.

■ The serving cutlery should be placed so that the handles face the nearest guest.

■ The serving dishes may be removed when they are empty at any time during the meal.

10.9 BUFFET SERVICE

In buffet service the food, hot or cold, is presented attractively on a separate table away from the guests and they come to the table to select what they require. Usually service staff serve the guests with the food they have selected, but sometimes buffets are arranged so that the guests can help themselves.

When service staff present the food they stand behind the buffet and assist the guests by plating their food for them as they select it. Silver service technique should be used for plating the food. Hold the guest's clean plate in your left hand and, using a serving spoon and fork held in your right hand, transfer the food items selected from the service plates to the guest's plate.

As in silver service at table you must carefully place the selected items on the plate so that it is visually well-balanced and convenient for the guest.

When the guests are helping themselves it is usual for them to select one course at a time and then come back for more. Food service staff should maintain the arrangement of the food on the service platters throughout service to ensure that the buffet is always attractively presented. They should also make sure there are plenty of plates and cutlery and that the guests have all they require including drinks.

10.10 CAFETERIA SERVICE

In cafeteria service guests collect their own meals on a tray as they select food items from the hot or cold counter. Modern food-hall operations often use this basic service technique.

Buffet and cafeteria waiting staff, like all other waiters, must have a good knowledge of the items they are serving.

10.11 QUESTIONS

(1) What is a tureen?

(2) How is soup served in individual cups?

(3) How is soup served from a large tureen?

(4) What is the difference between guéridon service and guéridon preparation?

(5) Describe guéridon service technique.

(6) How are the sauces served in guérudon service?

(7) What is family service?

(8) When should the serving dishes be removed during family service?

(9) What are the two different methods of buffet service?

(10) What is cafeteria service?

11 . Other Food Service Procedures

11.1 At various stages of the meal the waiter may be required
- to crumb (or brush) down the table
- to serve hot or cold towels
- to change ashtrays.

The necessary techniques and procedures for these services are detailed in this chapter.

The little touches make the difference.

11.2 CRUMBING/BRUSHING DOWN

Tables are usually crumbed down after the main course and sideplates have been cleared.

Although a variety of brush and pan sets are available for this purpose, the most commonly used equipment is a dinner plate and a folded service cloth (Fig. 11.1). This basic equipment is, of course, readily available in all styles of establishment.

11.3 *Use of service plate and cloth*

- Make sure the sideplates, cruets, and other items no longer required have been removed.
- Hold the plate on the flat of your left hand with your hand under the centre of the plate.
- Brush down from the guests' left (from where their sideplates were before they were cleared).
- Hold the plate just under the edge of the table with your left hand.
- Brush the crumbs onto the plate using a folded service cloth held in your right hand.
- Do not flick the crumbs, but brush them steadily towards you with the folded service cloth.
- Move anti-clockwise round the table crumbing down each guest's place as required, finishing with the host.

Fig. 11.1 Crumbing down.

11.4 SERVICE OF HOT OR COLD TOWELS

Hot or cold towels or flannels are sometimes offered to the guests – often in Indian and Chinese restaurants, for instance – for them to refresh themselves either before or after the meal. The towels are moistened and lightly sprayed with a cologne. They often come individually wrapped in plastic.

Whether the towels are hot or cold is likely to depend on the climatic conditions. Moistened and slightly scented towels, either hot or cold, provide a refreshing start or finish to the dining experience.

11.5 *The technique of serving towels*

- Stack the towels on a serving tray together with a set of tongs or service cutlery for service.
- Carry the tray of towels on the flat of your left hand.
- Offer the towels from the guests' right.
- Move anti-clockwise round the table offering towels to each of the guests, with the host last.
- Place the serving tray on the centre of the table so that the guests can put their towels on it after they have finished with them.
- Remove the tray with the used towels on it.

11.6 ASHTRAYS

Many restaurants now have smoking and non-smoking areas, and in some no smoking is allowed. The correct procedure for laying and handling ashtrays will therefore depend on the rules of the establishment.

In some establishments ashtrays are not placed on the tables before service begins as part of the mise-en-place but are only brought when they are requested by guests. When this is so the waiter must be observant so that ashtrays are brought immediately they are required.

It is the responsibility of all waiting staff to ensure that used ashtrays are removed and cleaned frequently and that clean ashtrays are always available to smokers.

11.7 *Changing ashtrays*

Waiting staff should make regular rounds of the service area, clearing used ashtrays and replacing them with clean ones. Never remove an ashtray unless a clean one is available to replace the one removed.

The procedure for changing ashtrays (Fig. 11.2) is the same whether serving at table or at the bar. When clearing a used ashtray it must first be covered to avoid the possibility of spilling ash on the table or the bar. When the dirty ashtray has been covered and removed, replace it immediately with a clean one.

- Hold a clean ashtray in your right hand and place it over the dirty ashtray.
- Remove the two ashtrays together using the one hand.
- Transfer the dirty ashtray to your left hand.
- Use your right hand to place a clean ashtray the right way up where the dirty one was.

Fig. 11.2 Changing ashtrays.

Dirty ashtrays should be held in the left hand or on a service tray well away from the guests.

11.8 QUESTIONS

(1) When are tables usually crumbed down?
(2) How is a table crumbed down using a service cloth and plate?
(3) What is the technique used to serve towels?
(4) How can an ashtray be changed without any danger of the contents spilling on the table?

12 . The Use of the Guéridon

Is there any reason why the use of a guéridon should suggest to guests that the restaurant is expensive? Or why the term should suggest a lot of extra work and extraordinary skills to waiters?

In fact the guéridon can be used effectively in a simple way and without much expense to give guests a 'visual' of the fare. A guéridon allows waiters to demonstrate a greater versatility in their service style.

12.1 Most people imagine that the term *guéridon* refers to table cooking as demonstrated in fine dining-rooms. In fact the guéridon is simply a piece of equipment on which we serve or prepare food in the dining environment.

In this chapter we shall show the basic uses of the guéridon as a simple means of offering appropriate services to guests, and greater profitability to the establishment.

On completion of this chapter you should have a basic understanding of:

- The definition of the guéridon and the uses to which it is put
- The use of the guéridon as an aid to making sales
- The selection of food for the guéridon
- Guéridon mise-en-place
- Guéridon food preparation techniques – tossing, cooking, boning, carving
- Guéridon preparation of liqueur coffees.

12.2 THE GUERIDON AND ITS USES

A guéridon is simply a trolley or side table used for the service or preparation of food in the dining-room.

A guéridon can be an elaborate piece of moveable furniture on castors made from exquisite timbers and provided with expensive build-in cooking equipment and silver fittings. Or it can simply be an ordinary small dining table.

As we have seen, guéridon *service* means no more than the transfer of food from a serving dish to a plate on a side table or trolley in the presence of the guests (see 10.5 and 10.6).

Guéridon *preparation* is the preparing or finishing of food on the guéridon.

12.3 THE GUERIDON AS A SALES AID

The guéridon can be used most effectively as an aid to sales. The display of food on a guéridon and the preparation of food in the presence of guests, rightly used, can be powerful generators of extra sales. At its simplest the guéridon can be used to display or to prepare:

- Hors d'oeuvres
- Salads
- Bakery items
- Desserts
- Fresh fruit.

12.4 FOOD SELECTION AND PRESENTATION

Food selection

When selecting food for display or preparation on the guéridon remember that the foodstuffs chosen should:

- Be prepared and kept hygienically according to the food hygiene regulations
- Be fresh and visually attractive
- Not discolour or break down easily
- Be simple to prepare and require a minimum of cooking time
- Maintain their quality in spite of the limited preparation or cooking time
- Not produce unpleasant smells or other offensive effects when they are prepared or cooked.

12.5 Salads

Some key points to consider when preparing salads on the guéridon are:

- Thoroughly clean salad items and drain them in the kitchen before they are brought to the guéridon
- Ensure that your hands are clean before touching the food.
- Prepare items in bite-size portions.
- Keep items chilled until they are needed for use.
- The salad dressing may be prepared either in the kitchen or on the guéridon.
- Salad items and the dressing should be tossed at the guéridon at the time of service.

12.6 Meat

Key points when selecting and preparing meat for the guéridon are:

- Select a product of premium quality.
- Remove all fat and sinews.
- Trim portions, allowing for one-minute cooking time.
- Keep prepared items chilled, ready for use.
- Seal meat items to conserve the juices.
- Complete the cooking in the minimum amount of time.

12.7 Fruit

Key points for consideration when preparing fruit for the guéridon are:

- Clean and portion the fruit.
- Take special care that fruits which may become discoloured when peeled or cut are kept in an appropriate juice to discourage discoloration.
- Keep prepared fruit chilled until it is needed for use.
- Avoid cooking fruit beyond the point at which it breaks down, taking special care of berries and soft fruit which break down easily.

12.8 GUERIDON MISE-EN-PLACE

To avoid any delay or confusion when preparing dishes at the guéridon in front of guests it is essential that the preparation (mise-en-place) of the guéridon should be complete.

The mise-en-place includes both the equipment used to prepare the food and the equipment needed to serve it, as well as the products required to create the dish.

12.9 VARIATION OF RECIPES

The recipes used in cooking at the guéridon may vary in detail from one establishment to another, but the essentials of the classic receipts must be maintained to ensure that they are clearly identifiable to the guest. For example, a Caesar salad always includes lettuce, eggs, anchovies, crisp diced bacon, and croûtons, but Parmesan cheese is optional, and the eggs may or may not be cooked.

New dishes can be created for preparation at the guéridon to suit the establishment's menu, but they must of course follow the basic rules for the selection and preparation of foods.

12.10 GUERIDON FOOD PREPARATION TECHNIQUES

The following food preparation procedures are appropriate for use at the guéridon, and will enhance guests' enjoyment of their meals and tempt others to try the same items.

12.11 *Tossing*

Salads, seafoods and fruit are often suitable for tossing in front of the guests as they can be simply prepared and will tempt others to order some for themselves.

The main ingredient may be displayed in its natural state and then tossed with previously prepared sauces, dressing or liqueurs.

If the sauces or dressings are prepared at the guéridon then their preparation must be completed before the main item is added and tossed.

12.12 *Cooking*

Major considerations when cooking on the guéridon are:
- choosing the appropriate cooking medium, for example clarified butter or cooking oil

Fig. 12.1   An inexpensive modern cooking lamp.

- the length of cooking time
- the ability to create the appropriate flavours in a minimum of time.

The majority of items cooked on the guéridon lend themselves to the additional effect of flaming (*flambé* work).

Table cooking no longer requires expensive cooking lamps, or guéridons with inbuilt cooking equipment, as a range of good but inexpensive table-top gas-cylinder cookers is now available. An example is shown in Fig. 12.1.

12.13   *Flambé work*

Flambé work involves lighting liquor (usually a spirit or liqueur) in a pan at the guéridon.

The procedure is:

- Light the cooking lamp.
- Pour the required quantity of the liquor into the pan (Fig. 12.2).
- Cover the lamp's flame completely with the pan.
- Leave the liquor to warm in the pan while you place the bottle of liquor well away from the flame.
- Move the pan back towards you, tilting it *away* from you (Fig. 12.3) until the liquor just comes into contact with the flame and ignites.
- As soon as the liquor is alight, lift the pan slightly and move it gently in a circular motion so that the flames move around the pan.
- When igniting the liquor hold your body upright. Do not bend your head and shoulders over the pan – flames can flare up unexpectedly.

Fig. 12.2   Pour the required quantity of liquor into the pan.

12.14   *Safety in guéridon cooking*

Cooking at the guéridon, particularly flambé work, obviously has its dangers because it involves naked flames in the dining-room, and fuel for those flames. Special precautions are therefore necessary.

- Regular checks of the cooking lamps and gas bottles will ensure that potential faults, in particular loose fittings or leaks, will be detected before the faults become dangerous.
- A fire blanket and a small hand-held extinguisher should be kept easily accessible, in a place well-known to all the waiting staff.
- When preparing to use the guéridon, position it at a sufficient distance from the guests' table to make sure that there can be no danger to the guests. The guéridon should be at least its own width away from the table. This has the added advantage that service can take place round the table without the guéridon getting in the way of the waiters.

Fig. 12.3   Tilt the pan away from you.

12.15 *Maintenance of cooking lamps*

■ Lamps should be stripped down and all parts cleaned regularly.
■ After cleaning always check that lamps work as soon as they are reassembled.
■ Gas bottles must never be replaced near a naked flame.
■ Always check bottles for leaks.
■ On spirit lamps always check the length of the wick and make sure it is trimmed.
■ Never check the spirit level in the reservoir near a naked flame.
■ Do not overfill the lamp.
■ Take care to wipe up immediately any spirit which may have been spilled.
■ Untrained staff must never use a cooking lamp.

12.16 *Boning*

If there is a side table or trolley the waiter can use it for boning meat and fish for guests in their presence. Fine dining rooms, employing staff with the necessary skills, are often able to offer a range of menu choices requiring this form of guéridon technique.

The technique is most commonly used when guests are offered the service of having their (already-cooked) fish boned for them (see Fig. 12.5).

12.17 *Carving*

The carving of the joint, poultry or game at the table was for centuries a traditional part of the dining experience. Nowadays, in restaurants when the carving is done in the presence of the guests, it is usually performed at a special carvery or, where there is one, on an elaborate beef trolley (Figs 12.4 and 12.6), rather than on an

Fig. 12.4 Carving trolley.

Fig. 12.5 Boning fish (courtesy Graham Brown and Karon Hepner).

Fig. 12.6 Carving at the trolley.

ordinary guéridon. The disadvantage of carving in front of the guests is that portion control is more difficult.

12.18 *Liqueur coffee*

Liqueur coffees are often prepared in front of guests on a guéridon because the process is visually interesting and provides an exciting finale to the dining experience. The technique of preparing liqueur coffees is explained later (15.25 and 15.26).

12.19 QUESTIONS

(1) How can use of the guéridon help sales?
(2) What six considerations should be borne in mind when selecting food for preparation on the guéridon?
(3) At what point should a salad be tossed if it is done at the guéridon?
(4) Why do meat portions have to be small for cooking at the guéridon?
(5) How can you prevent fruit from becoming discoloured?

(6) Why is it especially important that the mise-en-place is complete before cooking on the guéridon begins?
(7) What is the procedure for tossing a salad at the guéridon?
(8) What is the correct procedure for flambé work?
(9) What are three safety points to bear in mind when working at the guéridon?
(10) How would you bone a fish?

13 . Beverage Equipment and Service Knowledge

Our guests come expecting a pleasant and satisfying dining experience. All too often the expectations built up by an exciting menu, and all the good work of the chef in the preparation and presentation of the food and the good service of the food by the waiter, are thrown away by a lack of professionalism in the preparation and service of the drinks.

13.1 Beverages are as important as the food in the dining experience, and they should therefore be given as careful attention as the food when they are being prepared and served.

On completion of this chapter you should have a basic understanding of the following:

- Beverage equipment identification
- Equipment preparation and maintenance
- Beverage lists
- The handling and placement of equipment
- The co-ordination of food and beverage service.

13.2 ## BEVERAGE EQUIPMENT IDENTIFICATION

The service of beverages requires a wide range of equipment. The types of equipment used will vary depending on the tasks to be performed and the type of establishment. A waiter should be familiar with the full range of commonly-used equipment, including all the equipment described in this chapter.

13.3 ### Glassware

There is now an enormous range of commercial glassware available so that food outlets from the simplest to the most traditional and expensive can choose glassware to suit all their particular needs.

When selecting glassware, management will take various factors into account, such as size, shape, ease of handling and washing, durability, and price. The glassware selected should, of course, be appropriate to the style of the establishment and its menu.

While the designs of the glassware available vary considerably from manufacturer to manufacturer, there are standard basic shapes which identify the glasses as belonging to the various classical types (see Fig. 13.1).

13.4 *Service equipment*

Many specialist devices and types of equipment have been produced over the years to help the waiter with the extraction of corks, the carrying of drinks and the cooling of beverages. The 'waiter's friend' (Fig. 13.2) is the recognized device used by waiters to extract corks.

How these pieces of equipment are used is explained in chapter 15.

13.5 PREPARATION AND MAINTENANCE OF EQUIPMENT

The exact procedures to be adopted for the service of beverages will depend on the type of establishment, the styles of service offered, and the availability of service station areas.

Pre-service duties will include cleaning and polishing the necessary glassware, service station mise-en-place, preparation of ice buckets, and the handling and placing of equipment.

13.6 *Cleaning and polishing glassware*

Even when glasses are hygienically washed and sterilized by the high temperature of the washing cycle in a commercial dishwasher, it is still necessary to polish all glassware by hand before it is placed on the table or used to serve drinks. A lint-free polishing cloth should be used to polish glasses and make sure they are spotlessly clear.

13.7 *Service station mise-en-place*

Efficient service requires careful prior preparation of the service equipment. In some establishments this is done on a special piece of furniture in the dining-room known as the drink waiter's station. Often space does not allow this and a service station must be established behind the scenes; commonly the bar is used.

Here is a check-list of supplies and equipment that may be required for beverage service:

- Additional glassware
- Drinks trays
- Wine lists
- Table-napkins
- Straws
- Toothpicks (hygienically wrapped)
- Matches
- Ashtrays
- Service cloths
- Docket book
- Wine coolers
- Ice buckets.

Fig. 13.1 Standard glassware.

Cocktail glass

Worthington
(fruit squash) glass

Wellington

Colada

Highball

Old fashioned

Balloon

Copita

Elgin sherry glass

Port

Thistle

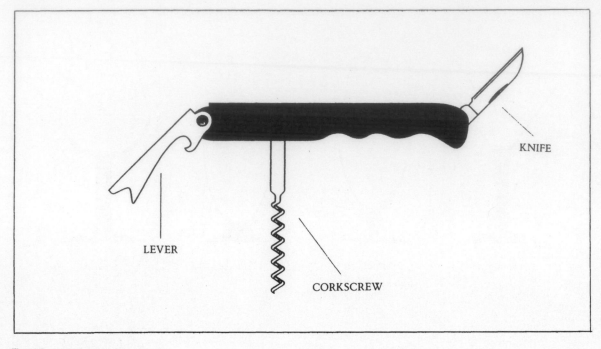

Fig. 13.2 Waiter's friend (open).

13.8 *Wine coolers and ice buckets*

Ice buckets are used to keep wine and sparkling wines cool in more formal and usually more expensive restaurants, while simple insulated wine coolers, sometimes placed on the table, are used in less formal establishments.

Ice buckets, when required for use, should be half filled with a mixture of crushed ice (two-thirds) and cold water (one-third). The water allows the bottle to sink into the ice instead of balancing on top of it. The bucket may be placed in a tripod stand.

13.9 **BEVERAGE LISTS**

Beverage lists come in many different formats (Fig. 13.3). Sometimes a so-called 'wine list' will contain the entire range of beverages available. This format can be extremely confusing for the guest. A better solution is to divide the various different types of beverage into separate lists. This helps guests to find and select the beverages they require more speedily. Possible lists may include:

- Cocktail list
- Drinks list (includes apéritifs, beers, spirits and non-alcoholic drinks)
- Wine list
- After-dinner drinks list (liqueurs, ports, brandies)
- Liqueur coffee list.

Fig. 13.3 A brief extract from a wine and beverage list.

Bin No	HOUSE SELECTION	Price Per Bottle
	CHAMPAGNE	
1	De Venoge, Cuvee Louis Dornier NV *Brut* *Fresh, light and crisp, the high proportion of the red Pinot Noir grapes in the blend give this champagne its rich, full style.*	£28.50
	WHITE	
2	Reynier Blanc *Antonin Rodet* *Blended in the classic Burgundian style, this wine has a light, fragrant bouquet and plenty of fruit, giving a clean, soft and rich flavour.*	£15.00
	RED	
3	Reynier Rouge *Antonin Rodet* *This red wine has rich raspberry fruit with the fuller, earthy characteristics reminiscent of a good Burgundy.*	£15.00
	NON VINTAGE CHAMPAGNE	
4	Moet et Chandon NV *Brut Imperial* *This champagne is pale straw in colour, with a fine mousse and a slight appley, yeasty nose. It is almost lemony on the palate with good length.*	£41.00
8	Laurent Perrier Rose NV *Brut* *Blended only from the wines of selected years, this dry rose champagne has a fresh ripe nose, with good fruit and a lively mousse. Very refreshing and a delightful colour.*	£65.00
	VINTAGE & PRESTIGE CHAMPAGNE	
9	Veuve Cliquot 1983 *Brut* *A mouthfilling and weighty champagne displaying great finesse. The ripeness of the grapes gives this wine great length.*	£75.00
11	Louis Roederer Cristal 1983/85 *A light, delicate champagne, soft with elegant fruit. In the traditional clear crystal bottle.*	£155.00
	WHITE BORDEAUX	
14	Chateau Magneau 1989/90 *Graves* *A smooth, crisp, dry white wine with soft, ripe, gooseberry fruit overtones.*	£18.00
15	Chateau Boyrein 1990 *Graves* *Dry with full flavour and pleasant rich finish.*	£21.00
	LOW ALCOHOL	
92	Masson Light (0.49% vol) *This light, clean tasting, de-alcoholised white wine has a pleasing freshness and can be enjoyed any time.*	£8.00
	MINERAL WATER	
	Tynant Original *Still or Carbonated*	£3.00

13.10 *The wine list*

Wine lists are usually divided into wines of different types, for example:

- White table wines
- Red table wines
- Champagne and sparkling wines
- Dessert wines.

See Fig. 13.3 and sections 14.3–14.6.

13.11 HANDLING AND PLACEMENT OF EQUIPMENT

In order to ensure good hygiene presentation it is essential that all glassware should be handled by the stem or base of the glass. When glasses are being moved in the presence of guests they should always be carried on a beverage tray (Fig. 13.4). Before the guests' arrival, when the tables are being laid, several glasses may be held upside down in one hand with their stems between one's fingers (Fig. 13.5).

Fig. 13.4 Carrying glasses in the presence of guests.

13.12 *Placing of glasses*

If a single glass is being laid at a dining table it should be placed 2.5cm above the main knife. If more than one glass is placed on the table, the glasses are positioned in a line at an angle of 45° in the order in which they will be required. See 4.11 and 4.14.

13.13 FOOD AND BEVERAGE CO-ORDINATION

Regardless of whether the establishment has decided to employ a specialist wine waiter, or to make all its waiters responsible for both food and beverage service, it is essential that the service of the food and the beverages should be co-ordinated.

The food waiter and the wine waiter must communicate if they are to provide a co-ordinated sequential service. The sequence of service requires both food and beverages to be served at the appropriate times throughout the meal without interfering with each other.

Fig. 13.5 Carrying glasses before the guests' arrival.

13.14 *Key points in food and beverage service co-ordination*

- Before the menu is presented guests are offered an apéritif (pre-dinner drink) to stimulate the appetite.
- Because the wines are selected to complement the food chosen, the wine list is usually presented after the food order has been taken.

- The wine selected to accompany each course is served just prior to the food in that course. It is usual to serve white wines before red, dry wines before sweet, young wines before old – but what wines are chosen and in what order is, of course, up to the guest; the 'right' wine is what the guest wants.
- Remind guests that dessert wines are available when the desserts are being ordered. Dessert wines are sweet, and complement sweet dishes.
- Orders for after-dinner alcoholic beverages are taken before coffee is served. This allows the coffee and other after-dinner drinks, such as port, cognac or liqueurs, to be served at the same time.

13.15 QUESTIONS

(1) What factors are taken into account when purchasing glassware?

(2) What three different shaped glasses are commonly used for beer?

(3) What sort of drink is a worthington glass commonly used for?

(4) What items should you check for when doing service-station mise-en-place?

(5) What proportions of ice and water go in an ice bucket?

(6) How are wines usually divided on a wine list?

(7) How should glasses be handled?

(8) Why is the wine list usually presented after the food order has been taken?

(9) What is the usual sequence of serving different types of wine?

(10) When can this sequence be broken?

14 . Beverage Product Knowledge

You may think that a bright personality and the ability to open a bottle of wine or beer is enough to make you a good drinks waiter, but without a basic knowledge of products, the job can only be half done.

Guests rely on us to assist them in making their selections and in educating them in their appreciation of wine and other beverages.

14.1 You cannot be a competent drinks waiter without a basic knowledge of the products you are selling and serving. This chapter lists and defines the various categories of beverages.

On completion of this chapter you should have a basic understanding of the following:

- Apéritifs
- Table wines
- Dessert wines
- Fortified wines
- Champagnes and sparkling wines
- Spirits
- Beers
- Liqueurs
- Cocktails
- Non-alcoholic beverages
- Aerated waters.

More information on particular beverage items may be found in the Glossary.

14.2 ## APERITIFS

An apéritif is a pre-dinner drink taken to stimulate the appetite. Most apéritifs are dry to taste because dry beverages stimulate the appetite, while sweet drinks tend to dull the appetite. In spite of this some guests may prefer to drink a sweet drink, such as a sweet sherry, before a meal as an apéritif.

A good waiter will never make guests feel uncomfortable because of the drinks they have chosen, no matter how inappropriate they may seem. Popular apéritifs include:

- dry champagne
- pre-dinner cocktails (acidic or dry rather than creamy)
- dry sherry
- dry ('French') vermouth
- a proprietary apéritif (for example, Campari, Fernet Branca, Dubonnet).

14.3 WINE

The term 'wine' indicates a type of beverage made from fermented fruit. Wine may be made from a variety of fruits, but wine as we generally know it is made from the fermented juice of grapes. When another fruit is used to produce the wine, the name of the fruit used is included on the label, for example 'strawberry wine'.

As a general rule red wine is made from 'black' (actually purple) grapes, while white wine is made from 'white' (actually green) grapes. Rosé wine, which is pink (rosé) is made from black grapes, but the skins of the grapes are removed early in the process of fermentation.

Traditionally, wine comes from Europe and the countries bordering the Mediterranean, with French wines being, perhaps, the most famous. However, good wines are produced all over the world wherever the soil and climate are favourable to grape growing. The main wine-producing countries are:

- European: France, Germany, Italy, Spain, Bulgaria, Austria, Hungary, Portugal, Greece, Romania.
- Non-European: Australia, New Zealand, North America (especially California), South America (especially Argentina and Chile) and South Africa.

Wine is produced in the UK, but the industry will never be very large here because the climate is not ideal for grape growing.

As a general rule red wines should be served at 'room temperature' (about 18°) and white wines should be served mildly chilled (about 6°C).

14.4 *Choosing wines*

The variety of different types of wine is extensive, and you will find that your guests often have strong preference, sometimes based on knowledge and sometimes not. You should never embarrass guests by criticizing their choice. It is their right to drink what they like, whatever the convention. However, when your advice is asked it is important that you have a good general knowledge of wine and of the wine list in your establishment so that you can help your guests to make a suitable choice.

Many wines, especially European wines, are described according to the region where the grapes are grown. France has many famous wine regions, for example, Burgundy, Bordeaux and Beaujolais; German examples are Rhine and Mosel wines. Wine from outside Europe is often described by the variety of the grape rather than the region of origin and grape variety has a strong influence on the character of the wine. Some famous grape varieties are:

- Chardonnay – full-flavoured, dry
- Riesling – delicate, crisp, fruit-flavoured
- Traminer – fruity, spicy

- Cabarnet sauvignon – dry
- Pinot noir – light, soft
- Gamay – fruity, light
- Shiraz – robust.

Wine producers often blend the different varieties to produce their own distinctive wines.

There are many traditions governing what wines are suited to various foods but the choice of which wine to drink with food is purely a personal one. If the client asks for advice in the choice of wine the sommelier should ask whether the customer prefers red, white or rosé, and whether sweet or dry. The sommelier can then base his recommendation around this. Figure 14.1 sets out examples of suitable wines for a range of dishes.

Food	Example of wine	Type
Hors d'oeuvre		
Smoked salmon	Muscadet	Medium dry white
Charentaise melon	Alsace Riesling	Light fruity white
Oysters	Champagne	Sparkling white
Fish		
Grilled sole	Chablis	Dry white
Poached salmon	Montagny Premier Cru	Dry white
Trout (pan fried)	Macon Villages	Dry white
Lobster	Pouilly Fuissé	Medium dry white
Farinaceous		
Pasta (no sauce)	Orvieto Classico Secco	Crisp white
Lasagne or pasta with a meat sauce	Chianti Classico	Full red
White meat, poultry	Moselle wines, Piesporter, Hock, Niersteiner, Australian Chardonay	Medium white
	Rosé d'Anjou	Rosé
Roast/grills	Nuits St Georges	Full red
	Médoc	Full red
Braised meats/stews	Chateauneuf du Pape	Rich red
	Burgundy	Rich red
	Julienas	Rich red
Sweets	Muscat de Beaumes de Venise	Heavy sweet white
	Champagne	Sparkling white
	Sauternes	Rich sweet white
Cheese		
Mild flavour	Port or Beaujolais Villages	Light red
Strong flavour	Port of Médoc	Full red

Fig. 14.1 Examples of suitable wines for various types of dishes.

14.5 *Wine quality*

The quality of wine is strictly controlled by law, though there are differences between the various wine-producing countries.

In France the *Appellation d'origine contrôlee* (AOC) specifies that wines must carry a label detailing their place of origin. The better the quality of the wine the more detailed the information on the label is. Thus the labels on ordinary table wines contain the name of the region; those on superior wines detail the name of the commune (French for parish) and the labels on the best wines give the name of the particular vineyard where the wine was produced. AOC also governs such factors as the precise area where the grapes may be grown, the types of vines that can be used and the levels of alcohol and sugar in the finished wine. If any of these conditions are not fulfilled the wine grower is not permitted to use the particular label for the wine.

The Germans and Italians have systems similar to the French appellation contrôlée. The German system is called *Qualitätswein mit Prädikat* (QMP) and the Italian system is called *Denominazione di origine controllata* (DOC).

Another way to tell the quality of wine is by its vintage. In years when the weather conditions are especially favourable to grape growing, the wine produced is superior. The wines produced in these years are known as vintage wines.

14.6 DESSERT WINES

Dessert wines are rich and sweet. They are designed to be consumed with sweet food items. Sauternes is a famous white dessert wine. Spätleses and ausleses are German styles of dessert wine.

14.7 FORTIFIED WINES

A fortified wine is a wine strengthened with the addition of spirit. The spirit also preserves the wine for longer periods after the bottle is opened. Fortified wines include sherry, vermouth, muscat and port.

There are various different styles of sherry, ranging from very sweet sherries to extremely dry. The sherries taken with a meal are usually dry. They are used as apéritifs or taken with soup.

Vermouths come in three main styles: rosso, bianco and dry. Rosso vermouth, sometimes called 'Italian', is light red, sweet and strong-tasting. Bianco is light golden, medium sweet, and spicy. Dry or 'French' vermouth is almost colourless and has a delicate flavour.

Ports come in several styles: ruby, tawny, and vintage. Ruby ports are the youngest and least rich. Vintage ports mature in the bottle and develop a sediment. They should therefore be decanted before they are served. Almost all ports are red wines, but there are white ports.

14.8 CHAMPAGNE AND OTHER SPARKLING WINES

Sparkling wines get their sparkle or effervescence from carbon dioxide. Carbon dioxide is produced naturally in the process of fermentation and can be retained to produce a sparkling wine.

Champagne is a region of France renowned for its sparkling wine, known as champagne. Champagne is made by a complex process called the *méthode champenoise* or champagne method. The most important feature of the méthode champenoise is that fermentation takes place in the bottle. Some other sparkling wines ferment in vats and are bottled later.

French champagnes are made from a blend of grapes, usually pinot noir (black) and chardonnay (white) grapes. Meunier, a grape variety similar to pinot noir, is also used.

In Europe only champagnes produced in the Champagne district by the méthode champenoise can be called champagne. If natural fermentation in a vat produces the sparkle, it can be called a 'sparkling wine' but if the carbon dioxide is injected into the wine it becomes a 'carbonated wine'.

The styles of sparkling wine include:

- Brut   dry
- Sec   medium dry
- Demi-sec   medium sweet
- Doux   sweet

The dry styles are much more popular than the sweet.

Champagne is sold in a variety of bottle sizes, each with a special name. The most common are:

- Magnum   two ordinary bottles
- Jeroboam   four ordinary bottles

The other large bottle sizes are listed in the Glossary (see champagne bottle sizes).

14.9 SPIRITS

Spirits are distilled alcoholic beverages. Distillation is the process of converting liquid into vapour by heating, and then condensing the vapour back to liquid form. Almost any fruit or vegetable can be crushed to liquid, fermented, and then distilled to make a spirit.

These are the most popular spirits, and their base ingredients:

Spirit	Base
Whisky	Grain (barley, wheat and maize)
Gin	Neutral spirit made from grain and then flavoured with juniper berries
Rum	Sugar cane
Vodka	Potatoes or grain
Brandy	Grapes

Scotch is the most popular kind of whisky. Bourbon is an American whisky made from maize. Cognac and armagnac are high-quality French brandies.

14.10 BEER

Beer is made from fermented grain by the process called brewing. The traditional ingredients are malt (barley soaked to germinate and then dried), yeast, hops and water. Beer is the general term for ales, lagers and stout. Ales and lagers are made by different techniques of fermentation: ales are top-fermented whereas lagers are bottom-fermented. In general lagers are paler and more highly-carbonated then ales. Stout is a dark heavy beer. Guinness is a kind of stout. Draught beer is beer drawn from a barrel, rather than bottled or canned.

14.11 *Service of beer*

Beer may be served from one of the following:

Pump (manual). This is the traditional way of serving beer from a cask. Special care is needed to make sure the beer is in good condition.

Free flow. This method is used with keg beers, a carbon dioxide cylinder is connected to the keg and the gas forces the beer to the tap.

Meters. These are also used with keg beers. They are sealed pumps which dispense beer in half pints.

Traditionally British beer is served at a temperature of 13–15°C. However, today many beers are served chilled.

Draught beer is often passed through a cooler before service. Keg beer pipes pass through a cooler to keep the temperature constant at 9–10°C for lagers and 13°C for bitters.

To maintain the quality of beer it is essential that all equipment is clean. A special pipe cleaning kit is provided by the supplier. This consists of a plastic bottle containing water or a diluted cleaning fluid which is pumped through the pipes flushing them clean. This should be done regularly.

Draught beer should be served with a small head. This can be achieved by tipping the glass at an angle when filling and levelling the glass when the desired amount has been poured. The same can be achieved with bottle beer by pouring slowly against the inside of the glass. The neck of the bottle must not come into contact

Container	Quantity (gallons)	(litres)
Pin	4½	20.457
Firkin	9	40.914
Kilderkin	18	81.828
Barrel	36	163.656
Hogshead	54	245.484
Keg	10	45.46

Fig. 14.2 Standard beer quantities.

Bloody Mary

Ingredients	Amount per drink
Vodka	1 × 3 out ($\frac{1}{6}$ gill)
Lemon juice	$\frac{1}{2}$ × 6 out ($\frac{1}{6}$ gill)
Tomato juice	4 ozs.
Tabasco sauce	1 dash
Worcester sauce	2 dashes
Salt and pepper	2 dashes each
Lemon segment	about $\frac{1}{6}$ lemon
Ice cubes	4–6 cubes

Method of preparation

Into an 8oz highball glass place ice cubes, cold vodka, fresh lemon, Tabasco, Worcester, salt and pepper. Top up with tomato juice. Stir.

Method of preparation

Into a shaker three-quarters filled with cubed ice pour Brandy, Crème de Cacao and cream. Shake well and strain into a small cocktail glass and add a sprinkle of nutmeg on top.

Brandy Alexander

Ingredients	Amount per drink
Brandy	1 × 6 out ($\frac{1}{6}$ gill)
Crème de Cacao (brown)	1 × 6 out ($\frac{1}{6}$ gill)
Cream	1 × 6 out ($\frac{1}{6}$ gill)
Nutmeg (ground)	Sprinkle

Method of preparation

Into a bar glass 3/4-filled with cubed ice pour Vermouth and gin, stir briskly and strain into small cocktail glass. Can also be served on the rocks in old fashioned glass.

Dry Martini

Ingredients	Amount per drink
Gin	2$\frac{1}{2}$ × 6 out
Vermouth (dry)	2 dashes
Olive	1
Stick	1

Fig. 14.3   Famous cocktails: Brandy Alexander; Bloody Mary; Tom Collins; Zombie; Dry Martini.

Tom Collins

Ingredients	Amount per drink
Gin	1 × 3 out
Lemon juice	1 × 3 out
Sugar syrup	1 × 6 out
Soda water	4 ozs
Ice	5 - 6 cubes
Angostura	2 dashes
Lemon slice	1
Cherry	1
Stick and stirrer	1 each
Straws	2

Method of preparation

Into a 12 oz highball glass place ice cubes, then add gin, lemon juice and sugar syrup, stir, then top up with soda water. Stir, add lemon slice and cherry on stick across top of glass, pouring 2 dashes of angostura over lemon slice.

Method of preparation

Mix in bar glass with cubed ice. Stir well and pour over cracked ice in 12 oz highball glass. Decorate with orange and lemon slice, pineapple chunk and cherry on long stick.

Zombie

Ingredients	Amount per drink
Rum Jamaica	1 × 6 out
Rum Puerto Rican	2 × 6 out
Rum 151° Proof	½ × 6 out
Orange Curacao	1 × 6 out
Lemon Juice	1 × 6 out
Orange Juice	1 × 6 out
Grenadine	1 × 6 out
Pernod	½ × 6 out
Orange slice, lemon slice, pineapple chunk, cherry	1 dash / 1 of each
Stick	
Straws	1
Cracked ice	2

with the beer. If the beer has a sediment a little beer must be left in the bottle to prevent the sediment going into the glass.

The standard beer quantities are shown in Fig. 14.2.

14.12 LIQUEURS

Liqueurs are spirit-based (or sometimes wine-based) liquors, sweetened and flavoured. They have been made for centuries and new ones are being devised all the time.

Some liqueurs are generic, that is they are liqueurs of a particular type, which anyone may make. Advocaat, crème de menthe and curaçao are popular generic liqueurs. Other liqueurs are proprietary, that is they may only be made by a single distiller who owns the right to make the liqueur of that name. Bénédictine, Cointreau, Drambuie and Grand Marnier are examples of proprietary liqueurs.

Liqueurs are often taken with the coffee at the end of a meal. They are usually served neat (without any mixer) in a liqueur glass. They may also be taken in black coffee, as a liqueur coffee (see 14.16 under 'coffee', and 15.25–15.26).

Liqueurs are also frequently used in cocktails.

14.13 COCKTAILS

Cocktails are mixed drinks. Two or more ingredients are mixed by one of the following methods:

- Shake and strain (in a cocktail shaker, with ice)
- Stir and strain (in a mixing glass, with ice)
- Blend (in an electric blender, with the quantity of ice specified in the recipe)
- Build (prepared directly in the glass).

Cocktails fall into three broad types:

- Pre-dinner cocktails. These are usually acidic or dry and make good apéritifs. A Dry Martini is a classic pre-dinner cocktail.
- After-dinner cocktails. These tend to be richer, often creamy and sweet. A Brandy Alexander is an example.
- Long drink cocktails. These often contain fruit juices, soft drinks or milk in addition to their alcoholic base. A Tom Collins is an example.

Most cocktails are served with a garnish, which may be as simple as a slice of lemon or a cherry. The garnish should be appropriate to the contents of the cocktail. Many classic cocktails are served with a standard garnish. For example a Dry Martini is served with an olive or a twist of lemon, whereas a Gibson, which otherwise has the same ingredients, is served with a pearl onion. The garnish is as much part of the cocktail as its liquid ingredients.

Most classic cocktails have a spirit base, but this is not necessary. Some cocktails contain no alcoholic component at all, in which case they are called virgin cocktails or mocktails.

Figure 14.3 shows examples of five famous cocktails.

14.14 NON-ALCOHOLIC DRINKS

The term non-alcoholic drinks includes a wide variety of beverage items, from cold to hot and from the simple to the exotic. Some are served from the kitchen/still area and some are dispensed from the bar.

Non-alcoholic drinks served from the kitchen/still area

14.15 *Tea*

A growing demand for a variety of specialist teas has made it necessary for establishments to expand the range of teas they offer.

The majority of teas are prepared using tea-bags, but some teas are prepared from loose leaves. When tea is served guests pour for themselves. The waiting staff provide the prepared tea, additional hot water, milk, lemon, and the appropriate sweeteners. Types of tea commonly requested include English Breakfast, Earl Grey, Darjeeling, China, and herbal tea.

14.16 *Coffee*

Good quality coffee can be a key issue in ensuring a good dining experience, or visit to a brasserie or bar, and the guests' decision on whether or not to come back. In a restaurant coffee is generally the last product consumed. In bars and brasseries it is either the last product consumed on a meal visit or it may be the whole purpose of the visit. The correct preparation and serving of coffee is of more and more importance to customers (see also 15.22 and 15.23).

Coffee is available in many blends, and is prepared in many styles. It can be instant, or prepared using a filter/drip, a percolator, a plunger, or in an espresso machine. Styles of coffee frequently requested are:

- **Long black.** Freshly percolated coffee served without milk or cream in a large (tea) cup.
- **Café au lait** or white coffee is coffee served with milk. Café au lait is usually made with hot milk (*au lait* is French for 'with milk'), whereas ordinary white coffee has cold milk added. Sometimes cream is used instead of milk.
- **Espresso** coffee (literally 'pressed out' coffee) is made in a machine which uses steam pressure. An 'espresso' (without qualification) usually means a small black coffee made using an espresso machine. Espresso coffee should have a creamy golden froth. This is the mark of a well-maintained machine, freshly-ground coffee, and the right quantity of coffee used in the process.
- **Cappuccino** coffee is made using an espresso machine, and has frothed milk added. It should be strong and milky with a

creamy frothed crest. It is usually garnished with a sprinkling of chocolate or cocoa. Cappuccino coffee is so called because its appearance is reminiscent of the white on brown *cappuccio* or cowl worn by Capuchin friars.

- **Macchiato** coffee is an extra-strong espresso served long or short in a glass with a dash of cold milk. *Macchiare* means to stain in Italian. A macchiato is a very strong coffee just 'stained' with a little milk, barely enough to change its colour.
- **Vienna coffee** is topped with thickened cream, very rich.
- **Turkish** or **Greek** coffee is strong, dark and sweet. It is made from a fine powder of pulverized coffee beans. Unlike other coffees, the water is not passed through ground coffee beans, rather the coffee and the water are 'cooked' together. Sugar is added during the preparation, rather than after it, since stirring the coffee would disturb the sediment which forms in the cups.
- **Decaffeinated** coffee is real coffee with the stimulant caffeine extracted. Some people prefer coffee substitutes which are not made from coffee beans. They are usually made of cereals such as barley with chicory.
- **Liqueur** coffees are those served with a spirit or liqueur. Irish coffee is the obvious example. Irish whiskey is added to hot sugared black coffee which is then topped with cold, fresh cream. A number of different liqueurs, for example Tia Maria or Galliano, are commonly served with coffee in the same way under a variety of names, for example 'Jamaican Coffee' or 'Napoleon Coffee'. (Liqueur coffees are, of course, alcoholic, but for convenience are described here with the other coffee variations. See also 15.25 and 15.26).

14.17 *Hot chocolate*

Nowadays chocolate is almost always made from pre-prepared (instant) powder. The quality of the chocolate used is the essential factor in the end product – the better the brand, the better the result. If good chocolate is to be served you must use a good product. The chocolate powder is mixed with hot (but not boiled) milk before service, usually in the cups in which it is to be served (see 15.24).

Non-alcoholic drinks dispensed from the bar

14.18 *Aerated waters*

Aerated water is simply water charged with gas, usually carbon dioxide, to make it effervescent. Aerated waters often contain a syrup for taste and colour. Soda water is a colourless and tasteless aerated water. Bitter lemon, Indian tonic, and dry ginger are flavoured aerated waters.

14.19 *Fruit juices*

Commercially-packed brands (canned, boxed or bottled) may be used or, for some varieties of fruit such as oranges, lemons and grapefruit, the juices may be prepared fresh. Serve chilled.

14.20 *Squashes*

These are preparations of fruit juices or syrups with sugar, water and other ingredients, usually described by the manufacturers as 'cordials'. Some use mineral water instead of ordinary tap water.

14.21 *Mineral waters*

Mineral waters are so-called because of the minerals they contain which are said to be good for health. They may be still or sparkling (effervescent). If they come unadulterated from a natural spring they are 'natural' mineral waters, and if their effervescence is also natural, rather than added by the injection of carbon dioxide, they are 'naturally sparkling'. 'Carbonated natural' mineral waters are made from spring waters with carbon dioxide added.

Natural mineral waters are often named after the place from which they come. Evian, Perrier and Vichy are natural mineral waters from France (Evian is still, while Perrier and Vichy are naturally sparkling). Appollinaris is a naturally sparkling variety from Germany. Some of the natural mineral waters most commonly for sale in the UK are shown in Fig. 14.4. Sometimes mineral waters are flavoured with fruit juices.

Mineral waters can be used as mixers or appreciated as refreshing, cleansing beverages. On their own mineral waters should be served chilled, but without ice unless it is requested by the customer. Sometimes they are served with a spirit, e.g. Whisky and Ashbourne.

14.22 *Non-alcoholic wines*

These are prepared from a fruit juice base, and can be still or aerated, with no alcohol content.

Country of Origin	Name	Sparkling/still
England	Ashbourne	Sparkling
England	Buxton	Still
England	Malvern	Sparkling
Germany	Appolinaris	Sparkling
France	Vittel	Still
France	Vichy	Sparkling
France	Perrier	Sparkling
England	Abbey Well	Still
Wales	Brecon	Sparkling
England	Buxton Spring	Sparkling
Italy	San Pellegrino	Sparkling

Fig. 14.4 Some natural mineral waters available in the UK.

14.23 *Non-alcoholic cocktails*

Current trends towards responsible drink-driving habits have led to an increase in the availability of non-alcoholic drinks, including many non-alcoholic mixed drinks or cocktails. Often these are simply 'virgin' versions of an already popular cocktail, e.g. ones with the alcoholic ingredient left out or with some other ingredient substituted for it. A Virgin Mary, for example, is a non-alcoholic variation of the Bloody Mary with the vodka omitted. Responsible beverage servers are now very conscious of the need to offer a good variety of non-alcoholic drinks.

14.24 **QUESTIONS**

(1) What is an apéritif?

(2) At what temperature should wine be served?

(3) What does AOC stand for?

(4) What is a fortified wine?

(5) What makes the bubbles in sparkling wine?

(6) How do you make a head on a draught pint of beer?

(7) At what temperature should lagers be served?

(8) What are the three broad types of cocktails?

(9) What is a macchiato coffee?

(10) What types of non-alcoholic drinks are usually available at a bar?

15 . Beverage Service Procedures

Do patrons purchase drinks simply to quench their thirst? Or do they really come to enjoy a total hospitality experience – the company, the atmosphere of the venue, and the service – as well as the food they eat and the beverages they drink?

15.1 Beverages may be served on their own (for example in bar or lounge service), or their service may be carefully co-ordinated with the service of the food so that the beverages complement the food, enhancing the guests' enjoyment of both.

The style of beverage service offered will depend on the character of the establishment and the type of beverages being served. The methods of service explained in this chapter reflect a common-sense approach to beverage service, but some establishments may require variations on these procedures.

On completion of this chapter you should have a basic understanding of the following:
- Selling beverages
- Licensing laws
- Measures
- Taking beverage orders
- Handling glassware
- Tray carrying and service
- Beer service
- Wine service
- Champagne service
- Liqueur, port and brandy service
- Coffee and tea service
- Changing glassware.

15.2 ## SELLING BEVERAGES
The way beverages are sold is a key part of the hospitality experience. Bar and beverage service staff must not only understand the products they are selling, but they must also know how to serve them, from both technical and psychological points of view.

15.3 ## *Licensing laws*
Food service staff must know how the licensing laws apply in their place of work because ignorance could lead to the establishment losing its licence.

Types of licence

Off licence. An establishment that sells liquor only for consumption off the premises.

Residential licence. A licence for establishments providing breakfast, accommodation and at least one main meal. Liquor must only be supplied to residents.

Restaurant licence. This allows the sale of liquor only as an accompaniment to food.

Restaurant and residential licence. This permits the sale of liquor to residents and non-residents eating a meal at a table in the establishment's restaurant.

Occasional licence. Used for special occasions (up to four in one year) on premises that are not normally licensed. The licence holder must be a representative of a recognized organization.

Full on licence. The broadest type of licence. The holder may sell liquor for consumption on and off the premises. Hotels and public houses use this licence. It may be granted for the sale of all liquor or restricted to certain types, e.g. wines or beers. Sometimes there are special restrictions on individual licences imposed in the public interest.

Permitted hours. Intoxicating liquor may only be consumed on licensed premises during the times permitted according to the licence:

Day	Hours
Monday–Saturday	11 AM–11 PM
Sunday, Good Friday and Christmas Day	12 noon–3 PM and 7 PM–10.30 PM

This applies in England and Wales. It also applies generally to Scotland and Northern Ireland, though local hours may differ. Some areas of Wales forbid the sale of alcohol all day on Sundays.

Drinking up time of twenty minutes is allowed at the end of any permitted period of consumption. No new alcoholic drinks can be bought from the bar during this period. If the alcohol has been purchased with a meal drinking up time is extended to thirty minutes after permitted hours.

In the Republic of Ireland, licensing hours are somewhat different:

	Day	Hours
Summer	Monday–Saturday	10.30 AM–11.30 PM
	Sunday	{ 12.30 AM–2 PM
		4 PM–11 PM }
Winter	Monday–Saturday	10.30 AM–11 PM
	Sunday	{ 12.30 AM–2 PM
		4 PM–11 PM }
	Christmas Day and Good Friday	All bars closed (but residential licence still applies as usual)
	St Patrick's Day	As Sunday but no afternoon closing

15.4 *Measures*

Wine, beers, cider, spirits, fortified wines and vermouths, must be sold in accurate measured quantities. This is not only a legal requirement but it is also good stock control.

Liquor	*Measure*	*Notes*
Wine	Carafe 25cl 50cl 75cl 1 litre	The measure used must appear on the wine list.
Beer and cider	⅓ pint ½ pint or multiples of ½ pint.	Either in a capacity container or through a metered pump. These measures do not apply to shandy.
Spirits: gin, rum, vodka, whisky	¼ or ⅕ or ⅙ of a gill (¼ pint or 5oz) or multiples of the above measures. The chosen measure must be used throughout the establishment	Either using an optic or thimble measure.
Fortified wines; vermouth	⅓ of a gill (3 out).	
Liqueurs	⅙ of a gill (6 out).	

New regulations on measures

The following regulations will apply in UK from 1 January 1995:

Wine: Wine must be served in 125ml or 175ml glasses (in public houses).

Spirits: Spirits should be served in 25ml or portions or multiples thereof.

Beer: No changes are planned for beer but *mixes* (e.g. shandy) will not have to be served in a specific measured glass.

Cocktails: If a cocktail contains more than three spirit ingredients no specific measure is required.

15.5 *Venues offering beverage service*

Venues offering beverage service include:
- Public houses and bars
- Lounges
- Restaurants
- Function facilities.

15.6 *Public houses and bars*

The traditional name 'public house' suggests a narrower range of skill in the bar staff than is required today. Pubs were traditionally a male domain, and most people drank beer there. In the past bar staff needed few technical skills beyond knowing how to pull a pint and how to mix basic spirits. Things have changed. Today's pub attracts both sexes; it may offer entertainment, and a complete range of beverages including beers, wines, cocktails, spirits and a growing range of non-alcoholic drinks.

There are also specialist cocktail bars, bars in clubs and hotels and bars at special events. Staff at all these types of bar need the skill to serve the full range of drinks correctly, and must know how to sell them.

Techniques and vehicles for selling beverages in bars include verbal recommendations, promotional displays, board listings, and the availability of a drinks list.

15.7 *Lounges*

Lounge services are offered in a wide diversity of types of venue, including pubs, hotels, restaurants, lounge bars, discos and clubs. Guests can sit away from the bar in a relaxed environment and may be served by floor staff.

In the lounge sales are made by verbal recommendation, or by using sales tools like tent cards (Fig. 15.1), or cocktail/beverage lists.

Fig. 15.1 A tent card.

15.8 *Restaurants*

When beverages are sold and served in a restaurant consideration has to be given to the integration of food and beverage service so that they enhance each other.

The methods used to sell beverages in restaurants vary to suit the type of establishment but they commonly include verbal recommendation, tent cards, cocktail/beverage lists, 'wine lists', and liqueur coffee lists.

15.9 *Functions*

The beverages served at a function are usually pre-arranged by the function host with the venue operator rather than sold at the function itself. The venue manager may make verbal recommendations or may offer a beverage list from which the host selects the drinks to be served. Should the host request a beverage not on the standard list, it may be purchased by the venue especially for the function.

15.10 *General points on selling beverages*

When selling beverages:

- Do not dictate your personal preferences.
- Offer a diversity of recommendations so that guests are prompted to choose what they personally prefer.
- Suggest beverages that complement the occasion, but do not convey any sense of disapproval if something 'unsuitable' is chosen. Guests have the right to drink whatever they choose, and have come to enjoy themselves, not to be 'corrected'. Your job is to make them feel comfortable and relaxed.

15.11 **TAKING BEVERAGE ORDERS**

Beverage orders should be taken as soon as guests are comfortably settled, be it a bar, lounge, or at a table in a restaurant. Remember the following points:

- When taking the orders (verbally or in writing) make sure you clearly understand them and that they are precise, so that the guests receive what they have ordered. If you are not quite clear what has been ordered, do not hesitate to confirm it with the guest.
- If there are several guests write the orders down in logical order (as the guests are seated, or with some other clear identification) so that you place the drinks correctly when they are served (see 6.9 and 6.10).
- Avoid the use of abbreviations; they can easily cause confusion.
- Different venues have different methods for recording sales. Whatever the system in use – hand-written dockets, a cash register, or a computer system – it is essential that you record all items sold in the appropriate way.
- In a restaurant the wine order is usually taken after the guests

have selected their food. Additional orders for wine may be taken throughout the meal; indeed, if the guests' glasses look nearly empty, discreetly ask the host whether another bottle of wine should be brought.

■ The order for after-dinner beverage items (such as port, brandy or liqueurs) should be taken prior to the service of coffee, so that the drinks can be served with the coffee.

15.12 GLASSWARE AND DRINKS TRAYS

All glassware, whether clean or used, should be carried upright on a drinks tray, except that wine glasses may be carried upside down by their stems, held between the fingers of the left hand, when setting covers before guests arrive (see 13.11).

All glassware (clean or used) must always be held only by the stem or base of the glass, never by the rim.

5.13 *Tray service (Fig. 15.2)*

A drinks tray is carried on a slightly cupped hand on the pads of the fingers (Fig. 15.3). This allows the waiter to adjust the balance of the tray as glasses are removed or added to the tray. When serving drinks from a tray to seated guests hold the tray behind the guest's head, and use your right hand to place the drink from the guest's right (see also 5.9 and 13.11).

Fig. 15.2 Tray service.

Fig. 15.3 Carrying the drinks tray.

15.14 BEER SERVICE

Beers, in particular the increasingly popular premium and imported beers, are often served at the table from individual small bottles.

15.15 *Serving small beer bottles (Figs. 15.4 and 15.5)*

The procedure for serving small bottles of beer at table is:

- Carry a clean cold beer glass and an open bottle to the table on a service tray.
- Hold the tray behind the head of the guest to be served.
- Pick up the glass at its base and place it to the guest's right.
- Take the bottle in your right hand with the label clearly showing to the guest.
- Pour the beer into the glass on the table so that the flow is directed to the inside opposite edge of the glass. Pour slowly so that a head can form.
- Continue pouring until the glass is full, with a well-rounded head.
- If the bottle still contains some beer, place it on the table to the right of the glass, with the label facing the guest.

Fig. 15.4 Beer glasses, left to right: lager glass; straight beer glass; tankard.

15.16 WINE SERVICE PROCEDURES

The service of wine whether it be over a bar or at table is a sequence of tasks involving basic skills. At table, in licensed restaurants of all types, the correct procedure does not vary. There may be some modification of the procedure, however, in busy bars. Always be sure to serve wine in the correct glass for its type (Fig. 15.6).

15.17 *Service of table wines (Figs 15.7 and 15.8)*

- Present the wine which the host has selected on a service cloth held on the flat of your left hand, with the label directed to the host so that it can easily be read. Identify the wine verbally in such a way that the host can easily recognize it and link it to the wording on the wine list. Do not open the bottle until the host has confirmed that the wine is the correct one.
- When the host has confirmed the wine is correct, take the bottle firmly in your left hand, holding it at a 45° angle at waist height. Cut the foil with the blade of the waiter's friend just above the raised ridge about 5mm (¼ inch) below the top of the bottle. Ease off the top of the foil with the point of the

Fig. 15.5 Serving beer at the table.

Fig. 15.6   Wine glasses left to right: Paris glass;
Champagne flute; white wine flute.

blade. Note that the foil should always be cut in this way even if a perforated pull-tab has been built into the foil; a clean cut prevents the wine from catching in the perforations and dripping when poured.

■ Close the blade of the waiter's friend and open the corkscrew. Hold the neck of the bottle firmly in the left hand. Insert the sharp tip of the corkscrew into the centre of the cork. Slowly turn the corkscrew in a clockwise direction, keeping it in line with the core of the cork. Stop turning when the last turn of the corkscrew is still visible to avoid piercing the base of the cork with the other end.

■ Tilt the arm of the waiter's friend so that the lever rests on the lip of the bottle. Hold the lever in place using the side of your index finger. Now extract the cork by raising the opposite end of the body of the waiter's friend, exerting leverage on the lip of the bottle until the cork starts to bend.

■ Now cease the lifting action and place your thumb and index finger at the base of the cork. Twist the cork gently onto its side to remove it from the bottle. This technique will prevent the cork from breaking and will allow the cork to be extracted without any distracting popping sound.

■ Remove the cork from the corkscrew and return the waiter's friend to the pocket.

■ In some establishments the cork is then presented to the host for inspection, particularly when fine red wines are being served. If it is the custom of the establishment to present the cork, a suitable small plate should be placed on the table in advance to accommodate it. If the cork has the name of the winery printed on it, the cork should be placed so that the writing can easily be read by the host.

■ Wipe the lip of the bottle with a service cloth.

■ The bottle is then held firmly in the right hand with the label directed toward the host. Pour a mouthful of wine into the host's glass for approval. The wine should be poured into the

Fig. 15.7 Presenting and uncorking a bottle of wine.

Fig. 15.7 *continued.*

centre of the glass with the bottle held above and not touching the glass. (Note: If the table is laid with more than one style of wine glass, the smaller glasses should be used for white wine and the larger for red.)

■ After the host has approved the wine, fill the guests' glasses (no more than two-thirds full) starting with the guest immediately to the right of the host. At table the wine is poured from the guests' right. Moving anti-clockwise round the table, complete the service by topping up the host's glass.

■ When all the glasses have been filled, bottles of white wine are placed in a cooler or ice bucket (if available), or placed on the table if the guests so request. Bottles of red wine should be placed on the waiter's station (if there is one) or placed on the table (if there is not, or if the guests request it).

■ Bottles of red wine may be collared with a napkin to improve their presentation (Fig. 15.9). White wine bottles, if placed in an ice bucket, may have a napkin draped over them.

■ The discarded cap, foil and cork must not be left at the table or dropped into the ice bucket. Put them in your pocket and dispose of them at the bar.

■ Keep an eye on the guests' glasses. When they are only one-third full top them up.

■ When the bottle is empty, ask the host whether they require another bottle of the same wine, or whether you should bring the wine list for them to select another. If another bottle of the same type of wine is ordered it is not necessary to change the glasses unless you are asked by the host to do so. Nor, in most establishments, is it necessary to repeat the tasting procedure. Simply open the bottle, and continue to top up the guests' glasses as before. If a different wine is selected, the glasses must be changed (see 15.27), and the tasting and opening procedures are repeated in the same way as they were performed for the original bottle.

Fig. 15.8 Service of wine.

Fig. 15.9 Bottles of red wine may be collared to improve their presentation.

15.18 CHAMPAGNE AND OTHER SPARKLING WINE

Except that the technique of opening a bottle is different, the procedure for serving a sparkling wine (Fig. 15.10) is essentially the same as that for a still white table wine.

- If a sparkling wine is selected place suitable glasses (narrow 'champagne flutes') in position.

- Present the bottle on a service cloth held on the flat of your left hand, with the label directed to the host so that it can easily be read. Identify the wine verbally so that the host can confirm that the correct wine has been brought – 'Your Domain Chandon, Sir?'

- When the host has confirmed that the wine is the correct one, proceed to open the bottle. Extraordinary pressure can build up in a bottle of sparkling wine, especially if it is shaken. People can be injured by the cork exploding violently out of the bottle, so opening must be undertaken with care. Never allow the bottle to point at your face or at anyone else; make sure it is pointing at the ceiling. During the opening procedure

(a)

(b)

hold the bottle at an angle rather than straight up. This reduces the pressure on the cork.

- Take the bottle firmly in your left hand, holding it at a 45° angle at waist height. With your right hand locate the wire ring on the neck of the bottle, and untwist it.
- Remove foil and the cage, holding the cork in place with the thumb of your left hand as an extra precaution.
- Take a service cloth in the palm of the right hand and with it cover and firmly hold the cork. Hold the base of the bottle with your left hand and twist it to loosen the cork. Ease the cork gently out of the bottle into the palm of your right hand.
- Wipe the lip of the bottle with the service cloth.
- Hold the bottle in the right hand so that the label faces the host, and pour a mouthful of the wine into the glass for approval.
- Alternatively, the bottle may be held with the thumb in the punt (the indentation at the base) with the fingers spread out to support the body of the bottle (Fig. 15.11).
- When the host has approved the wine, fill the guests' glasses (no more than two-thirds full), starting with the guest immediately to the host's right and moving anti-clockwise round the table. Complete the service by topping up the host's glass. You may have to pause while pouring to allow the bubbles to settle.
- Place the bottle in an ice bucket unless the host requests otherwise. The bottle may be collared with a napkin to enhance its presentation (Fig. 15.12).
- Top up the guests' glasses, and offer an additional bottle, as for ordinary table wines.

(c)

(d)

(e)

Fig. 15.10   Serving a sparkling wine.

Fig. 15.11 Alternatively, the bottle may be held with the thumb in the punt.

Fig. 15.12 The bottle may be collared with a napkin.

Fig. 15.13 Brandy balloon.

15.19 LIQUEURS, PORT AND BRANDY

Liqueurs, port and fine brandies (usually cognac, but sometimes armagnac) are commonly served with coffee at the conclusion of a meal. The waiter may suggest them verbally or offer the drinks list after the sweets or desserts. Glasses are usually pre-poured and served at table off a tray, but in some establishments the bottle is presented at the table and then poured for the guest or served from a beverage trolley.

The normal measures for brandy or liqueurs and for port or other fortified wines are explained in section 15.4.

Fine brandies are served in wide-bottomed glasses (balloons) (Fig. 15.13). It is usual for guests to warm their own brandy glasses in the palms of their hands but the waiter may be requested to warm the glasses before the brandy is served. Some establishments have special warming lamps for this purpose. Note that the glass is empty when warmed on a lamp; the brandy itself is not warmed for the guest.

15.20 COFFEE AND TEA

The exact procedure for serving coffee and tea at table will vary, depending on the venue, the style of service and the equipment available.

The preparatory steps for coffee and tea service are the same. They are:

- Take the order.
- Place the accompanying items (milk, sugar, and, if required, cream and lemon) on the table. An underliner may be used to present these items. Make sure the sugar bowl has a clean spoon with it.
- Place a cup and saucer, and a teaspoon from each guest's right. If coffee or tea are being served with cheese or dessert, or for afternoon tea, the cup and saucer are placed to the right of the cover.
- If tea or coffee are being served at the end of a meal after the table has been cleared, the cup and saucer should be placed near the centre of the cover.
- The handle of the cup should be to its right, and the teaspoon should be placed at a 45° angle on the saucer just behind the handle.

15.21 TEA (Fig. 15.14)

The ritual for serving tea allows the guests to pour for themselves. Present the teapot and its accompanying hot water pot on an underplate with a tea-strainer, and a small napkin.

The strainer and the napkin may not be provided in all establishments. A strainer is unnecessary if tea-bags have been used, but one still may be asked for by guests. If tea-bags have been used they should be served with tea-bag strings and labels hanging

Fig. 15.14 Tea service.

out so that the customer can see the type of tea being used. The napkin is to assist the guest to hold the hot pots while pouring.

Place the underplate to the right of the guest, with the handles of the teapot and hot water pot directed to the guest.

15.22 COFFEE

The way in which coffee is prepared and served depends on which kind of coffee it is. The many different kinds of coffee were described in the previous chapter (14.16). Regardless of which kind of coffee is being served there are no points to be won by serving insipid, thin coffee. Most people prefer rich and flavoursome coffee, with only a minority preferring their coffee weak. Most people who drink black coffee, particularly short black espresso, want high quality, rich and strong coffee. Coffee can always be diluted if it is too strong. However, unless it is made with a plunger, it cannot be strengthened if it has been made too weak. The amount of water pushed through the coffee determines its strength, without (up to a point) compromising its richness and aroma. The less water, the richer and stronger the coffee.

Good coffee is essential in modern brasseries and cafes. It is often prepared in rather different ways but the keys to successful espresso coffees are:

- Fresh coffee
- Hot cups
- A well-serviced machine
- An understanding of what makes good coffee good.

Espresso coffee, especially when served in a small cup, should have a creamy golden-brown froth. This is a sign of a well-maintained machine, freshly ground coffee and the right quantity of coffee used in the process.

A **cappuccino** requires the correct ratio of coffee to milk. Fill the 'arm' of the espresso machine according to the instructions, or as advised by your colleagues. About a third of the coffee cup is then filled with coffee, and the rest with frothed milk. The key to a good cappuccino is not the crest of froth but the coffee/milk ratio. A cappuccino should be strong and milky with a creamy frothed crest.

An important point to remember is that hot milk does not froth. Frothing is achieved by forcing steam through cold milk, boiling it in the process. To achieve well-frothed milk only add enough milk for the coffees you are making.

A cappuccino is usually served in a cup, but it is sometimes served in a glass. The chocolate sprinkled on top as a garnish is an option, not an essential part of a good cappuccino.

15.23 *Service of coffee (Fig. 15.15)*

Except when guests have ordered a full pot of coffee, or when espresso coffee is being served, coffee is normally poured for them at table.

Fig. 15.15 Serving coffee from a coffee pot with a long spout.

Coffee is served from the right of the guest. If the coffee pot has a short spout, pick up the cup and bring it up to the pot to fill it. If the pot has a long spout enabling you to direct the flow accurately, you should pour the coffee straight into the cup on the table.

In formal silver service present the coffee pot and milk jug on an underliner and then pour both coffee and milk for the guests.

Coffee and tea can both be prepared on and served from a guéridon. If speciality coffees and teas are served, the guéridon enables you to make the most of their presentation (see 10.5, 10.6 and chapter 12). Liqueur coffees are particularly suited to preparation on the guéridon (see 15.25 and 15.26 below).

15.24 HOT CHOCOLATE

Hot chocolate is usually served in cups prepared in the still area rather than poured from a pot at the table. The cups are served from the guests' right. For chocolate preparation see 14.17.

15.25 LIQUEUR COFFEE

Liqueur coffees can provide an additional highlight to the dining experience. When prepared and served correctly they will not only impress the guests but encourage them to order more. The simplicity of the technique involved, and its impressive visual effect, make liqueur coffees particularly appropriate for preparation in front of guests, either on a guéridon or at the bar.

The preparation of a perfect liqueur coffee is a simple process in which fresh, cold, pouring cream is floated on hot liqueured coffee. The result should be a dramatic visual contrast of white on black.

A liqueur coffee is not only enjoyed for its eye appeal, aroma and for its taste; there is also the special sensation of drinking the hot liqueured coffee through the layer of cold, fresh, cream. If a liqueur coffee is to be fully appreciated it is therefore essential that the cream should not be semi-whipped, whipped, or dispensed from a pressure-pack can.

Although different establishments may make minor variations to the recipes, and may use their own names for the various liqueur coffees they offer, the simple technique used to create the perfect liqueur coffee should not be altered.

15.26 *Liqueur coffee preparation*

To prepare a perfect liqueur coffee:

- Choose an appropriate glass, preferably one made of clear, toughened glass, with a stem or with a handle. Pour a measure of the selected spirit or liqueur into the glass.
- For additional visual effect, the spirit or liqueur can be warmed (Fig. 15.16) and flamed in a spirit warmer before it is poured into the glass.
- Add sugar, if required.

Fig. 15.16   Pouring from a spirit warmer.

Fig. 15.17   Add aerated pouring cream.

- Pour hot, black, percolated or filtered coffee into the glass, filling the glass up to 1.5cm (¾ inch) from its top.
- Stir.
- Lightly aerate the cream by shaking it in a closed container for about three seconds.
- Pour the cold, aerated cream into the bowl of a spoon placed at the level of the top of the coffee (Fig. 15.17). Continue until the cream is about 1cm (½ inch) deep
- Remove the spoon and serve.

15.27 CHANGING GLASSWARE

The original glassware may be used if additional bottles of the same type of wine as was originally ordered are required, unless a change of glasses is requested. If wine of a different style or type is ordered then fresh glasses must be placed before the new wine is served.

Select the style of glassware appropriate to the style of wine chosen (for example, champagne flutes for a sparkling wine), and take the glasses to the table on a drinks tray. Place the glasses a little further away from the guests than the original glasses and at an angle of 45° to the right of them.

Remove the original glasses when the guests have finished the wine in them.

Remember that the glasses should be handled by their stems whether they are being placed or removed.

After-dinner drinks (liqueurs, ports and after-dinner cocktails) should be served in fresh glasses for each new order.

15.28 ASHTRAYS

The drinks waiter must see that guests' ashtrays are clean and, if necessary, frequently replaced. For the technique of changing ashtrays see 11.6 and 11.7.

15.29 QUESTIONS

(1) Name two places where beverages are served other than the restaurant.

(2) Why should abbreviations be avoided when taking a beverage order?

(3) Should the wine order be taken before the food order?

(4) How should glassware be handled?

(5) When should the selected wine be opened?

(6) Why is a little wine served to the host before the guests?

(7) At what stage of the meal are liqueurs, brandies and ports offered?

(8) What is the name of the glass used for the service of brandy?

(9) In the service of coffee, what is a demi-tasse?

(10) What is a liqueur coffee?

(11) List the equipment required for the service of tea.

16 . End-of-Service Procedures

'First-rate meal, well served, but if we could only find a waiter to give us our bill we would be able to leave. The show begins in ten minutes.'

16.1 We have already stressed the importance of greeting and receiving guests warmly and professionally and ensuring that effective and efficient meal service takes place. However the total experience for the guest does not end there; an equal emphasis must be placed on the end-of-service procedures.

When you have read this chapter you should have a basic understanding of the correct ways to deal with:

- Preparing and presenting a bill
- Payment procedures and methods
- Tips (gratuities)
- Saying goodbye to the guests
- Tidying, cleaning and resetting after service.

16.2 ## PREPARING AND PRESENTING A BILL

The methods by which bills are prepared and processed vary from one establishment to another. They range from hand-written dockets to high-tech computerized systems.

The two purposes of a guest's bill are to inform the guest of the amount to be paid (giving details of what is charged for), and to act as a control system for the establishment. To make sure that their control systems operate effectively establishments must make sure that their new service staff understand how the billing system works before they begin to serve guests.

Guests' bills may be presented at the table, at the bar, or at a cashier's desk. No matter where it is presented, the bill should be kept up to date at all times. Where possible, the bill should be kept ready for presentation as soon as the guest requires it. This may not always be possible, particularly when beverages are being served right up to the time of the guests' departure.

16.3 ### Presenting the bill

It is essential that you should be alert to signs that guests may want their bill. Nothing is more irritating to guests than to be kept waiting while they try to attract the attention of a waiter to ask for their bill. This is particularly so for busy business-people at lunchtime. Many a promising restaurant has failed because it earned a reputation for slow service, and the fatal slowness may well have been in the bringing of the bill rather than in the actual food service.

Generally speaking, bills should not be presented until they are asked for, but some establishments, which specialize in quick service and a high turnover of guests, place the bill on the table before the end of the meal.

When a bill is presented at table it is placed in front of the host (probably the person who has asked for the bill) on a small plate from the right. Either the bill is folded so that the amount to be paid cannot be seen by the other guests, or it is placed in a billfold which serves the same purpose. If there is no obvious host you may place the bill in the centre of the table.

Bills presented at bars should be presented on a plate, folded, or in a billfold.

If the establishment requires guests to pay at a cashier's desk as they are leaving, make this clear to the guests to avoid confusion and delay.

Do not hover around waiting for your guests to pay; leave them alone to pay in their own time. Remain alert though, so that when they have paid (or signed) for their meal, there is no unnecessary delay while they are kept waiting for you to collect the payment.

16.4 METHODS AND PROCEDURES FOR PAYMENT

Common payment methods include cash, credit cards, cheques, luncheon vouchers, and charge accounts. You must be familiar with the procedures for these various methods of payment and know which methods of payment are acceptable to the establishment.

Cash payments are very simple, only requiring the settling of the bill and the tendering of the guest's change.

Credit cards The precise procedure for use with credit cards will vary from establishment to establishment. When the card is placed on the bill you should collect it and, before processing it, check:

- That the establishment accepts the kind of card presented
- Its expiry date
- That it has been signed.

It is also wise to check the number against the current warning bulletin.

Credit card companies set a 'floor limit' for the 'merchants' accepting their cards. Any card transaction for a sum above the floor limit must be approved by the company. If the amount of bill to be settled is above the floor limit then either the waiter or the cashier must telephone through to the credit-card company for approval. You must therefore know the floor limit of the establishment.

When phoning for approval you must have the card with you so that you can quote its number and expiry date. You will also be asked for your establishment's 'merchant number' so you must have that at hand also.

Processing credit cards involves either the traditional manual completion of a voucher for signature by the guest, or for the card to be run through an electronic imprinter which will produce a transaction slip for the guest to sign. When vouchers are prepared it is usual not to complete the Total line so that the guests can confirm the amount signed for and add a tip if they so wish (see 16.5 below) unless a service charge (usually 10%) has been already included in the bill.

After you have checked that the guest has clearly completed the Total line on the voucher with the sum due (or more), and you have checked that the signature on the voucher is the same as that on the card, the card should be returned to the guest along with the customer's copy of the voucher. The guest's voucher should either be returned upside down or (better) in the billfold which was used to present the bill.

Cheques are usually not accepted without the support of a banker's card. Check that the details (name and bank's name) on the banker's card match those on the cheque and that the bill being paid does not exceed the limit stated on the card. If the bill is higher than the card limit, ask the customer to pay at least the excess by a different method.

Check that the customer has filled in the correct amount for payment on the cheque in both writing and numbers. Check that the correct date has been filled in at the top right-hand corner and that the customer has signed the cheque with a signature that matches the one on the banker's card. Many establishments have a name stamp to complete the payee section on the cheque, but if not, it is helpful to tell the customer exactly what to write in order to avoid confusion.

The cheque card, like a credit card, should be returned to the customer with the receipt.

Luncheon vouchers are often given to office workers as a supplement to their salaries. Some sandwich bars and restaurants accept them in payment or part-payment of bills. The value of the voucher is written clearly on it. Make sure that the establishment accepts luncheon vouchers before you accept them in payment of a bill.

Charge accounts Before a guest can be allowed to charge the cost of a meal (or drink) to a charge account the transaction must have been authorized by management. It may be necessary to check the guests' signatures against a charge record or, if it is in a hotel, the guest's name against a room number. Procedures for recording information on charge account transactions vary from establishment to establishment. You must, of course, strictly follow house procedures.

16.5 TIPS (GRATUITIES)

Tips are a bonus for especially satisfying service and should not be thought of as a right. There are no hard-and-fast rules on the amount of the tip or, indeed, on whether one is left or not. In many establishments a service charge is automatically added to the bill, usually of about 10 per cent. Never expect or anticipate a tip. If the guest has paid in cash always place the full change on the table unless the guest has very clearly indicated that the excess payment is intended as a gratuity.

Never ever allow guests to leave with the humiliating impression that you think they should have tipped you, or that their tip could have been more generous. If you do, they will not come back. Remember, the waiter has absolutely no right to a tip.

In some establishments it is house policy that all tips should be pooled and distributed among all the staff. This is called the 'trunk system' or tronc. Where this system is in place it must be very strictly adhered to or there will be bitter disputes. In other establishments individual waiters keep the tips they have been given.

16.6 SAYING GOODBYE TO THE GUESTS

The last impression guests are given as they leave after a meal is as important as their first impression on arrival. The farewell should be warm and friendly, and as personal as possible. If you are not too busy serving other guests, assist those departing by moving their chairs for them, collecting their personal belongings (not forgetting coats, hats, and bags!), and offering to call for a taxi.

If it is not physically possible to assist your guests to leave because you are busy serving others, at least acknowledge their departure with a nod and a smile. If you can, wish them 'Good evening' and thank them for coming. You should have taken the trouble to note their names (the credit card is an invaluable reminder for names); if you know the name, use it: 'Good night, Mrs Hill. We look forward to seeing you again soon'.

16.7 TIDYING, CLEARING AND RESETTING

The waiter's responsibilities do not end with the departure of the guests. When the guests have left, the tables and service areas must be cleared of used and soiled items and the tables prepared for use again.

The procedure for resetting the tables and work areas will vary from one establishment to another. In some establishments each table is reset for the same meal service as soon as the guests sitting at that table have left. This allows the table to be used again, increasing the number of covers served in that meal service. In other less hurried establishments, after the guests from one meal service have left, the tables are reset for the next service – for example, when one set of guests has finished their lunch the table may be reset for dinner.

16.8 *Procedure for clearing and re-setting*

- Remove coffee cups and centre items, glassware and ashtrays. (If you have kept the table tidy throughout the service of the meal, these should be the only items left on the table when the guests depart.)

  The cups and saucers should be carried using either the two- or the three-plate carrying technique (see 7.5 and 7.6). Do not stack the cups. Glassware should be removed on a drinks tray. The remaining centre items are removed by hand.

- If tablecloths are used in the establishment, the table must be reclothed. If the table is reclothed after service (when the restaurant is empty) use the clothing procedure described in 4.6. If the table is reclothed during service, follow the procedure in 4.7. If tablecloths are not used, all tables must be carefully wiped down.

- Whether the table is reset or not, ensure that all the chairs are returned to their original positions round the table. Do not forget to check the chairs for crumbs.

- The procedures for setting or resetting covers are described in chapter 4, particularly in 4.10–4.15.

- In most establishments workstations are restocked with cleaned, polished equipment immediately after the completion of service in preparation for the next service. (See 4.8.)

QUESTIONS

16.9
(1) What are the two purposes of a bill?

(2) Why is it important to present the bill promptly?

(3) What should you do with the bill if it is not clear who is the host?

(4) What is the procedure for accepting payment by credit card?

(5) What do you need to look for when checking that a cheque has been correctly completed by the customer?

(6) How should credit cards and banker's cards be returned to the customers?

(7) Why should you never stand and wait for a tip?

(8) How can you make a good impression when saying goodbye to guests?

(9) How should you carry cups and saucers when clearing a table?

(10) How should work stations be left?

17 . Function Operations

17.1 Functions offer people who lack formal training their greatest opportunity to gain part-time employment and establish themselves in the hospitality industry. The relatively simple skills required of a waiter for a specific function can easily be demonstrated by the employer, and working at the function will ensure that those skills are practised repeatedly over a short period.

By the end of this chapter you will have a basic understanding of:

- Styles of functions
- The variation of function covers
- Food and beverage service in function operations
- Function staff organization.

How often do we attend a function where the standard of service is not only unsatisfactory for the guests but an embarrassment to the staff employed to provide it?

Far too often function staff are left to survive as best they can when prior knowledge of the simplest of skills would have given them a sense of pride, and the service expectations of the guests would have been fulfilled.

17.2 STYLES OF FUNCTION

Function catering can involve anything from the simple service of sandwiches and coffee or tea to gala banquets, and the functions can take place anywhere, indoors or out-of-doors, from the garden of a private home to a grand ballroom.

The precise tasks required of service staff at functions requiring food-and-beverage service are defined by:

- The customer's needs
- The occasion
- The types of food and beverages to be served
- The amount the customer is prepared to spend.

Within these constraints the only limits to the diversity of function operations and what services are provided are the physical facilities available and the imagination of the caterer.

17.3 FUNCTION COVERS

The cover for a function is dictated by the menu items to be served. Functions usually have set menus and the cutlery items are set in the order in which they will be used (see 4.10 and 4.12 and Figs. 17.1 and 17.2).

Fig. 17.1   A possible function cover.

Fig. 17.2   Set menu cover with dessert cutlery.

17.4 *Dessert covers*

Dessert cutlery presents special problems for which there is more than one acceptable solution. At functions it is very likely that there will be pressure on space on the table, which adds to the advantages of bringing the dessert cutlery to the table only when it is needed for the sweet course (see 4.13). If the dessert cutlery has been laid with the original cover it will have to be corrected. For the procedure for correcting dessert covers see 6.17.

17.5 *Glassware*

At functions, there may also not be room to place all the glasses in a single line in order of their probable use. If there are more than two glasses they may have to be arranged in a triangle (see 4.14).

17.6 *Cups and saucers*

If cups and saucers are required when the cover is laid they are placed above and slightly to the right of the main knife, with the handle of the cup turned to the right so that it may be conveniently grasped by the guest without any need to turn it. Alternatively (and more usually for dinner functions) cups and saucers may be placed immediately before they are required for use (see 15.20).

17.7 FUNCTION SERVICE

The basic styles of service offered at functions are no different from those in restaurants – plate service, silver service, etc. The skills required for each style of service have been described in previous chapters (see chapter 7 for plate service and chapter 8 for silver service).

17.8 *Function service skills*

The basic skills required for function service are:
- Providing hospitality (see 1.3, 1.4)
- Setting tables (4.10 onwards)
- Carrying a tray or platter (5.9, 13.11, 15.13)
- Use of a service cloth (7.4)
- Carrying or clearing plates (7.2–7.6, 9.2–9.7)
- Pouring wine (15.17, 15.18).

17.9 *Function staff organization*

The number and organization of the staff at a function will depend on the particular requirements of different functions. Different styles of functions demand different staff arrangements and procedures. In some circumstances the waiting staff work as a team serving all of the guests at a number of tables, in others they have particular stations allocated to them and they are responsible for serving a set number of guests.

In most circumstances the team organization best satisfies the needs and expectations of the guests and lightens the load on individual serving staff.

17.10 *Team operations*

At large functions, to preserve a smooth and quick level of service, the service staff is often divided into teams.

Each team is made up of the number of staff needed to handle the service of a complete table. For example, tables setting ten guests may require a team of five staff. The team of five is itself divided into two groups with different functions – a serving group of three and a 'running' group of two.

The runners are responsible for the picking up of plated items from the kitchen and their transfer to a service area within the dining room. The serving group collects the plates (or other items) from the service area and serves them directly to the guests.

When one table has been served, the whole team – servers and runners – moves on to another table.

Clearing is done in the same way. The serving group clears the table and carries the used items to the service area, and the runners remove them from the service area to the washing-up area.

The number of tables a service team can handle depends on the complexity of the menu, the style of service and the facilities at the venue. A food-service team of five, plate-serving an 'average' three-course dinner, might be expected to serve up to twenty tables of ten guests, i.e. up to 200 guests.

17.11 *Beverage service at functions*

Responsibility for beverage service is normally pre-arranged by a station drinks waiter. The precise duties involved will depend on the selection of beverages and the way they are to be served. They may range from serving a variety of beverages from a tray to table service of apéritifs (15.13), table wines (15.17), sparkling wines (15.18), after-dinner drinks (15.19), and coffee (15.20, 15.22).

If food and beverage service at functions is to be co-ordinated, the beverages must be served alternately with the food. The beverages for each course should usually be served before that course.

At functions there will usually be separate teams responsible for serving the beverages, alternating at the table with the food-service teams. Even if there are not, and the same waiters are responsible for serving both food and beverages, the beverages and the food are not served simultaneously but separately, to avoid confusion.

Glossary

This glossary is not simply an explanation of the technical words used in the text. It also covers a large number of the terms used in food and beverage service and which are frequently used in menus in the *descriptions* of the dishes on offer. It therefore covers much of the food product knowledge with which every waiter should be equipped.

The headwords are in **bold** type. After the headword, if it comes from a language other than English, its language of origin is given in brackets in abbreviated form in *italics*, e.g. (*Fr.*) for French. Most of these are obvious enough, but some are a little rare, e.g. (*Heb.*) for Hebrew or (*Yid.*) for Yiddish. Occasionally the reference is to a culture rather than to a particular language, e.g. (*Ind.*) for Indian (which is not the name of a language).

For words of non-English origin, especially the many French words, there follows in square brackets a simple pronunciation guide. This is not as simple as it may seem because some languages make use of sounds for which there is no equivalent in English, for example the nasal **in** in the commonly-used French word *vin* (wine) which we have tried to indicate by using brackets: [vi(n)]. there is also the problem of the soft **j** sound in French which we have indicated by -zj,

as in *jus* [zjoo] (meat juice) or *aubergine* [oh-bear-zjeen] (eggplant).

All French nouns have a gender – masculine or feminine – as well as a number – singular or plural. Adjectives used to describe nouns have to agree with them in both gender and number, the adjective following the noun, as in *marrons glacés* (candied chestnuts). Most plurals are easy, just add s, but some are less obvious as in *gâteaux* (cakes). When the plural is not obvious we have included it after the headword, therefore **gâteau(x)**.

Because French words are so common in food service, and because French adjectives have to agree with their nouns, we include the gender when a French noun is explained, for example – **crème** (*Fr.*) (fem.). Because *crème* is feminine any qualifying adjective must also be feminine, as in **crème brulée**.

As French adjectives have both masculine and feminine forms we have included both when you are likely to encounter them. In most cases all the feminine form requires is to add **e** to the masculine form. We have indicated this by putting the additional **e** for the feminine form in brackets, for example **gratiné(e)**.

Most words used in definitions which are themselves defined in this glossary are printed in **bold** type.

abalone [aba-lony] Large **mollusc** (genus *Haliotis*) in rough ear-shaped shell.

abats (*Fr.*) (masc. pl.) [a-ba] Offal (always referred to in the plural – **les** *abats*). (*See also* **sweetbreads**.)

accompaniment **Condiment** offered by the waiter to add relish to the dishes served. Many condiments are traditional, e.g. red currant jelly with lamb or **Parmesan** cheese with **pasta**.

acidity Wine-tasting term indicating tartness.

advocaat **Liqueur** of egg yolks, sugar, and brandy; egg nog. (In Dutch 'advocate' or 'lawyer'.)

aflatoxin Food poison (toxin) derived from the yellow mould *Aspergillus flavus*.

agneau (*Fr.*) (masc.) [anyo] Lamb.

ail (*Fr.*) (masc.) [ahyuh] **Garlic**.

aïloli/ailloli (*Fr.*) (masc.) [ahyuh-oh-lee] **Provençal**

garlic mayonnaise. (From *ail* 'garlic' and provençal dialect *oli* 'oil'.)

à la (*Fr.*) [ah lah]   With, in the manner of, when referring to a feminine noun, e.g. *à la carte* (*see* **carte, à la**), *à la russe* (*see* **russe, à la**) etc. (*A la* is the feminine equivalent of **au**).

al dente (*Ital.*) [al dentay]   Cooked so as to be firm not soft, when bitten, esp. referring to **pasta**. (*Dente* means 'tooth'.)

ale   Top-fermented **beer**.

alfalfa sprouts [al-fal-fa]   Lucerne; fine hairy sprouts used in salads and sandwiches.

al fresco (*Ital.*)   Informal (meal) in the open air.

almond paste   *See* **marzipan**.

à maison   *See* **maison**.

amande (*Fr.* fem.) [amah(n)d]   Almond.

amandine (*Fr.*) [amah(n)deen]   With almonds.

amaretto (*Ital.*)   (1) Bitter almond-flavoured **liqueur**. (2) Small almond biscuit or **macaroon** served at the end of the meal or with desserts.

amontillado (*Span.*) [amon-till-ahdoh]   Medium-dry style of **sherry**.

ananas (*Fr.*) (masc. sing.) [a-nah-na]   Pineapple.

anchovy   Small very strongly-flavoured fish, usually preserved in salt.

anglaise, à l' (*Fr.*) [ah longl-ayz]   English-style; means different things with different items, but is most commonly applied to boiled vegetables served simply with chopped parsley and a knob of butter. (*See also* **crème anglaise**.)

Angostura Bitters   Proprietary brand of aromatic bitters used as a flavouring, by the addition of a few drops only, in drinks, e.g. **Pink Gin** or **champagne cocktail**, and in cooking. (Angostura is the former name of Cuidad Bolivar, Venezuelan town where first made.)

Anna   *See* **pommes Anna**.

antipasto (*Ital.*) (*pl.* antipasti)   Selection of **appetizers** served before a meal. Italian equivalent of **hors d'oeuvre**. (Literally 'before' (*anti*) 'the meal' (*pasto*).)

apéritif (*Fr.*) (masc.) [apay-rit-eef]   A drink served before a meal to stimulate the appetite.

à point   *See* **point, à**.

appetizer/appetiser   Food served before a meal to stimulate the appetite.

apple/apricot Danish   *See* **Danish pastry**.

Appolinaris   Brand of mineral water.

arborio rice   Italian rice used for **risotto**.

armagnac (*Fr.*) (masc.) [ar-man-yak]   Fine **brandy** made in the Armagnac district, S. France.

aroma   (1) Fragrance, smell. (2) Wine-tasting term. Scent of the grapes in a young wine. As wine matures the aroma decreases and the **bouquet** increases. (*See also* **nose**.)

aromatic   Fragrant, sweet-smelling.

artichoke   Two quite different vegetables:
(1) **globe artichoke**   Thistle-like plant with a large flower. The 'heart' and the base of the scaly leaves of the immature flower are eaten, usually with **vinaigrette**. (French *artichaut* [arti-show].)
(2) **Jerusalem artichoke**   Vegetable used in soups, stews, etc. It looks like a knobbly potato or piece of fresh **ginger**. (The name has nothing to do with Jerusalem but is a corruption of *girasole*, Italian for sunflower. French *topinambour* [topi(n)-am-bore].)

aspic   Savoury jelly (natural **gelatine**) made from meat **stock**. Used for setting cold fish or meat in a mould with vegetables, and for garnishing.

assiette (*Fr.*) (fem.) [assy-ett]   Plate, e.g. *une assiette de viandes*.

au (*Fr.*) (masc.) [oh]   With, in the manner of, when referring to a masculine noun, e.g. *au beurre* (*see* **beurre, au**), *au poivre* (*see* **poivre, au**), etc. (*Au* is the masculine equivalent of **à la**.)

aubergine [oh-bear-zjeen]   Eggplant.

auslese (*Ger.*) [ows-layz-uh]   Sweet dessert wine made from selected late-picked **riesling** grapes. (*Auslese* means 'selected'.) (*See also* **spätlese**.)

aux (*Fr.*) (plural) [oh]   With. (Plural of **au** and **à la**, e.g. **feuilleté** *aux* **pommes, soupe glacée** *aux* **moules**.)

B and B   Cocktail of **brandy** and **Bénedictine**.

baba (*Fr.* from *Polish*) [baa-baa]   Small light yeast cake, usually containing raisins. *Babas au rhum* (**rum** babas) are soaked in **rum** syrup.

Bacardi   Proprietary brand of white **rum**.

back of house   The parts of the **establishment** not seen by the guests; the kitchen, **stillroom** and accounts department as opposed to the dining room. (*See also* **front of house**.)

bacteria   Plural of bacterium. Tiny single-celled organisms often dangerous to health, but sometimes useful, e.g. in cheese-making.

bagel (*Yid.*) [bay-gul]   Ring or doughnut-shaped hard bread roll.

bagna cauda (*Ital.*) [banya cowda]   Hot **anchovy** dip. (Literally 'hot bath', from Piemont in N. Italy.) (*See also* **crudités**.)

baguette (*Fr.*) (fem. [bag-ett]   French bread stick.

bain-marie (*Fr.*) (masc.) [ba(n) maree]   Large open dish partly filled with hot water, in which pans stand so that their contents are kept hot without over-cooking. (Literally, 'bath of mary'.)

baklava/baclava (*Grk. & Turk.*)   **Filo** pastry cake containing almonds and spices and dipped in honey. Traditionally it is cut into triangular shapes.

ballotine (*Fr.*) (fem.) [ba-yot-teen]   Meat or fish boned, stuffed, rolled and served cold with an **aspic** glaze, or in a **chaudfroid**. A ballotine may also be served hot, **glazed** in its own **reduced** juices. (*Ballot* means 'bundle'.)

balsamic vinegar Fragrant, matured, sweet, wine **vinegar** with intense flavour used in **vinaigrette** dressings and to enhance the flavour of fruit, e.g. strawberries. (*See also* **malt vinegar**, **rice vinegar**, *and* **wine vinegar**.)

balthazar Very large bottle of **sparkling wine**, the equivalent of 16 standard 75cl bottles. (Balthazar was one of the three wise men who visited the infant Jesus.) (*See also* **champagne bottle sizes**.)

baron of beef Very large joint of beef, including **loin** and rump, often spit-roasted.

barquette (*Fr.*) (fem.) [bar-ket] Small boat-shaped pastry which can be filled with various ingredients. (Literally, 'little boat', 'little barque'.)

basil Pungent, sweet leaves from related plants (species *Ocimum*) used as flavouring herb, esp in Italian and SE Asian cookery. (*See also* **pesto** *and* **pistou**.)

basmati rice [bass-mutee] Long-grain rice in Indian cuisine, esp. **pilau** and **biryani**.

batter Fluid dough of flour and water or milk, usually with egg, used in cooking. It may be poured, e.g. to make **pancakes**, **waffles**, or **Yorkshire pudding**, or it may be used as a coating, e.g. to make fritters or deep-fried fish.

bavarois (*Fr.*) (masc.) [bavah-rwah] Dessert of custard stiffened with **gelatine**, mixed with whipped **cream**, shaped in a mould and served cold. (*Bavarois* means 'Bavarian', from Bavaria, region in S. Germany.)

bay leaf Leaves of the bay tree used, fresh or dried, to give flavour to **casseroles**, **stocks** and **marinades**. They are also used in a traditional **bouquet garni**.

bean curd Bland curd made from **soya beans** and rich in minerals and protein. (*See also* **tofu**.)

béarnaise (*Fr.*) [bay-airnayze] Sauce made of beaten egg yolks and lemon juice or **reduced wine vinegar** mixed with butter, shallots and served warm, usually with fish or grilled meat. (The French is *sauce béarnaise*. Béarn is a province in SW France.)

beaujolais (*Fr.*) [bow-zjol-lay] French wine from the Beaujolais region of E. France, or a **generic** wine in that style. The wine is red, fruity and light, and drunk while still young. (*See below*.)

beaujolais nouveau (*Fr.*) [bow-zjol-lay noo-voh] Beaujolais wine from the latest **vintage**. Britain has borrowed from the French tradition of racing the new vintage to particular restaurants as soon as it is bottled to see who can serve it first.

beef olive *See* **paupiette**.

beef bourguignon *See* **boeuf bourguignon**.

beef Stroganov *See* **boeuf Stroganov**.

beef Wellington Beef **fillet**, liver **pâté** and mushroom

duxelles baked in **puff pastry**. (Named in honour of the Duke of Wellington, 1769–1852, British general and Prime Minister.) (*See also* **croûte, en**.)

béchamel (*Fr.*) (fem.) [bay-sha-mel] Sauce made by adding milk to a **roux**; it is the foundation of many other sauces. (Attributed to Louis de Béchameil, Lord Steward to Louis XVI.)

beef rendang *See* **rendang daging**.

beer Alcoholic beverage made from **fermented** malted barley (sometimes wheat) flavoured with hops; general term for **ales**, **lagers** and **stouts**.

beignet (*Fr.*) [bay-nyay] **Fritter**.

Belgian endive *See* **chicory**.

Bénédictine (*Fr.*) [benny-dick-teen] **Proprietary liqueur**, very sweet and spicy, from Normandy (N. France). (*See also* **B and B**.)

bergamot Orange-scented herb (*Monarda didyma*) used in savoury and sweet dishes. It gives a distinctive flavour to **Earl Grey tea**.

beurre (*Fr.*) (masc.) [burr] Butter.

beurre au (*Fr.*) [oh burr] Cooked in butter.

beurre blanc (*Fr.*) (masc.) [burr blo(n)] Smooth sauce made by whipping butter into a **reduced** mixture of white wine, **wine vinegar** and finely chopped onions. (*Blanc* means 'white'.)

beurre fondu (*Fr.*) (masc.) [burr fon-doo] Butter melted slowly with lemon juice, white **pepper** and salt, often served with boiled or steamed vegetables and poached fish. (*Fondu* means 'melted'.)

beurre maître d'hôtel (*Fr.*) (masc.) [burr may-truh doh-tell] Softened butter added to mushroom **duxelles**, chopped parsley and lemon juice. Usually served with fish or grilled meat. (*See* **maître d'hôtel**.)

beurre meunière (*Fr.*) (masc.) [burr murn-ee-yair] **Beurre noisette** with lemon juice added. (*See also* **meunière, à la**.)

beurre noisette (*Fr.*) (masc.) [burr nwa-zet] Sauce of butter heated until brown (nutty) and served very hot. (*Noisette* is French for 'hazelnut'.)

bianco (*Ital.*) [bee-yan-ko] Golden medium-sweet style of **vermouth**. (Literally, 'white'.)

bien cuit (*Fr.*) (masc.) [bee-an cwee] Over-cooked (steak). (Literally, 'well cooked'.) (*See also* **bleu**, **point (à)**, *and* **saignant**.)

bifteck (*Fr.*) (masc.) [biff-tek] Beef steak, e.g. *bifteck au poivre*, 'pepper' steak. (*Bifteck* is a French corruption of the English words 'beef steak'.)

billfold (*USA*) Wallet or folder used for presenting bills, change, etc.

bill of fare **Menu**.

biryani/biriani (*Ind.*) [birry-ahnee] **Pilau**, usually spiced and coloured yellow with **saffron** and garnished with hard-boiled egg.

biscotte (*Fr.*)   Toasted slice of **brioche** or a rusk, served at afternoon tea.

bisque (*Fr.*) (fem.) [beesk]   Thick creamy soup, usually based on **seafood**, e.g. prawn bisque. (*See also* **chowder** *and* **potage**.)

bistro (*Fr.*) [bees-troh]   Small informal restaurant.

bitters   Flavoured alcoholic spirits of varying strengths. Different brands have very different characters and uses. (*See* **Angostura Bitters**, **Campari**, **Fernet Branca**, *and* **Underberg**.)

black bean   Salted **soya bean** available dried or bottled. (*See also* **black bean sauce** *below*.)

black bean sauce   Sauce made from fermented **soya beans** used in Chinese cooking.

black pepper   *See* **pepper**, **peppercorn**.

black pudding   Savoury pork sausage stuffed with oatmeal, blood, seasoned meat, etc. The French equivalent is **boudin noir**.

blanc(he) (*Fr.*) [bla(n)sh]   White.

blanch   To place briefly in boiling water and then drain to remove excess salt, bitterness, etc. before normal cooking. (Literally, to whiten.)

blanquette (*Fr.*) [blahn-ket]   Delicate but creamy stew of **veal**, lamb or chicken with vegetables, e.g. *blanquette de veau* (From *blanc*, 'white'.)

blend   To mix, usually in an electric blender. Common technique for mixing **cocktails**.

bleu (*Fr.*) [bluh]   Extremely **rare** (steak, etc.). (Literally, 'blue'.) (*See also* **bien cuit**, **point** (à), *and* **saignant**. *See also below*.)

bleu, au (*Fr.*) [oh bluh]   Way of cooking freshly-killed fish, particularly trout, so that skin has a bluish tinge. (*Bleu* means 'blue'.)

blini (*Russ.*) [blee-nee]   Small thick savoury **pancake**, in Russia traditionally served with **soured cream** to accompany **caviare**.

blintz (*Yid.*)   Small savoury **pancake** like a **blini**, but often filled with cheese, etc.

Bloody Mary   Cocktail of **vodka** in **tomato juice**, flavoured with lemon juice, **Tabasco**, and **Worcestershire sauce**.

blue   Extremely **rare** (steak, etc.). (*See also* **bleu**.)

blue vein   Blue mould in blue or green cheese (*See* **gorgonzola**, **roquefort**, *and* **stilton**.)

bocconcini (*Ital.*) [bokon-cheenee]   Small balls of fresh white **mozzarella** preserved in **whey** to retain moisture. Bocconcini are often served as part of the **antipasto** or in salads. (Literally 'little mouthfuls'.)

body   As wine-tasting term describes the consistency or 'thickness' of the wine.

boeuf (*Fr.*) (masc.) [burf]   Beef. (*See also* **bifteck**.)

boeuf à la ficelle (*Fr.*) [burf ah lah fee-sel]   Beef **fillet** tied with string to keep its shape, and cooked in **stock**. (*Ficelle* means 'string'.)

boeuf bourguignon (*Fr.*) [burf boor-gee-nyo(n)]   Beef bourguignon. A **casserole** made with braising steak and red wine. (*Bourguignon* is French for 'Burgundian' or 'from **Burgundy**'.)

boeuf en daube (*Fr.*) [burf o(n) dobe]   Beef **braised** in a red wine **stock**. (*See also* **daube**, **en**.)

boeuf Stroganov/Stroganoff   Strips of beef in a creamy sauce garnished with mushrooms. (The Stroganovs were a wealthy merchant family ennobled by Peter the Great of Russia.)

bok choy (*Chin.*)   White cabbage with fleshy white stems and light green leaves.

bolognais(e) (*Fr.*) [bol-on-ayz]   With a thick meat-and-**tomato** sauce; properly *à la bolognaise* in French, meaning 'in the style of Bologna' (city in NE Italy).

bolognese (*Ital.*) [bolon-ayz-ay]   Italian for **bolognaise**. (In Italy a bolognaise sauce is usually called *ragu*.)

bombe (*Fr.*) (fem.) [bombuh]   Frozen dessert (*bombe glacée*) made in a spherical mould (or one with a rounded top) lined with ice-cream and various fillings. (*Bombe* is French for 'bomb', or 'spherical container'.)

bon appétit! (*Fr.*) [bo(n) apay-tee]   Enjoy your meal! (Literally, 'good appetite'.)

bonne femme (*Fr.*) [bon fam]   Simply cooked; home-style, with potato, e.g. **potage** *bonne femme*. (Literally, 'good woman'.)

bordelaise, à la (*Fr.*) [ah lah bord-eh-layz]   In the style of Bordeaux (town in SW France); cooked with **shallots** and wine, e.g. *poulet* sauté à la bordelaise.

bortsch/borsh (*Russ.*) [borsch]   Beetroot soup served with **soured cream**.

botrytis   Fungus or mould (*Botrytis cinera*), sometimes called **noble rot**, which shrivels late-picked grapes and makes them intensely sweet. Botrytis-affected grapes are used to make many excellent sweet **dessert wines**.

bottomless cup   System used for **coffee**, etc. whereby customers may have their cups refilled as often as they like at no additional charge.

botulism   Food poisoning found principally in canned food and sausages caused by the bacterium *Clostridium botulinum*. (*Botulus* is Latin for 'sausage'.)

bouchée (*Fr.*) (fem.) [boo-shay]   Small **savoury** consisting of a round **puff pastry** with various fillings. (Literally, a 'mouthful'; *bouche* means 'mouth'.)

boudin (*Cajun*) [booda(n)]   Sausage made of pork liver, cooked pork, rice, and seasonings.

boudin noir (*Fr.*) [booda(n)nwa]   **Black pudding**; sausage made from pig's blood, **cream**, fat, and seasonings. (*Noir* means 'black'.)

bouillabaisse (*Fr.*) (fem.) [boo-ya-bayss]   Rich **provençal** stew of fish, mussels, etc. simmered with **herbs**. (*See also* **gumbo** *and* **pochouse**.)

bouillon (*Fr.*) (masc.) [boo-y-o(n)] Plain unclarified meat or vegetable **broth** used as **stock** in cooking. (*See also* **consommé, julienne, potage,** *and* **soupe.**)

bouquet (*Fr.*) (masc.) [boo-kay] Wine-tasting term. The smell of a maturing wine (as opposed to the **aroma** of the grapes). (*See also* **nose.**)

bouquet garni (*Fr.*) (masc.) [boo-kay gar-nee] Bunch of herbs, traditionally consisting of **thyme, marjoram,** parsley and **bay leaves,** used for flavouring sauces, **stock,** etc.

bourbon [burbun] American **whiskey** made principally from fermented maize grain. (Originally from Bourbon County, Kentucky.)

bourguignon *See* **boeuf bourguignon.**

braise To stew meat etc. slowly in very little liquid in a closed pan.

brandy Distilled **spirit** made from fermented grapes. (*See* **armagnac, cognac;** *see also* **calvados** *and* **cherry brandy.**)

Brandy Alexander **Cocktail** of brandy, brown **crème de cacao,** and cream.

brandy snap Golden-brown lacy biscuit flavoured with **ginger** and rolled into a cylindrical shape; they are sometimes made to form a basket in which to serve ice-cream desserts.

brasserie A small (and usually cheap) restaurant or a bar in which food and drinks are served. The word originally meant a brewery. (*Brasser* is French for 'to brew'.)

bratwurst (*Ger.*) [brat-voorst] Uncooked highly-seasoned sausage made from pork and **veal.** (Literally, 'frying sausage'.)

brawn Pieces of meat, esp. calf's or pig's head, cooked and set in **aspic,** shaped into a loaf and served cold. (*See also* **galantine.**)

bread and butter pudding (*UK*) Sweet **pudding** of bread layered with sultanas, candied (mixed) peel and sugar, cooked in egg custard.

breathe Wine-tasting term. To allow a wine to 'breathe' is to allow it to come into contact with air by removing the cork from the bottle some time before the wine is drunk in order to enhance the **bouquet.**

brie (*Fr.*) [bree] Soft creamy cows' milk cheese with a soft edible crust. (Brie is a small town near Paris.) (*See also* **camembert** *and* **chèvre.**)

brine Solution of salt and water usually used as a preservative. (*See also* **cure, pickle,** *and* **smoke.**)

brioche (*Fr.*) (fem.) [bree-osh] Light soft roll, often in the shape of a ring, made from yeast dough with eggs and butter.

brochette (*Fr.*) (fem.) [bro-shett] Skewer on which pieces of meat, etc. are cooked, as for **kebabs.**

brodo (*Ital.*) [brohdoh] **Clear soup; stock.** (*See also* **minestra** *and* **zuppa.**)

broil To grill.

broiler Young chicken bred for broiling.

broth Meat, fish, or vegetable **stock.**

brunch Substantial late-morning meal, replacing breakfast and lunch. (*Compare* **yum cha.**)

brunoise (*Fr.*) (fem.) [broon-warze] **Diced** vegetables, often **braised** in butter, used as a **garnish** for soups, sauces, etc. (*Brun* means 'brown'.)

bruschetta (*Ital.*) Baked or toasted slices of bread, oiled and sprinkled with herbs and served as an **appetizer.** **Tomato** and **garlic** are sometimes added. (*See also* **canapé** *and* **crostino.**)

brush down To remove crumbs, etc. from tables or tablecloths prior to service of next course, also called **crumbing down.**

brut (*Fr.*) [broot] Very dry (**champagne**).

bubble and squeak (*UK*) Mashed potatoes mixed with cooked cabbage and fried. (*See also* **réchauffé.**)

buckwheat Not strictly speaking a **cereal,** but the round plump seeds of an annual plant (*Fagopyrum esculentum*) used in a similar way. It has a strong, distinctive taste and is much used in Chinese, E. European, and Jewish cuisine. Buckwheat flour is used to make **blini** and **piroshki.**

buffet [boof-ay] (1) Meal consisting of a number of dishes set out so that guests can select what they want for themselves. (2) Room or counter where snacks or light meals may be bought.

buffet froid (*Fr.*) (masc.) [boof-ay fwah] Cold meats or shellfish; one of the later courses of the **classic menu,** following the salads and preceding the sweets (**entremets**).

buffet, turkey *See* **turkey buffet.**

build Cocktail-mixing term. To add ingredients one to the other in the glass in which they will be served.

burghul (*Mid. East & Grk.*) Style of **cracked wheat,** whereby the grains are hulled (removed from their husks), steamed and cracked. (*See also* **kibbeh.**)

burgundy Smooth, soft red wine from Burgundy (province in W. France) or similar in style. There are also white burgundies, always so-called. (*See also* **boeuf bourguignon, chablis,** *and* **pinot noir.**

bus (*USA*) To perform general clearing duties in a food-or-beverage service area.

busboy/busgirl (*USA*) Person who clears crockery, glassware, etc. from a food-and-beverage service area.

butterfly (-ied) Cut of meat or fish, esp. prawns, split so that one side remains intact while it is opened flat on the barbecue or grill.

buttery An informal restaurant with bar seating.

cabernet sauvignon (cab-air-nay so-vee-nyon] Grape variety used to make red wines, especially **claret.** Called simply 'cabernet' when blended with other varieties, e.g. cabernet-**malbec**.

cacciatore/cacciatora (*Ital.*) [cat-cha-toray] Cooked with **tomatoes**, **mushrooms**, herbs and, usually, wine, e.g. *pollo alla cacciatora*, chicken cacciatora. (*Cacciatore* means 'hunter'.) (*See also* **chasseur**.)

Caesar salad Salad consisting of **cos** lettuce, dressing, almost raw eggs, **Parmesan** cheese, diced crisp bacon, **anchovy fillets** and **croûtons**, often served as a substantial first course. (Devised by Caesar Cardini, chef in Tijuana, Mexico *c.* 1925.)

café au lait (*Fr.*) (masc.) [caffay oh lay] White **coffee**; coffee with hot milk or **cream** added.

café complet (*Fr.*) A pot of coffee and milk served with **croissants**, butter and **preserve**.

caffeine [caf-feen] Mild stimulant found in **coffee** and **tea**.

Cajun/Cajan [kay-jun] Cuisine developed by **creole** French-speakers in Louisiana (state in S. USA). The key ingredients are **capsicum**, onion, and celery with plenty of **pepper**. (*See also* **gumbo**.)

calamari (*Ital.*) (pl.) [kal-a-maar-ee] Squid.

calcium Mineral, found esp. in cheese and milk, necessary for the building of bones and teeth.

call away/call up To request the kitchen to plate up the next **course**.

calorie Measure of the energy in food. Short for kilocalorie. 1 Calorie = 4.2 **kilojoules**.

calvados Apple **brandy** made in Normandy (province in N. France famous for apples). (*See* **normande**.)

calzone (*Ital.*) [kal-zohny] Savoury pasty made with **pizza** dough.

camembert (*Fr.*) [cam-embear] Soft cheese made from cows' milk, with a downy skin. (Camembert is a village in Normandy, N. France.) (*See also* **brie** and **chèvre**.)

Campari Brand of Italian **bitters**. Bright red, it is often served as an **apéritif** mixed with **soda**.

canapé (*Fr.*) (masc.) [can-a-pay] Small piece of bread (usually toasted) or biscuit, garnished with **caviare**, cheese, **pâté**, **smoked** salmon, etc. Cold canapés are usually served as savoury **appetizers** with drinks before a meal. (*See also* **bruschetta**, **crostino**, *and* **Melba toast**.)

canard (*Fr.*) (masc.) [can-ar] Duck. (*See also* **caneton**.)

cane spirit Clear spirit distilled from sugar, often used in **cocktails**.

caneton (*Fr.*) (masc.) [can-uh-to(n)] Duckling. (*See also* **canard**.)

cannelloni (*Ital.*) (pl.) Form of **pasta** in large tubular rolls filled with cheese or meat, etc. and **baked**.

cantaloup/cantaloupe Rock melon.

canteen Type of restaurant in a factory or school. Also the name for a cutlery box or container.

Cantonese One of the five main styles of Chinese cuisine; *Cantonese* cuisine is the style usually encountered in Westernized restaurants. (*See also* **Fukien**, **Honan**, **Peking**, *and* **Szechwan**.) (Canton is a city in S. China near Hong Kong, now called Guangzhou.)

caper **Pickled** bud or young berry of a Mediterranean shrub (*Capparis spinosa*) used as a garnish or seasoning.

caponata (*Sicily*) [capon-ahtah] Dish of aubergine, tomatoes, and celery flavoured with **capers**, **anchovies** and **olives** fried together in olive oil but served cold, usually as an **hors d'oeuvre**.

cappuccino (*Ital.*) [cap-poo-chee-no] Popular style of **espresso coffee** served with frothy milk.

capretto (*Ital.*) [kap-rettoh] Milk-fed kid (young goat).

capricciosa (*Ital.*) [caprit-chosa] Sauce containing **tomato**, cheese, ham, **mushrooms**, **olives**, and usually **anchovies** commonly served as pizza topping. (*Capriccioso* means 'naughty' or 'capricious'.)

capsicum Family of plants otherwise called **peppers**, including **chillies** and **sweet** (or bell) **peppers**. The word, used alone, usually refers to the latter.

carafe (*Fr.*) (fem.) [ca-raaf] Glass bottle or spoutless jug used for water or wine.

caramel Melted sugar heated slowly until it is brown.

caramelize (1) To turn sugar into **caramel** by heating. (2) To pour melted sugar over food to brown it.

carbohydrate Essential energy-giving nutrient; an organic compound of carbon, hydrogen and oxygen. (Starch, sugar, and cellulose are groups of carbohydrates.)

carbonara (*Ital.*) Bacon-and-**cream** sauce served on pasta.

carob Pod of *Ceratonia siliqua* (locust bean) used ground as a sugar or chocolate substitute.

carpaccio (*Ital.*) [car-patchy-o] Thin slice of raw beef (or tuna) with a **vinaigrette** sauce, served cold.

carpet bag steak Fillet steak filled with oysters, sewn up and grilled.

carré (*Fr.*) (masc.) [caray] Cut of meat, e.g. *carré d'*agneau (**rack** of lamb), *carré de* **veau** (neck of **veal**).

carte, à la (*Fr.*) [ah lah kart] Type of **menu** which offers a choice of items which are individually priced and cooked to order.

carte du jour (*Fr.*) (fem.) [cart doo joor] **Menu** of the day.

cassata (*Ital.*) [kass-ahta] Layers of different ice-creams, one of which is flavoured with **liqueur** and contains **glacé** fruits. (Literally 'little case' because of its traditional brick shape.)

casserole (1) Pan with a lid for cooking stews. (2) Stew cooked in a casserole.

cassis (*Fr.*) (masc.) [cass-ecce] (1) Blackcurrant. (2) Blackcurrant **liqueur**.

cassoulet (*Fr.*) (masc.) [cass-oo-lay]   **Râgout** of haricot beans and meat with a **gratin** topping.

caviare/caviar   Salted sturgeon's eggs. Other fish **roe**, esp. **lump-fish**, is often used as a substitute.

cayenne pepper   Hot spice made from dried, ground red **chillies**, sometimes placed on the table in a small **cruet**. Also called 'red pepper' or 'chilli powder'. (Originally from Cayenne, city in French Guyana.)

cep [sep]   Kind of edible mushroom with thick stalk (*Boletus edulis*). French *cèpe* [saip].) (*See also* **morel, oyster mushroom, pine mushroom,** *and* **truffle**.)

cereal [serial]   (1) Any grain used as food; corn: wheat, barley, maize, oats, rye, etc.
(2) Packaged pre-cooked breakfast food made from such grain.
(Ceres was the Roman goddess of corn crops.)

cervelles (*Fr.*) [fem. pl.] [sur-vel]   Brains.

cevapcici (*Serb.*) [sevap-chee-chee]   Skinless spicy sausage or meatball made of several different meats minced with **capsicum** and **garlic**.

chablis [shablee]   Dry white **table wine** made in the northern **Burgundy** district of France.

chafing dish [chay-fing dish]   (1) Portable pan with a source of heat used for cooking at table, or on a **guéridon**.
(2) Hotplate for keeping dishes warm; a **réchaud**.

cha gio (*Viet.*) [chah zo]   **Spring rolls**; small **pancake** parcel filled with minced crab, pork, and mushroom deep-fried and wrapped in a lettuce leaf with **Vietnamese mint** and dipped in **nuoc cham**.

champagne   **Sparkling wine** from the Champagne region (N. France).

champagne bottle sizes   Champagne and other sparkling wines are often available in extra large bottles; the different sizes have these traditional names: **magnum** (2 bottles), **jeroboam** (4 bottles), **rehoboam** (6 bottles), **methuselah** (8 bottles), **salmanazar** (12 bottles), **balthazar** (16 bottles), and **nebuchadnezzar** (20 bottles). (The 'bottles' are multiples of the standard 75cl bottle.)

champagne cocktail   **Cocktail** of **champagne** with a small measure of **brandy**, a sugar cube and a few drops of **Angostura Bitters**.

champignon (*Fr.*) (masc.) [shom-pee-nyo(n)]   Mushroom.

chantilly   *See* **crème chantilly**.

chapati/chupatty (*Ind.*)   Thin unleavened bread; **roti**.

charcoal grill   To grill food over a 'natural' heat source of burning charcoal. (*See also* **char grill**.)

charcuterie (*Fr.*) (fem.) [shar-coot-er-ee]   (1) Pork butchery.
(2) Cooked meats, e.g. **terrines, smoked** ham, **salamis,** etc., made primarily from pork. (*See also* **smallgoods**.)

charcutière, à la (*Fr.*) [ah lah shar-coot-ee-air]   Served with a **demi-glace** containing wine and thin strips of **dill pickle**.

chard, rainbow.   *See* **silverbeet**.

chardonnay [shar-don-ay]   Grape variety used to make white wines, e.g. white **burgundy**.

char grill   To cook food on a grill which has coke or coals over an 'artificial' electric or gas heat source. (*See also* **charcoal grill**.)

charlotte (*Fr.*) (fem.) [sharl-ot]   Hot baked dessert of **puréed** fruit cased in or layered with bread or spongecake, cooked in a mould. (Named in honour of Queen Charlotte, consort of George III.)

charlotte russe [sharl-ot rooss]   Cold dessert of custard prepared in a **charlotte** mould lined with jelly and sponge fingers. (*Ruse* means 'Russian'.)

Chartreuse   Old French **proprietary liqueur** with very complex flavours. There are two styles: green and yellow. The green is stronger and less sweet. (Named after *La Grande Chartreuse* monastery near Grenoble, France, where the liqueur is made.)

chasseur (*Fr.*) (masc.) [shass-ur]   Cooked with white wine, **shallots**, mushrooms, and tomatoes, e.g. **tournedos** *chasseur*. (*Chasseur* means 'hunter'.)

châteaubriand (*Fr.*) (masc.) [shat-oh-bree-ond]   Tender thick **fillet** steak, usually served with a **béarnaise** sauce. (Devised by the chef to the Vicomte de Châteaubriand, 1768–1848, French diplomat, writer, and gourmet.)

chaud (*Fr.*) [show]   Hot.

chaudfroid (*Fr.*) (masc.) [show-frwah]   Cold dish of fish or meat served in a solidified coating of **gelatine** (**aspic**) sauce; cooked hot and served cold. (*Chaud* is French for 'hot' and *froid* is French for 'cold', so literally 'hot– cold'.)

chawarma/shwarma (*Leb.*) [sha-warma]   *See* **döner kebab**.

cheddar   The most popular kind of tasty cheese (originally made in the village of Cheddar in Somerset, England).

chef (*Fr.*) (masc.) [shef]   Senior or head cook. (*Chef* is French for 'chief' or 'head'.)

chef de rang (*Fr.*) (masc.) [shef duh rung]   Traditional term for a senior waiter; the waiter immediately under the station head waiter in an **establishment** with a full service brigade. (*See* **rang**.)

cherry brandy   Cherry-flavoured **liqueur**, usually made by **macerating** cherries in neutral spirit. (*See also* **kirsch**.)

cherry tomato   *See* **tomato**.

chervil   Small plant with parsley-like leaves used as a herb for seasoning, esp. in French cuisine; one of the ingredients of **fine herbes**.

chèvre (*Fr.*) (fem.) [shevruh]   (1) She-goat.
(2) Goat's cheese.

chevreuil, en (*Fr.*) [ahn-shev-ruyee]   Cooked to taste like venison; **marinated** meat served with *sauce* **poivrade** or *sauce* **venaison**. (*Un chevreuil* is a roe-deer.) (*See also* **salmis**.)

chiboust   *See* **crème chiboust**.

chick-pea   Seed of the **legume** *Cicer arietinum*. It is a staple of Middle Eastern cooking, and is used in dishes such as **hummus** and **falafel**.

chicory   (1) Belgian or white **endive** (*Cichorium intybus*); vegetable with tightly-wrapped white leaves which may be thinly sliced and served raw in salad or cooked by steaming or boiling. Its roots are ground and mixed with **coffee** and it is used in coffee substitutes.
(2) Curly **endive** (Cichorium endivia); sharply-flavoured spinach-like vegetable. (Italian *cicoria*; Greek *rathikia*.)

chiffonnade   (*Fr.*) (fem.) [shiffon-ard]   Leaves of salad vegetables (lettuce, **chicory**, etc.) cut or shredded into thin strips, used as a **garnish**.

chilli   Pod and seeds of varieties of the **capsicum** plant used as a very hot spice, particularly in SE Asian, Indian and Mexican food. Chillies are red or green. When dried and powdered red chillies become **cayenne pepper**. (*See also* **pepper** *and* **sweet pepper**.)

chilli con carne   (*Mex.*) [chilly con car-nay]   Stew of **chillies**, **minced meat** and beans. (*Con carne* is Spanish for 'with meat'.)

China tea   Green **tea**, often served without milk. (*See also* **jasmine tea**.)

chipolata [chipoh-lahta]   Very small sausage.

chives   Thin green flavouring **herb** related to onion and garlic, but without a distinct 'bulb'; it is one of the ingredient of **fines herbes**.

chlorophyll   Substance which makes plants green. (Literally, 'green leaf' in Greek.)

choi   *See* **choy**.

cholesterol [kolesterol]   Fatty substance found only in animals, high levels of which are associated with heart attacks.

chop suey   (*Chin.*) [chop sooee]   Shredded meat cooked with vegetables.

chorizo (*Span. & Mex.*) [koreet-soh]   Spicy pork sausage usually eaten cooked, esp. with **paella**.

chou (*Fr.*) (masc.) [shoo]   Cabbage. (*See also* **choy**.)

choux (*Fr.*) (masc. pl.) [shoo]   Small light buns made of **choux pastry**. Choux are served either cold as a **sweet** with a **cream** filling, or with a savoury stuffing as **hors d'oeuvre**.

choux pastry [shoo]   Very light pastry used to make **choux**, **éclairs**, **profiteroles**, etc; **pâte à choux**.

chowder (*USA*)   A creamy soup made from seafood, usually molluscs, e.g. clam chowder. (*See also* **bisque**.)

chow mein (*Chin.*) [chow meen]   Fried **noodles** with green vegetables and, usually, meat.

choy (*Chin.*)   Cabbage. (*See also* **bok choy** *and* **choy sum** below.)

choy sum (*Chin.*)   Pretty variety of cabbage with long stem and yellow flowers. The stems are particularly tasty, with a mildly bitter flavour.

Christmas pudding (UK)   Rich steamed pudding containing dried, fresh, and **glacé** fruits, spices, nuts, eggs, **suet**, and **brandy**. It is made months in advance and reheated on Christmas Day.

chutney (*Anglo-Ind.*)   Thick mixture of fruits and vegetables preserved in **vinegar**, sugar and spices, served as a **condiment**.

cider   Alcoholic drink made from the fermented juice of apples.

citronelle   *See* **lemon grass**.

citrus   Fruit from any citrus tree – lemon, lime, orange, grapefruit, cumquat, etc.

cl   Centilitres (hundredths of a litre).

clafoutis (*Fr.*) [claff-ootee]   Baked **pudding** of **batter** spread thickly on a base of fruit, esp. black **morello** cherries, and served warm.

claret   Red wine either from the Bordeaux region of SW France or of similar type. Clarets are medium-bodied and have a distinctively astringent aftertaste because of their high **tannin** content. (The English word 'claret' comes from the French word *clairet* meaning 'clear, bright' (wine). (*See also* **cabernet sauvignon**.)

clarify   To make clear; to remove the impurities from stocks, etc. so that they are no longer cloudy. **Stocks** may be clarified by boiling egg whites in them which coagulate and trap the particles to be removed. (*See also* **ghee**.)

classic menu   The full traditional banquet menu as it developed in France in the nineteenth century, with courses offered as follows: (1) **hors d'oeuvre** (2) soups (**potages**) (3) fish (poisson) (4) **entrées** (meaning small, preliminary meat dishes, the first of the meat courses (5) **relevés** (6) **sorbets** (7) roasts (**rôtis**) (8) vegetables (**légumes**) (9) sweets (**entremets**) (10) **savouries** (11) cheeses (**fromages**) (12) desserts (in the sense of fresh fruit and nuts (13) beverages (coffee, tea, etc. – not, strictly speaking, a course).

clear soup   Consommé. (*See also* **brodo**, **julienne**, **marmite petite**, **steamboat**, *and* **tom yam**.)

cloche   Dish cover, usually metal, often semi-spherical with a handle at top, serving to keep food warm. A cheese cloche (to protect from flies, etc.) is usually made of glass or transparent plastic.

clotted cream   *See* **cream, clotted**.

cocktail   Mixed drink, almost always alcoholic, often with a **spirit** base.

coconut   Edible flesh of the fruit of the coconut palm. It can be **desiccated** (dried), shredded and used in **curries**, cakes, **puddings** and confectionery.

coconut cream Thick mixture of processed **coconut** flesh and **coconut milk** used in **curries** and Asian dishes.

coconut milk (1) Liquid from inside the **coconut**.
(2) Processed milky mixture of **coconut** flesh with **coconut milk** used as a drink or in Asian cooking.

cocotte (*Fr.*) (fem.) [cock-ot] Small round or oval oven-proof cooking dish in which food may be both cooked and served. (*See below.*)

cocotte, en (*Fr.*) [ahn cock-ot] Cooked and served in a small **cocotte** dish (e.g. **oeufs** *en* **cocottes**).

coeur à la crème (*Fr.*) [cur ahlah crem] Dessert of **fromage blanc**, drained and set in a perforated heart-shaped mould and turned out to serve with fresh fruit or a **coulis**.

coffee Drink made from the ground beans of the coffee (*Coffea*) plant, usually served after a meal. There are many ways of serving it. (*See also* **café au lait, cappucino, Cona, decaffeinated, espresso, Greek, iced, liqueur, macchiato, mocha, Turkish** *and* **Vienna coffee**.)

cognac (*Fr.*) (masc.) (con-yak] Fine **brandy** from the Cognac region of SW France.

Cointreau (*Fr.*) [kwi(n)-troh] Popular **proprietary** French **triple sec curaçao liqueur**.

Colada One of a group of **blended** long-drink **cocktails**, all including white **rum, coconut cream**, pineapple juice and cream.

collation A light meal, usually cold, served out of normal hours.

com chien (*Viet.*) [kom chin] Fried rice.

commis (*Fr.*) (masc.) [commie] Assistant or trainee. Short for commis cook or **commis de rang**.

commis de rang (*Fr.*) (masc.) [commie duh rung] Assistant or trainee waiter, below the **chef de rang** in the traditional service brigade.

commis waiter [commie] Ordinary assistant waiter or trainee waiter. (*See* **commis** *and* **commis de rang**.)

compote (*Fr.*) (fem. [kompot] Fruit cooked in syrup; stewed fruit.

com tam (*Viet.*) [kom tum] 'Broken' rice topped with pork. (*Com* is 'rice', *tam* 'crushed'.)

Cona coffee Method of making **coffee** by **vacuum infusion**, similar in principle to the percolator method. The equipment consists of two bowls which are placed one above the other. Water is boiled so that it rises from the lower bowl through a tube into the upper bowl where it passes through ground coffee and a filter before returning to the lower bowl from which it is served. Cona is a trade name.

Condé (*Fr.*) [conday] Various dishes dedicated to the Prince de Condé, great French general, 1621–86 or his descendants. A Condé is usually a cold dessert of poached fruit, esp. pears, arranged in and around a ring of sweet, creamy rice and served cold.

condiment Seasoning (e.g. **mustard, soya sauce,** or **pickle**) used to give relish to food, usually added to the food after it has been served at table.

confit (*Fr.*) (masc.) [con-fee] Piece of almost boneless meat, usually duck, goose, or **game**, cooked in its own fat and juice and sealed in a pot, immersed in the same fat, for preservation, e.g. *confit d'oie*.

consommé (*Fr.*) (masc.) [con-som-ay] A clear soup made from beef or chicken **stock** which has been clarified. It is usually served hot but may be chilled in which case it will be jelly-like but not solid. (*See also* **bisque, bouillon, garbure, julienne, marmite petite, pistou, potage, soupe,** *and* **vichyssoise**.)

contaminate (verb) hence **contamination** (noun) (1) To pollute or infect.
(2) To blend different mixtures thus spoiling both. This often occurs when one utensil is re-used in the preparation of different dishes.

continental breakfast Light breakfast of fruit juice, **croissants** or toast with butter, preserves and coffee.

coq au vin (*Fr.*) [cock oh va(n)] Chicken **casseroled** with bacon, onion, **garlic** and **mushrooms** in **brandy** and red wine. (Literally 'cock in wine'.)

coquille (*Fr.*) (fem.) [coh-kee] Shell (of fish etc.).

coquilles Saint (St) Jacques (*Fr.*) [coh-kee san zjak] **Scallops** served cooked in a creamy sauce and presented in a scallop shell with mashed potato **piped** around the edge. (The scallop shell was the symbol of the pilgrims who visited the tomb of St Jacques – St James – of Compostella, N. Spain.)

corbeille (*Fr.*) A basket, usually of fruit.

cordial (1) Any stimulating beverage.
(2) Concentrated fruit squash, e.g. lemon cordial.
(3) (*USA*) **liqueur**.

coriander Fragrant herb or spice with a bitter flavour. Both the leaves and seeds are commonly used in S and SE Asian **cuisine**.

corkage Charge made by an **establishment** for opening bottles brought by customers.

corked/corky wine Wine which has been spoiled because the bottle has a faulty and mouldy cork. Seriously corked wine becomes bitter and foul-smelling but mild corking may be difficult to detect. The word has nothing to do with pieces of cork which may fall into the wine when the bottle is opened.

corn (on the cob)/sweet corn/maize Cluster of small yellow grains on a central core or cob covered with fine silky threads and a green sheath. If served whole a **fingerbowl** is required. Miniature baby corn is used whole esp. in Chinese dishes. (In French *maïs*.) (*See also* **polenta**.)

corn chip Thin crisp wafer made from maize (**corn**)

flour and served with **nachos** or eaten as a snack.

Cornish pasty   Mixture of meat and vegetables (potatoes, onions, turnips etc.) wrapped in pastry case.

cos [koz]   Lettuce with crisp, long leaves.

côte (*Fr.*) (fem.) [coat]   Rib, e.g. *côtes de* **veau**.

coulibiac (*Fr.*) [cooly-bee-ahkee]   French adaptation of a Russian fish pie, traditionally layered salmon, rice, and chopped hard-boiled eggs rolled in pastry.

coulis ((*Fr.*) (masc.) [coo-lee]   Thin **purée** of fruit, seasoned cooked vegetables, or fish.

coupe (*Fr.*) (fem.) [coop]   (1) Stemmed bowl, usually made of glass.
(2) Dessert served in such a bowl (*coupe* **d'ananas**, *coupes* **glacées**).

courgette (*Fr.*) (fem.) [koor-zjet]   Variety of marrow also known as **zucchini**. The flowers can be stuffed with a **farce**.

course   Stages of a meal, e.g. **entrée**, main course, **dessert**. (*See* **classic menu**.)

court-bouillon (*Fr.*) (masc.) [coar bwee-yon]   **Broth** of white wine, herbs, and vegetables in which fish is simmered; a seasoned fish **stock**.

couscous (*Arab.*) [koos koos]   N. African dish of steamed **semolina** served with meat or vegetables.

couvert (*Fr.*) [koo-vair]   **Cover**

cover   (1) Place setting for one guest.
(2) The number of guests at a **function** or **establishment**.

cover charge   A charge added to the bill for rolls, butter, laundry etc.

cracked wheat   Whole wheat grains cracked and broken open by crushing to produce a coarse meal. *See also* **burghul** *and* **kibbeh**.)

crackling   Crisp baked skin or rind of pork, usually served sliced.

crawfish   Large salt-water **crustacean** without large claws, also known as spiny lobster.

crayfish   Freshwater crustacean resembling a small lobster. (French **écrivisse**).

cream   (1) Thick fatty part of milk. Light or reduced cream has a lower fat content. Thickened cream has a thickening agent (e.g. **gelatine**) added to enhance whipping.
(2) Food resembling pure cream in consistency; dessert containing cream; creamed soup, e.g. butter cream, custard cream, cream of mushroom soup. (*See also* **crème** *etc.*, *and below*.)

cream cheese   Soft, spreadable cheese.

cream, clotted   Cream, skimmed from **scalded milk**, cooled and traditionally served with **scones** and jam for cream tea. (*See also* **Devonshire tea**.)

cream, soured   Thick **cream** to which a culture has been added to give a sharp taste. (It is not cream that has gone 'off'.)

crème (*Fr.*) (fem.) [cream]   **Cream**, custard.

crème, à la (*Fr.*) (fem.) [ah lah crem]   Cooked with **cream**, cream sauce, or custard.

crème anglaise (*Fr.*) [crem on-glaze]   Custard of a pouring consistency cooked slowly over a **bain-marie**. (Literally, 'English cream'.)

crème brûlée (*Fr.*) [crem broo-lay]   Thick, smooth custard covered with a thick crust of sugar which has been grilled until **caramelized** and crisp. (*Brûlée* means 'burnt'.)

crème caramel (*Fr.*) [crem cara-mel]   Custard set in a mould containing a **caramel** sauce. Once turned out the sauce sits on top and slips down the sides.

crème chantilly (*Fr.*) [crem shahn-tee-yee]   Fresh **cream** whipped and sweetened with **vanilla sugar**. (Chantilly is a town near Paris.)

crème chiboust (*Fr.*) [crem shiboost]   Custard similar to **crème pâtissière** but with **gelatine** added. The eggs are separated and the whipped whites are added to the warm custard. (Chiboust was a pastry cook in 19th-century Paris.)

crème d', de . . . (*Fr.*) [crem duh]   Cream **liqueurs** (*crème* **d'amandes**, *crème de* **cacao**, *crème de* **menthe**).

crème de cacao (crem duh kakau)   **Liqueur** made from **vanilla** and cocoa beans. There are white and brown styles. (*Cacao* is French for 'cocoa'.)

crème de menthe (*Fr.*) [crem du mah(n)th]   Peppermint-flavoured **generic liqueur**, usually bright green. (*Menthe* means 'mint'.)

crème fouettée (*Fr.*) [crem foo-ettay]   Whipped **cream**.

crème fraîche (*Fr.*) [crem fraysh]   Thick **cream** to which a culture has been introduced resulting in a sharp taste and almost solid consistency. (Literally, 'fresh cream'.) (*See also* **mascarpone**.)

crème pâtissière (*Fr.*) [crem paht-ees-see-year)   Thick custard thickened with flour to which beaten egg white is added to provide a **mousse**-like texture which will hold its shape in cakes and desserts. (*Pâtissier* (fem. *~-ière* means 'pastry cook' or 'confectioner'.) (*See also* **crème chiboust**.)

creole [cree-yoal]   In the style of the West Indies. Typically savoury dishes contain **capsicums** or bananas, and sweet dishes contain sugar, **rum**, or bananas. (French, *créole* [cray-oal].) (*See* **Cajun**.)

crêpe (*Fr.*) (fem.) [krep]   Very thin **pancake** cooked on both sides, usually filled and rolled up when served. *Crêpes* can be sweet or savoury.

crêpes Suzette (*Fr.*) (fem. pl.) [krep soo-zet]   Sweet **crêpes** flavoured with orange juice and orange **liqueur** (e.g. **curaçao** or **Grand Marnier**). They are often cooked at the table in a **chafing dish** and served **flambé** in lighted **rum**. (Invented by chef Henri Charpentier *c.* 1900, and named in honour of a child dinner guest of the Prince of Wales.)

crépinette (*Fr.*) (fem.) [krep-in-ett]   Finely minced meat with seasonings cooked in a caul (thin membrane); a flat sausage.

cress   (1) Salad greens from the mustard family.
(2) *Lepidium sativum*, a tiny green seedling with little black seeds commonly known as garden or mustard-and-cress. (*See also* **rocket** *and* **watercress**.) (French, *cresson*.)

croissant (*Fr.*) (masc.) [kwa-sahn]   Crescent-shaped sweet roll usually made of **puff pastry**, commonly served at breakfast with butter and jam or chocolate. (Literally 'crescent'.) (*See also* **pain au chocolat**.)

croquembouche (*Fr.*) [crockem-boosh]   Conical tower of small **choux** buns filled with custard or **cream** and coated with spun sugar, traditionally served at weddings. (Literally 'crisp in the mouth'.)

croque-monsieur (*Fr.*) (masc.) [crock muss-yure]   Toasted sandwich, esp. one filled with ham and **gruyère** cheese. (*Croque-madame* has a fried egg on top.) (*Croquant(e)* means 'crunchy' from *croquer* 'to crunch', 'to devour'.)

croquette (*Fr.*) (fem.) [kro-ket]   Minced mixture, usually meat or fish, with vegetables and seasoning, prepared with a sauce to bind and shaped into a small ball, tube, or **patty**. It is rolled in egg and breadcrumbs before it is fried.

cross-contamination   Spoiling of food by germs passing from one organism to another.

crostino (*Ital.*) (*pl.* **crostini**) [cross-teeno/ee]   **Canapé** or small savoury toast served as an appetizer; a **croûton**.

croustade (*Fr.*) (fem.) [kroo-stahd]   Case of pastry, or deep-fried bread, mashed potato, or rice containing a savoury mixture in a cream sauce or a **purée**, e.g. *croustades à la* **marinière**. (*See also* **vol-au-vent**.)

croûte (*Fr.*) (fem.) [kroot]   (1) Pastry case.
(2) Slice of fried bread on which **appetizers** are served. (*See also below*.)

croûte, en   Cooked in a pastry case (e.g. **pâté** *en croûte*, **poulet** *en croute*). (*See* **croûte** *above*.)

croûton (*Fr.*) (masc.) [kroo-ton]   Small cube of fried or toasted bread used to **garnish** soups and some salad and vegetable dishes. (*See also* **crostino**.)

crudités (*Fr.*) (fem. pl.) [kroo-di-tay]   Small pieces of vegetable served as an **appetizer** with an accompanying savoury dip. Typical vegetables include carrot, celery, mushroom, cauliflower, broccoli and **capsicum**. Many sauces are used: avocado dip, **mayonnaise**, **taramasalata** or any with a soft consistency.

cruets   Salt and **pepper** set, and containers for oil and **vinegar**.

crumb down   To brush the tablecloth between courses thus removing all debris. A table is usually crumbed down after the main course and before **dessert**.

crumble   A baked pudding made up of a crumbly mixture of flour, sugar and fat covering stewed fruit such as apples.

crumpet   A light yeast cake, toasted and served with butter at tea.

crustacean(s)   Type of shellfish, including **crayfish**, **lobsters**, prawns, shrimps, and crabs. (French *les crustaces*.)

cuisine (*Fr.*) (fem.) [kwi-zeen]   (1) Kitchen or kitchen staff (**chef** *de cuisine*).
(2) (Style of) cookery or food (e.g. French cuisine, Thai cuisine, **cuisine naturelle**).

cuisine minceur (*Fr.*) [kwi-zeen mansur]   Style of cooking using low-calorie ingredients and replacing the rich sauces of traditional French **cuisine** with vegetable **purée**, **fromage blanc**, or **crème fraîche**. (Created by Michel Guérard, *b.* 1933; *minceur* means 'slenderness'.) (*See also* **cuisine naturelle**, **haute cuisine**, **nouvelle cuisine**, *and* **Pritikin**.)

cuisine naturelle (*Fr.*) [kwi-zeen natoor-ell]   Style of cooking using fresh ingredients prepared so that the natural flavour is evident. Fats, alcohol, salt, and sugar are used sparingly. (Created by Anton Mosimann, *b.* 1947, at the Dorchester Hotel in London.) (*See also* **cuisine minceur**, **haute cuisine**, **nouvelle cuisine**, *and* **Pritikin**.)

Cumberland sauce   Sweet-and-sour sauce made of orange and lemon juice and zest, red currant jelly and **port**, usually served cold with roasted or **braised** strong-tasting meats like mutton, **venison** or duck. (From Cumberland, county in N. England.)

curaçao [cure-a-soh]   Orange **liqueur**, either white or blue in colour. (Originally made with oranges from Curaçao, W. Indian island.) (*See also* **triple sec**.)

curd   Rich creamy fattening part of milk which can be separated from the watery part or **whey**.

cure   To **preserve** food by drying, salting, **pickling**, or **smoking**. (*See also* **brine**.)

curry (*Anglo-Ind.*)   Dish of meat or vegetables prepared with spices, particularly **turmeric**; general term for Indian dishes. The English word curry comes from a Tamil (S. Indian) word meaning sauce, but the word is little used in Indian cookery.

custard apple   Soft fruit of W. Indian tree (*Anona reticulata*) shaped like large apple with flesh tasting like custard.

cutlet   (1) Thick slice of meat on the bone from the neck of lamb or **veal**. (*See also* **papillote**.)
(2) Thick slice of fish on the bone. (*See also* **darne** *and* **trançon**.)

cuvée (*Fr.*) [koo-vay]   Batch of wine or a blend of wines from different vats.

dahl/dal (*Ind.*) [dahl]   Thick **purée** of **lentils**. With **roti** it is the staple food of N. India.

daikon radish [dye-ko(n)]   Giant white radish which is **pickled** and served beautifully sliced or shredded as a

garnish with many Japanese meals. (*See also* **horseradish** *and* **wasabi**.)

Danish pastry Flaky yeast cake topped with icing, nuts and fruit and usually baked in a scroll shape. (Also known as Apple Danish, Apricot Danish etc.)

dariole (*Fr.*) (fem.) [da-ree-ole] (1) Small steep-sided mould used in making small pastries and **puddings**.
(2) Food that is baked or set in a *dariole*.

Darjeeling tea Fine black Indian **tea**. (Darjeeling is a hill town in the tea-growing area of NW India.)

darne (*Fr.*) [darnuh] Steak or **cutlet** of large round fish such as schnapper or cod, cross cut through the bone, e.g. *darne de saumon* (salmon steak). (*See also* **trançon**.)

daube, en (*Fr.*) [ahn dobe] Cooked slowly in a pan; **braised**, e.g. **boeuf en daube**. (*Une daubière* is a stewpan.)

de (*Fr.*) (masc.) [duh] Of, as in *côte de boeuf* ('side of beef'), *pâté de foie* ('pâté of liver'); spelt **d'** when next word starts with a vowel, as in **mignonnettes** *d'***agneau** ('mignonnettes *of* lamb').

débarrasseur (*Fr.*) Assistant waiter who clears tables and does other chores in the dining room.

decaffeinated coffee/tea **Coffee** or **tea** from which **caffeine** has been extracted.

decant To pour a **liquor**, especially wine, carefully without raising sediment from a bottle into a **decanter**, **carafe** or jug.

decanter Narrow-necked glass jug, usually with a stopper, used for storing or serving wines or **spirits**.

deglaze To remove fat from a pan in which meat has been cooked by pouring alcohol into the pan and boiling briskly. **Stock** or **cream** is then added to form a **jus** or sauce. (French *déglacer*.)

dégustation (*Fr.*) (fem.) [day-goo-stah-seeo(n)] (1) Tasting; sampling food and drink.
(2) Wine-tasting.
See also **menu dégustation**.

déjeuner (*Fr.*) Lunch.

de la (*Fr.*) (fem.) [duh la] Of the, when used with a feminine noun, as in *de la* **maison** ('*of the* house'). Note that **du** is the masculine form of *de la*, used with masculine nouns.

delicatessen (Ger.) Shop selling cheeses, cooked meats and groceries, casual restaurant. (Literally 'delicacies' in German.) (*See also* **charcuterie**.)

délice (*Fr.*) [day-leece] Trimmed and folded fillet of fish.

demi-glace (*Fr.*) (fem.) [demee gluss] Rich brown sauce made by **reducing stock** to half its original volume. **Madeira**, **sherry**, or **brandy** is often added after the reduction. (Literally, 'half glaze'.)

demitasse [demee tass] Very small **coffee** cup for after-dinner coffee. (*See also* **espresso**, **Greek**, and **Turkish**.) (French, literally 'half cup'.)

des (*Fr.*) (pl.) [day] Of, when used as a plural, e.g. **purée** *des* **marrons**.

desiccate To preserve by drying, e.g. desiccated **coconut**.

dessert (1) Final, **sweet** course of a meal.
(2) Fruit and nuts served at the end of a meal. (*See* **classic menu**.)

dessert wine Sweet wine usually served with dessert. (*See* **auslese**, **muscat**, **spätlese**, and **sauternes**.)

devilled **Marinated** meat in a thick, slightly sweet, spicy sauce. A devil mixture usually contains one or all of the following: **mustard**, **Worcestershire sauce**, sugar, and **tomato** sauce. (*See* **diable**.)

Devonshire tea Afternoon **tea** with **scones**, **clotted cream**, and jam.

diable, à la (*Fr.*) [ah lah dee-ah-bluh] **Devilled**, as in **boeuf** *à la diable*. (*Diable* means 'devil'.)

dice To cut up into small even cubes. (*See also* **macédoine**.)

digestif (*Fr.*) (masc.) [dee-zjes-teef] A digestive; an after-dinner drink, particularly a **liqueur**, said to aid digestion, whence the name.

Dijon (*Fr.*) [dee-zjo(n)] **Mustard** which is prepared with verjuice (acid from unripened grapes) and white wine. (Dijon is a city in Central W. France.)

dill Fragrant annual plant, the feathery leaves of which are used as a **garnish** and as a flavouring herb. The seeds are used in **pickles**. (*See* **dill pickle** *below*.)

dill pickle Baby cucumber pickled with **dill** seeds.

dim sum (*Chin.*) Small savoury **dumpling** containing meat and cabbage wrapped in a **won ton** wrapper and steamed or deep dried.

distillation Process used to make **spirits** from **fermented** 'wine'.

doily Lace-like paper mat used to decorate plates, particularly under cakes, or on an **underliner**.

dolcelatta (*Ital.*) (doll-che-lah-tah) Moist, creamy, mild, blue-veined cheese made from cow's milk.

dolmas (*Grk.* & *Turk.*) [doll-mahth] (*pl.* **dolmades** [doll-mah-thess]) Vine (or cabbage) leaves stuffed with oily rice, sometimes with nuts, currants and minced lamb, etc. in the rice. Dolmades are often served with **meze**.

döner kebab (*Turk.*) [doaner kuhbabb] **Marinated** lamb, thinly sliced from a vertical **salamander**, rolled with salad, **tahini** and **hummus** in **pitta** bread. (Lebanese equivalent is **chawarma**.)

Drambuie Proprietary **liqueur** made from Scotch **whisky**, heather, honey, and herbs.

draught beer Beer drawn from a barrel rather than bottled or canned.

dredge To sprinkle with castor sugar, flour, etc.

dredger Sugar castor, sugar shaker.

dressing *See* **French dressing** *and* **vinaigrette**.

dry ginger (ale) Non-alcoholic drink of carbonated water flavoured with **ginger** extract. Often called 'dry' as in '**brandy** and dry'. (*See* **ginger**.)

Dry Martini **Cocktail** of gin with a little dry (French **vermouth**, **garnished** with a green **olive** or a twist of lemon.

du (*Fr.*) (masc.) [doo] Of the, when used with a masculine noun, as in **carte** *du jour* ('**menu** *of the* day'). Note that **de la** is the feminine form of **du** and **des** is the plural.

Dubonnet French brand of aromatized wine or **vermouth** commonly served with **soda** or with ice as an **apéritif**.

duchesse *See* **pommes duchesse**.

du jour (*Fr.*) [doo zjoor] Literally 'of the day', e.g. **poisson** *du jour* ('fish of the day').

dumb waiter A small lift for sending food from the kitchen to the dining room. Alternatively, a sideboard in the dining room.

dumpling Ball of dough, either baked or simmered in a **casserole**; they may be sweet or savoury and flavoured with sugar, syrup, or herbs, etc. (*See also* **dim sum**, **gnocchi**, **quenelle**, *and* **won ton**.)

duxelles (*Fr.*) (fem. pl.) [dook-sel] **Sautéed** mixture of finely chopped onions or **shallots** with mushrooms, seasoned and **reduced**. Duxelles are used as a **garnish** or stuffing. Such dishes are described as **à la** *duxelles* (as in **omelete** *à la duxelles*).

Earl Grey tea Smoky-tasting blended **tea** flavoured with **bergamot**. (Earl Grey, 1764–1845, was Prime Minister 1830– 4.)

échalote (*Fr.*) (fem.) [ay-shallot] **Shallot**.

éclair (*Fr.*) [ay-clair] Small cylindrical cake made from **choux** pastry, split and filled with **cream** and iced with chocolate icing.

écrivisse (*Fr.*) (fem.) [ay-cree-veece] European fresh-water crayfish.

egg-nog/egg flip Alcoholic drink of liquor mixed with eggs and milk served either just warm or cold.

eggs Benedict Poached eggs with grilled ham served on a **muffin** or toast covered in **hollandaise**.

émincé (*Fr.*) (masc.) [ay-mah(n)-say] Thin slice, esp. of meat; rasher (of bacon). (*Emincer* means 'to slice finely'.) (*See also* **émincés** *below*.)

émincés (*Fr.*) (masc. pl.) [ay-mah(n)-say] Thin slices of left-over meat reheated in **jus** or sauce. (*See also* **émincé** *above, and* **réchauffé**.)

en (*Fr.*) [ahn] In, as in *en* **cocotte**. (*See also* **chevreuil**, **cocotte**, **croûte**, **daube**, **gelée**, *and* **papillote**.)

enchilada (*Mex.*) [en-chill-ahda] Fried **tortilla** filled with cheese and/or meat and rolled. Served with **chilli** sauce and, possibly, **guacamole**.

endive [en-dive] (1) *Cichorium endivia*, sometimes referred to as curly endive, a bitter green-leaf vegetable used in salads.

(2) Belgian endive, **chicory** (*Cichorium intybus*), used in salads or as a cooked vegetable.

English Breakfast tea Blended Indian and Ceylon (black) **teas**.

en pension (*Fr.*) Full board, with all meals provided.

entrecôte (*Fr.*) (masc.) [ahn-truh-coat] Rib steak of beef, often pounded and served as **minute steak**. (Literally, 'between the rib'.) (*See also* **filet mignon**, **porterhouse**, **rump**, **sirloin**, *and* **T-bone**.)

entrée (*Fr.*) (fem.) [ahn]tray] Small cuts of butcher's meat or poultry, served with a sauce or garnish, a main dish. In the **classic menu** the entrée was the first (and smallest) of the meat courses, following the fish course. (Literally, 'entrance'.)

entremets (*Fr.*) (masc. pl.) [ahn-truh-may] Sweet course. (*See* **classic menu**.)

épinards (*Fr.*) (masc. pl.) [ay-peenard] Spinach. (*See also* **silverbeet**.)

escalope (*Fr.*) (fem.) [ess-cal-op] Thin slice of boneless meat, e.g. *escalope de* **veau**.

escargot (*Fr.*) (masc.) [ess-car-go] Snail.

espagnole (*Fr.*) [ess-pan-yol] Spanish, as in **omelette farcia** *à la espagnole* ('Spanish omelette'). (*See also below*.)

espagnole, sauce (*Fr.*) (fem.) [sohs ess-pa(n)ol] **Reduced** brown sauce flavoured with **tomatoes** and **sherry**. (*See also* **salmis**, **sauce**.)

espresso (*Ital.*) [ess-press-oh] Strong black **coffee** made by forcing steam through ground coffee beans. (*Espresso* is Italian for 'pressed' or 'forced out' and, incidentally, for 'express' or 'fast'.)

essence Concentrated extract from fruit, flower, or nut used for flavouring, e.g. **vanilla essence**.

establishment A business in the hospitality industry – restaurant, hotel, etc.; a hospitality operation.

Evian Brand of **mineral water** (from Evian-les-Bains, spa town in French Alps).

extra virgin *See* **virgin olive oil**.

falafel/felafel (*Arab.*) [fell-a-fell] **Chick-pea** ball flavoured with spices.

farce (*Fr.*) [farse] Savoury stuffing; **forcemeat**.

farci(e) (*Fr.*) [farsee] Stuffed; a stuffed dish. (*Farcir* means 'to stuff'.)

farinaceous [farin-ay-shus] Consisting of cereals, beans, or pulses. (*Farina* is Latin for flour.)

felafel *See* **falafel**.

fennel (1) Large bulbous plant with a slightly aniseed taste. It is **braised** and served as a vegetable or can be sliced raw and mixed with salad greens.

(2) Feathery fronds of the fennel plant used as a herb or **garnish**, especially with fish.

(3) Fennel seeds, aromatic and used as a flavouring, especially in **pickled** foods.

fermentation   Process of converting a liquid containing sugar into alcohol by the action of yeast.

Fernet Branca [fair-nay brankah]   Brand of Italian **bitters**, usually served as an **apéritif** with **soda**.

feta/fetta (*Grk.*)   Cheese (traditionally made from ewes' milk) preserved in **brine**. It is a solid white cheese with a sharp and slightly salty taste. (*Fetes* means 'blocks' or 'slices', the curd being cut into blocks before being preserved.)

fettuccine (*Ital.*) (pl.) [fett-yu-cheeny]   Thin ribbons of **pasta** cut to a length of about 30cm. Very similar to **tagliatelle**.

feuilleté (*Fr.*) [foo-ee-et-ay]   **Puff pastry** case, traditionally cut into a leaf shape or triangle, but now any shape, e.g. *feuilleté de* **coquilles**, scallops cooked in a puff pastry case. (*See also* **pâte feuilletée**.)

ficelle, boeuf à la   *See* **boeuf à la ficelle**.

filet (*Fr.*) (masc.) [fill-ay]   **Fillet**. (*Filet de* **boeuf** is 'fillet of beef').

filet mignon (*Fr.*) (masc.) [fill-ay mee-neeyon]   Small, round **fillet** steak. (*See also* **entrecôte**, **minute steak**, **porterhouse**, **rump**, **sirloin**, *and* **T-bone**.)

fillet   (1) (noun) Thick boneless piece of meat or fish, usually the prime cut (e.g. fillet steak).
(2) (verb) To remove from the bone.

filo pastry [feel-oh]   Very thin paper-like pastry, buttered, and cooked in layers.

fine champagne   Description of the finest kind of **cognac** (**brandy**, *not* **sparkling wine**).

fine dining (**room**)   High-class dining (room) with formal service, typically found in **five-star** hotels.

fines herbes (*Fr.*) (fem. pl.) [feen airb]   Herbs (**chervil**, parsley, **tarragon** and **chives**) chopped up and mixed together, used to flavour food, typically **omelettes**, meat, and various sauces.

fingerbowl   Small bowl filled with water (and perhaps a piece of lemon) placed on the table so that guests can clean their fingers.

finish   Wine-tasting term. The last taste impression from a mouthful of wine.

fino [fee-noh]   Style of Spanish **sherry**.

five-star   First class (of hotels); top of the market, offering the full range of facilities and services.

flambé(e) (*Fr.*) [flahm-bay]   Flamed. Food served *flambé* has had **spirits** poured over it and then been ignited.

flan   Open tart containing a filling (of custard, fruit, etc.) (*See also* **frangipane**.)

fleuron (*Fr.*) (masc.) [flur-o(n)]   Crescent- or flower-shaped decorative edible (e.g. a *fleuron* of **puff pastry**).

float   (1) (verb) Cocktail-mixing term; to place one liquid above another in the glass so that they do not mix but one 'floats' above the other.
(2) (noun) Change placed in the till before trading begins.

floating islands   Soft balls of **meringue** poached in milk and served in custard sauce. (In French, **oeufs à la neige**.)

florentine [flo-ren-teen]   Thin biscuit of **glacé** fruit and nuts coated on one side with chocolate, often served after dinner with coffee.

florentine, à la (*Fr.*) [ah lah flo-ren-teen]   In the style of Florence (Italian city). Cooked or served with spinach and (usually) **mornay** sauce, e.g. **suprêmes** of chicken *à la florentine*.

flute   (1) (noun) Narrow-stemmed glass used for serving **sparkling wines**.
(2) (noun) Long thin French roll.
(3) (noun) Groove made on the outside of a food item for decoration.
(4) (verb) To make grooves on the surface of a food item, such as a pie crust or a **mousse**.

focaccia (*Ital.*) [fok-ah-cheea]   Flat bread similar to a **pizza** base. It is often spread with **garlic**-herb butter and served warm with **antipasto**.

fondant   Soft mixture of flavoured sugar used as icing on cakes or served as a **sweetmeat**, sometimes coated with chocolate.

fondue (*Swiss*) (fem.) [fon-doo]   Dish cooked at table by dipping small pieces (usually of meat or bread) into a bowl containing hot oil or melted cheese. (*Fondu* is French for 'melted'.) (*See also* **raclette**.)

fool   Cold dessert made of **puréed** fruit and whipped **cream**.

forcemeat   Meat chopped and seasoned for use as a stuffing; a **farce**.

forestière, à la (*Fr.*) [ah lah foress-tee-air]   Served with **sautéed** mushrooms. (*Forestière* means 'forester's wife' or 'female forester'.)

fortified wine   Wine strengthened by the addition of some **spirit**. Fortified wines include **muscat**, **sherry**, and **port**.

four, au (*Fr.*) [oh foor]   Oven-baked; roasted. (*Four* means 'oven'.)

framboise (*Fr.*) (fem.) [frahm bwaz]   Raspberry.

française, à la (*Fr.*) [ah lah frahn-sez]   In the French style; usually served with **demi-glace** sauce. *Petits pois à la française* are cooked with lettuce and onion.

frangipane (fronzji-pahn)   Custard made with ground almonds or crushed **macaroons**. (In French *crème frangipane*.) (*See also* **crème pâtissière**.) (Named after an Italian marquis, Muzio Frangipani, who lived in Paris in the 16th century and devised a bitter-almond scent for sprinkling on gloves.)

frangipane tart/flan   Jam-lined pastry case filled with **frangipane** cream and decorated with fresh **cream** and **pistachio** nuts.

frankfurter   Smoked beef-and-pork-sausage usually

simmered and served in a bread roll as a hot dog. Tiny **cocktail** frankfurters are served as **appetizers**. (Frankfurt is a city in central Germany.)

frappé (*Fr.*) [frappay]   Cocktail-mixing term; chilled with crushed ice, e.g. **crème de menthe** *frappé*. (Literally, 'crushed' or, more exactly, 'beaten'.)

French   Dry white **vermouth** (as in **gin**-and-**French**).

French dressing   Cold dressing for salad, etc. made with oil and **wine vinegar**, and seasonings like **pepper**, salt, **garlic** and **Dijon mustard**. Lemon juice is sometimes used instead of vinegar. (*See* **vinaigrette**.)

friandises (*Fr.*) (fem. pl.) [free-on-deez]   Dainties, e.g. fruits dipped in chocolate, or **petits fours**, often served at the end of a meal with the **coffee**.

fricassee [frik-a-see]   Pieces of meat, usually a white meat like chicken, cooked in **stock** and served in a white sauce. Fricassee has been adopted as an English word; the French is *fricassée* [frik-a-say]; so you should say 'chicken fricassee' (pronounced *see*) but *fricasseée* (pronounced *say*) *de* **poulet**.

frite (*Fr.*) [freet]   Fried. (*See* **pommes frites**.)

frittata (*Ital.*) [frit-ahta]   **Omelette**; beaten eggs fried on both sides to form a cake. Vegetables are sometimes beaten into the egg mix.

fritter   Food, either sweet or savoury, dipped in **batter** and deep-fried. (*See also* **pakora**.)

fritto misto (*Ital.*)   Mixed vegetables deep fried in **batter**. (Literally, 'fried mixed'.)

fritto misto de pesce (*Ital.*) [fritoh mistoh dee pescay]   Mixed **seafood** deep fried in **batter**. (Literally, 'fried mixture of the sea'.)

froid (*Fr.*) [fwah]   Cold, as in **buffet froid**.

fromage (*Fr.*) (masc.) [from-ahje]   Cheese.

fromage blanc (*Fr.*) [from-ahje bla(n)]   Low-fat fresh cheese made from skimmed milk. It is used in place of **cream**, or as an accompaniment to fruit. (*See also* **cuisine minceur**.)

frontignac (fron-ti-nyak)   Grape variety. *See* **muscat**.

front of house   The part of the **establishment** seen by the guests; the dining room as opposed to the kitchen. (*See also* **back of house**.)

frost   (1) To cover with sugar, esp. a cake. Frosted fruit is first dipped in egg white or lemon juice. (*See also* **frosting**.)
(2) To garnish a glass by dipping the rim in lemon juice and sugar or salt.

frosting   Soft icing used to decorate cakes.

fruits de mer (*Fr.*) (masc. pl.) [frooee duh mair]   **Seafood** (Literally, 'fruits of the sea'.)

fruity   Wine-tasting term. Pleasing taste of a young wine; description of its **aroma**.

Fukien [foo-kyen]   One of the five main styles of Chinese cuisine. Fukien cuisine is known for its **clear soups** and

seafood. (Fukien, now called Fujian, is a coastal province of China.) (*See also* **Cantonese**, **Honan**, **Peking**, and **Szechwan**.)

fumé (*Fr.*) [foomay]   (1) **Smoked**.
(2) Style of white wine, usually a **sauvignon blanc**, cloudy and piquantly tasty, called fumé blanc.

function   Pre-arranged occasion (banquet, dinner, cocktail party, etc.) for a known number of guests.

funghi (*Ital.*) (pl.) (*sing.* **fungo**) [foon-gee]   Mushrooms, e.g. **risotto** *alla funghi*.

gado-gado (*Indon.*) [gahdo gahdo]   Vegetables cooked in peanut sauce with hard-boiled egg.

galantine [galan-teen]   Boned meat, usually stuffed with **forcemeat**, pressed into shape and covered in **aspic** jelly. It is served cold. (*see also* **brawn**.)

galette (*Fr.*) (fem.) [ga-let]   Flat cake; **pancake**; thick shortbread biscuit.

Galliano   Golden-yellow herb **liqueur** from Milan (city in N. Italy). (Named after Major Galliano, a hero of the Italian–Abyssinian war of 1896.)

game   All wild animals and birds which are hunted. (In French *gibier*.) (*See also* **venison**.)

gammon   Ham, usually served hot as gammon steak.

garam masala (*Ind.*) [garram ma-sah-la]   Ground spices used as a flavouring in Indian cooking. Different mixtures are used for different purposes. (*Garam* means 'hot'.) (*See also* **curry** and **masala**.)

garbure (*Fr.*) (fem.) [gar-boor]   A very thick, hearty soup containing cabbage, beans, and **pickled** meat (typically **confit d'oie**), served ladled over wholemeal bread. (*See also* **potage** and **soupe**.)

garde-manger (*Fr.*) (masc.) [gard marnge-ay]   Specialist cook in charge of cold items and decorative work in a large kitchen.

garlic   Strong-smelling flavouring herb from the same family as onions. The garlic bulb consists of segments called cloves, the juice from which is used to flavour savoury foods.

garni (*Fr.*) (masc.) [gar-nee]   Decorated. (*See also* **bouquet garni**.)

garnish   (1) (noun) Items placed in or around a dish (or drink) for decoration or taste.
(2) (verb) To place such items on a dish or in a drink.

garniture   Items in a **garnish**; the trimmings.

gastronome   An expert on good eating and drinking; an epicure.

gastronomy   Science or art of good eating and drinking.

gâteau(x) (*Fr.*) [gah-toe]   Cake(s).

ga xao sa ot (*Viet.*) [gah saow shah u(t)]   Chicken with **lemon grass** and **chilli**. (*Ga* is 'chicken', *xao* means 'fried', *sa ot* is 'lemon grass'.)

gazpacho (*Span.*) [gaz-pah-cho]   Cold soup of **puréed**

tomatoes, cucumber, onions, **garlic** and **red pepper**, often garnished with **croûtons**.

gelatine/gelatin [jell-a-tin] Almost colourless, odourless, tasteless, soluble substance extracted from animal skin, bones and cartilage, etc. used to make jellies and various cold desserts. (*See also* **aspic**.)

gelato (*Ital.*) [jel-ahtoh] Whipped soft ice-cream.

gelée (*Fr.*) (fem.) [zjelay] Jelly.

gelée de cuisine [zjelay duh kwi-zeen] **Aspic** jelly.

gelée, en [ahn zjelay] In jelly, e.g. **oeufs poché** *en gelée*.

generic Of a general type (which anyone may make), as opposed to **proprietary** (particular brand, the exclusive property of a person or business); also as opposed to **varietal** in reference to wine.

genever [jenny-vur] Style of Dutch gin. (It has no connection with Geneva, the Swiss city, but is derived from the French word for 'juniper', *genièvre*.)

génoise (*Fr.*) (fem.) [gay-nwaz] Genoese sponge; light sponge cake.

Gentleman's Relish (*UK*) **Proprietary anchovy** paste usually spread on toast. (Also known as patum peperium, or patum for short.) (*See also* **relish**.)

gewürztraminer [geh-vurts-tram-eener] Variety of the **traminer** grape used to produce spicy white wine. (*Gewürtz* [gewoortz] is German for 'spicy'.)

ghee (*Ind.*) [gee] Clarified cow- or buffalo-milk butter used as a cooking medium, especially in Indian cookery. There is a much cheaper vegetable-oil ghee substitute, called *vanaspati* (vegetable) ghee.

gibier (*Fr.*) (masc.) [zjee-bee-ay] **Game** (wild animals and wildfowl). (*See also* **venison**.)

giblets [jib-lets] Innards of poultry and **game** birds, the edible portions of which are the liver, heart, etc.

Gibson Cocktail of gin with a little dry (French) **vermouth**, **garnished** with a pearl (cocktail) onion. (*Compare* **Dry Martini**.)

gigot (*Fr.*) (masc.) [zjee-go] Leg (of mutton or lamb).

gin Spirit made from grain alcohol distilled with selected herbs and fruit, in particular juniper berries. The most popular style, used in **cocktails**, is London Dry. The other main style, hollands (or **genever**) gin has a strongly distinctive flavour which makes it less suitable for mixing.

ginger The root of *Zingiber officinale*, used freshly grated in **curries**, dried and powdered as a sweet or savoury spice, or preserved in syrup and **glacéed**.

ginger ale *See* **dry ginger ale**.

ginger beer Slightly alcoholic, aerated drink made of **ginger**, **sugar syrup**, and yeast.

gingerbread Golden-brown soft biscuits or cake made into shapes and decorated with sweets (e.g. gingerbread man, gingerbread house).

Ginger Wine, Green *See* **Green Ginger Wine**.

girella Boneless cut of lamb or veal from the top of the leg.

glace (*Fr.*) (fem.) [gluss] (1) Ice (cream); iced drink. (2) **Glaze**, e.g. *glace de* **viande** ('meat glaze').

glacé(e) (*Fr.*) [gluss-ay] (1) Iced, icy. (2) Glazed. Preserved in sugar (e.g. glacé fruits).

glaze To make shiny, usually by coating with beaten egg or with a **reduced stock**. (*See also* **miroir**.)

globe artichoke *See* **artichoke**.

glühwein (*Ger.*) [gloo-vine] Spicy **mulled wine**.

gluten Elastic protein substance found in wheat flour. Sticky when wet, it holds the dough together and traps the air bubbles produced by the **fermenting** yeast so helping the bread to rise.

gnocchi (*Ital.*) (pl.) [nee-o-kee] Small **pasta dumplings** made from potato or **semolina**.

goi cuon (*Viet.*) [goi kuon] Chewy, soft, transparent **rice-paper** rolls containing rice **noodles**, prawns, and pork. They are eaten cold dipped in a peanut and bean sauce. (*Goi* means 'raw food', *cuon* is a roll.) (*See also* **cha gio** *and* **spring roll**.)

gomme syrup **Sugar syrup**.

gorgonzola (*Ital.*) Moist, creamy **blue-veined** cheese made from cows' milk. (Gorgonzola is a village near Milan, N. Italy.) (*See also* **dolcelatta**, **roquefort**, *and* **stilton**.)

gougère (*Fr.*) (fem.) [goo-zjair] Cheese-flavoured **choux** puff served warm. In **Burgundy** they are traditionally eaten cold when wine-tasting.

goujon (*Fr.*) (masc.) [goo-zjon] Thin strip of fillet of fish or chicken (a *goujon* is literally a gudgeon, a small freshwater fish).

goulash (*Hun.*) [goo-lash] Red stew of meat and onions seasoned with **paprika** and garnished with potatoes.

gourmand (*Fr.*) (masc.) [goor-mond] Lover of food; a glutton. (*Compare* **gourmet**.)

gourmet (*Fr.*) (masc.) [goor-may] Expert in food and wine; an epicure or **gastronome**. (*Compare* **gourmand**.)

Grand Marnier [gron marny-ay] **Proprietary liqueur**, **cognac**-based, with an orange flavour.

granita (*Ital.*) [gran-ee-tah] Crushed ice drink.

grappa (*Ital.*) Italian **spirit** made from the remnants of grapes (skins, stalks, pips, etc.) after the **fermented** juice or **wine** has been removed.

gras (*Fr.*) (adj.) [grah] Fat (as in **pâté de foie gras**).

gras, au (*Fr.*) [oh grah] With ham or bacon.

gratin, au (*Fr.*) [oh grat-i(n)] With a golden crust; sprinkled with breadcrumbs and/or grated cheese, and baked or grilled. (*See also* **gratiné(e)** *below*.)

gratiné(e) (*Fr.*) [grat-ee-nay] Cooked, usually with breadcrumbs and grated cheese, to form a golden crust. The word can be anglicized into 'gratinated'.

grazing Practice of eating modest snacks at different

places instead of having substantial regular meals.

grecque, à la (*Fr.*) [ah lah grek] In the Greek manner, mushrooms and vegetables with **coriander** seeds cooked in olive oil, served cold.

Greek coffee Strong, dark, sweet **coffee** served in small cups. **Turkish** coffee.

Green Ginger Wine **Proprietary fortified wine** made from dried grapes and flavoured with **ginger**.

green pepper *See* **sweet pepper**.

green peppercorn *See* **peppercorn**.

grenadine [grenna-deen] Red pomegranate-flavoured **cordial**, used for sweetening or colouring drinks.

grissino (*Ital.*) (*pl.* **grissini**) [griss-eenoh] Long, thin, crisp bread-stick served with **antipasto**.

gros sel (*Fr.*) (masc.) [grow sell] Rock salt. (Literally 'coarse salt'.)

gruyère (*Swiss & Fr.*) [groo-yair] Cows' milk cheese, firm and smooth in texture with small holes or eyes. The rind is not usually eaten. (Gruyère is a village in Switzerland.) (*See also* **raclette**.)

guacamole (*Mex.*) [gwah-kah-mo-lay] Spicy avocado sauce. (*See also* **enchilada** and **nacho**.)

guéridon [geri-don] Trolley or table on which food is prepared in the dining room.

guéridon service Service from a **guéridon**.

Guinness Famous Irish **stout**, originally brewed in Dublin, but now also elsewhere under licence.

gumbo (*Creole & Cajun*) (1) **Okra** or **lady's fingers**.
(2) Spicy **casserole** of **seafood** and vegetables (including okra). (*See also* **bouillabaisse** *and* **pochouse**.)
(3) (*USA*) **Okra** soup, or other preparations made using okra.

hâché(e) (*Fr.*) [ah-shay] Minced; mashed, *e.g.* **bifteck** *hâché*, **minced beef**, hamburger.

haggis Scottish dish, consisting of oatmeal and chopped offal stuffed and sewn into a sheep's stomach and steamed or poached.

halal (*Arab.*) [ha-laal] Lawful for Muslims; meat killed and prepared according to Muslim law. (Muslim equivalent of the Jewish **kosher**.)

haldi (*Ind.*) **Turmeric**.

halva (*N. Africa & E. Medit.*) Light, crunchy **sweetmeat** of ground **sesame** seeds, sugar, almonds, etc.

haricot (*Fr.*) (masc.) [arry-coh] Bean, esp. the small white navy bean used, for example, in a **cassoulet** or for baked beans. (*See also* **haricot vert**.)

haricot vert (*Fr.*) (masc.) [arry-coh vair] French or string (runner) bean. (*Vert* means 'green'.)

hash browns (*USA*) Cake of **puréed** potato and onion, bound with egg, and fried.

haute cuisine (*Fr.*) (fem.) [ote kwiz-een] French cooking and service of a very high standard. (*Haute* means 'high'.) (*See also* **cuisine**.)

Hawthorn strainer Cocktail strainer; it has two prongs which fit over the side of the blender with a wire coil which fits inside the rim.

herb Aromatic plant used in cookery to flavour food, e.g. **chervil**, **tarragon**. (*See also* **fines herbes**.)

herbal tea An **infusion** or 'tea' made by adding boiling water to the leaves or flowers of various herbs. Most, but not all, herbal teas are **caffeine**-free. Also called **tisane**.

hermitage Grape variety. (*See* **shiraz**.)

highball (1) Any **spirit** mixed with ice and soda or ginger ale served in a highball glass, e.g. a **Whiskey Highball**.
(2) A style of tall, straight-sided glass.

high tea Substantial meal combining tea and supper. Includes a hot course, followed by cakes, bread, butter and jam etc. Sometimes served instead of dinner to children.

hock English name for German Rhine wine; **riesling**; **generic** wines made in that style. (From Hochheim, German town from which hocks were shipped.)

hoi sin sauce (*Chin.*) Sweet and spicy sauce made of **soya beans**, **garlic**, and spices and served as a **condiment**, esp. with **Peking duck** and pork dishes.

hollandaise [oll-and-ayz] Rich sauce made from the careful **blending** of egg yolk, butter, and lemon juice or **vinegar**. The French term is *sauce hollandaise* [sohs oll-and-ayz].

hollands Dutch style of **gin**.

homard (*Fr.*) (masc.) [om-ahr] **Lobster**. (*See also* **crayfish** and **langouste**.)

hommos *See* **hummus**.

Honan [hoe-nan] One of the five main styles of Chinese cuisine. **Sweet-and-sour** dishes are typical of spicy *Honan* cooking. (Honan, now called Henan, is a province in central China.) (*See also* **Cantonese**, **Fukien**, **Peking**, *and* **Szechwan**.)

hors d'oeuvre(s) (*Fr.*) (masc.) [or-durv] **Appetizer** or small **savoury** served before or at the beginning of a meal. (Literally, 'before the work'.)

horseradish Pungent root of the mustard family (*Cochlearia armoracia*), usually used grated. (*See also* **daikon**, **horseradish sauce**, *and* **wasabi**.)

horseradish sauce Grated **horseradish** mixed with **cream**, **vinegar**, and seasonings and traditionally used as a **condiment** with roast beef, **smoked** trout and mackerel.

host(ess) (1) Patrons who are entertaining their own guests in an **establishment** and who are responsible for paying.
(2) Person who greets the restaurant's patrons, takes their coats, and shows them to their table, 'mine host'.

house wine Moderately priced wine usually bought in bulk by an **establishment** and often served from **carafes**. (*See* **vin ordinaire**.)

huître (*Fr.*) (fem.) (ooee-truh) Oyster.

hummus/houmos (*Grk. & Arab.*) [hoomuss] **Purée** of **chick-peas** and **sesame seed** paste, often served with **pitta** bread as a **meze** or **hors d'oeuvre**.

iced coffee Strong black **coffee** mixed with ice-cold milk, usually garnished with ice-cream.

iced tea Tea, usually Indian, poured over ice and served cold garnished with slices of lemon or **mint** leaves.

Indian tonic water *See* **tonic**.

infusion (1) The immersion of vegetables, herbs, **tea** or **coffee** in boiling liquid or wine until the flavours have been absorbed, so producing an aromatic fluid.
(2) Method used to give **liqueurs** their flavour.
(3) Beverage given its flavour by infusion.

insalata (*Ital.*) [insal-ahta] Salad.

insalata mista (*Ital.*) [insal-ahta-mista] Mixed salad.

Irish coffee **Liqueur coffee** made using Irish whiskey.

jaggery (*Anglo-Ind.*) Dark, crumbly sugar made from sugar-cane or the sugar palm and tasting of treacle. It is used in Indian cuisine. (*See also* **palm sugar**.)

jambon (*Fr.*) (masc.) [zjom-bo(n)] Ham.

jardinière, à la (*Fr.*) [ah lah jar-danee-air] Garnished with vegetables, esp. carrots, turnips, French beans, cauliflower, and peas. (A *jardinière* is a 'female gardener'.)

jasmine tea **China tea** scented with jasmine flowers.

jeroboam [jerruh-boh-am] Large bottle of **sparkling wine** (e.g. **champagne**) containing the equivalent of 4 standard (75cl) bottles. (Jeroboam was King of Israel, 931–910 BC. (*See also* **champagne bottle sizes**.)

Jerusalem artichoke *See* **artichoke**.

jugged hare Jointed hare **casseroled** in its own blood with wine, vegetables, and seasonings.

julienne (*Fr.*) (fem.) [zhoo-lee-en] (1) Vegetables or meat cut into thin, evenly-sized strips for preparation in cooking, or for use as a **garnish**, especially for **consommés**. (Perhaps named after a French chef called Jean Julien. The word julienne has been used in cooking since the early 18th century.)
(2) Clear vegetable soup.

jus (*Fr.*) (masc.) [zjoo] Meat juice, or unthickened pan juices, gravy, **stock**. (*See* **jus (au)** *and* **jus-lié**, *below*.)

jus, au (*Fr.*) [oh zjoo] (Meat) dressed with its own juice.

jus-lié (*Fr.*) [zjoo lee-ay] Thickened meat juice, gravy. (**Lié** means 'bound'.) (*See also* **jus** *above*.)

kabana/cabanossi (*Pol.*) [ka-bahna] Long, thin **smoked** sausage made from pork and beef seasoned with herbs and served cold.

Kahlua **Proprietary** Mexican **liqueur** based on cane spirit flavoured with coffee.

Kalamata olive Large black **olive** from Greece. (Kalamata is a town in S. Greece.)

kartoffel (*Ger.*) [car-toff-ell] Potato.

kassler/kasseler (*Ger.*) [kass-lair] **Pickled, smoked** pork cutlets thinly sliced and served cold, or carved in thicker pieces and fried. (Named after a butcher from Berlin, named Kasel.)

kebab/kabab/kebob (*Turk. & Ind.*) Small pieces of meat or fish, with vegetables, cooked on a skewer. (*See also* **brochette**, **döner kebab** *and* **shish kebab**.)

kedgeree (*Anglo-Ind.*) Dish of cooked rice, **smoked** fish, hard-boiled egg, and parsley flavoured with **turmeric** or **saffron**, usually served for breakfast.

ketchup **Sauce** made from **tomatoes**, mushrooms, **vinegar** and spices and used as a **condiment**. (In USA known as 'catsup'.)

kibbeh (*Arab.*) General term for the many dishes made from **burghul** used in the Middle East, especially Lebanon.

kilojoule Metric measure of the energy in food (abbreviation kJ.)

kimchee (*Korea*) [kim-chee] Hot **pickled** cabbage served with almost all Korean meals.

kirsch [keersh] Style of **cherry brandy**. (*Kirsche* is German for 'cherry'.)

Kobe beef [kohbay] Fine grain-fed and milk-fattened beef prized in Japanese cuisine. (Kobe is a city near Osaka, S. Honshu.)

kohlrabi [coal rah-bee] Turnip-like vegetable with a swollen, edible stem.

korma (*Ind.*) [kor-mah] Spicy meat **casserole** cooked in a rich **coconut** sauce.

kosher (*Heb.*) [koh-sher] Lawful for Jews; meat killed or food prepared according to Jewish law. (*See also* **halal**.)

kümmel [kewmel] Dutch **liqueur** flavoured with caraway seeds, usually served on ice as a **digestif**.

la (*Fr.*) (fem.) [lah] The, when used with a feminine noun, e.g. *la maison*. (*See also* **le** *and* **les**.)

ladyfinger Finger-shaped sponge cake. (In French *langues de chat*, literally 'cat's tongues'.)

lady fingers/lady's fingers (1) **Okra** *or* **gumbo**.
(2) Small stubby bananas.

lager (*Ger.*) [laag-er] Bottom-fermented **beer**. Most Australian beers are lagers.

lait, au (*Fr.*) [oh lay] With milk, as in **café au lait**. (*Lait* means 'milk'.)

laksa (*Singa.*) Spicy **seafood** soup with rice **noodles**. (*See also* **tom yam kung**.)

langue (*Fr.*) (fem.) [lahn-guh] Tongue.

langouste (*Fr.*) (fem.) [lahn-goost] **Crawfish**.

langoustine(s) (*Fr.*) (fem.) [lahn-goose-teen] **Scampi.**

lapin (*Fr.*) (masc.) [lapi(n)] Rabbit.

lard Rendered fat from the pig.

lardon (*Fr.*) (masc.) [lardo(n)] Strip of pork fat or bacon inserted into raw meat to enhance flavour while cooking or cooked and served as a garnish with salads and vegetables.

lasagne (*Ital.*) (pl.) [laz-an-yuh] Large flat pieces of **pasta**; the dish comprising layers of lasagne alternating with layers of meat sauce and cheese sauce.

layer Cocktail-mixing term. To pour the ingredients into the glass so that they do not mix but remain one above the other in clear layers.

le (*Fr.*) (masc.) [luh] The, when used with a masculine noun, e.g. *le* **jus**. (*See also* **la** *and* **les**.)

legume Vegetable with seeds in a pod, e.g. bean, **lentil**, and pea. (*See also* **légumes** *below*.)

légumes (*Fr.*) (masc. pl.) [lay-goom] Vegetables (*See also* **classic menu** *and* **legume** *above*.)

lemon grass Bushy grass-like herb used to flavour food, esp. in Thai cooking. (In French *citronelle*.)

lentil Bean (*Lens esculenta*) rich in nutrients including **protein**, one of the earliest cultivated foods known to man; the basic ingredient of **dahl**.

les (*Fr.*) (pl.) [lay] The, when used with a plural noun, e.g. *les* **légumes**. (*See also* **la** *and* **le**.)

liaison (*Fr.*) (fem.) [lee-ay-zon] Mixture, typically egg yolks and **cream** or flour and butter, used for thickening sauces and soups.

lié (*Fr.*) [leeay] Thickened (as in **jus lié**). (*Lier* means 'to bind', 'to thicken'.)

Ligurian olive Tiny black Italian olive. (Liguria is a province in NW Italy.)

linguini (*Ital.*) (pl.) [lingweenee] Type of **pasta** cut into long, very thin strips with square-cut edges.

liqueur (li-cure) **Spirit**- or wine-based **liquors** sweetened and flavoured with aromatic substances often served as **digestifs** (e.g. **Grand Marnier**).

liqueur coffee Coffee served with a **nip** of **spirit** or **liqueur**.

liquor (li-cur) Any liquid, but usually an alcoholic drink.

lobster Large salt-water crustacean with big claws, genus *Homarus* (**homard** in French).

lobster thermidor *See* **thermidor**.

loin Joint of meat that includes some or all of the ribs. (*See also* **carré**, **rack** *and* **saddle**.)

Lorraine *See* **quiche Lorraine**.

lumpfish roe Eggs of the lumpfish, often referred to as **caviare** (which is actually the much superior sturgeon's roe.) Lumpfish roe is dyed red or black in imitation of real caviare.

lyonnaise, à la (*Fr.*) [ah lah lee-on-nayze] In the style of Lyons (large city in SE France); garnished with onions, and often potatoes. (*See also below*.)

lyonnaise, sauce (*Fr.*) [sohs lee-on-nayze] **Reduction** of white wine, **vinegar** and golden onions added to a **demiglace**. (*See also* **lyonnaise (à la)**, *above*.)

macchiato [makee-ahto] Extra-strong **espresso coffee** served long or short with a dash of cold milk, usually in a glass.

macadamia (*Austral.*) Nut from rainforest tree of the genus *Macadamia* used in both sweet and savoury dishes and available ready-salted.

macaroon Small almond-flavoured cake or biscuit.

macédoine (*Fr.*) (fem.) [mass-ay-dwan] **Diced** fruit or vegetables; fruit thus cut and set in jelly; fruit salad. (Macédoine is French for 'Macedonia'.)

macerate [mass-errate] To steep in liquid; to soak food, particularly fruit, in alcohol. (*See also* **marinate**.)

madeira **Fortified wine** with a distinctive 'burnt' taste (from the Portuguese island of Madeira). (French, **madère**.

madeleine (*Fr.*) (fem.) [madel-ayn] Small sponge cake shaped like a **scallop** shell.

madère (*Fr.*) (adj.) [mad-air] **Madeira**.

magnum Large bottle of **sparkling wine** (e.g. **champagne**) containing the equivalent of 2 standard (75cl) bottles. (*Magnum* means 'big thing' in Latin.) (*See also* **champagne bottle sizes**.)

maison/à la maison/de maison (*Fr.*) (fem.) [ah lah/duh may-zo(n)] Home-made; made to the **establishment's** own special recipe, e.g. **pâté** *maison*. (*Maison* means 'house'.)

maître d'hôtel (*Fr.*) [met-ruh doe-tel] Steward, headwaiter. (*Maître* means 'master'.) (*See also* **beurre maître d'hôtel** *and* **maître d'hôtel (sauce)** *below*.)

maître d'hôtel, sauce (*Fr.*) (fem.) [sohs metruh dohtel] Sauce of melted butter, parsley, and lemon juice. (*See also* **beurre maître d'hotel** *and* **maître d'hôtel**.)

maize/sweet corn *See* **corn**.

malbec [mahlbek] Black grape variety popular in blends, e.g. **cabernet**-malbec, because it softens the effect of the **tannin**.

malt Grain, esp. barley, steeped in water to germinate and then dried. The process converts starch into maltose. Malt is used for brewing **beer** and to make **malt whisky**. (*See also* **malt vinegar** *below*.)

malt vinegar Strong, dark brown **vinegar** distilled from **malt** and used mostly as a **pickling** agent and traditionally sprinkled over fish and chips. (*See also* **balsamic vinegar**, **rice vinegar**, **vinaigrette**, *and* **wine vinegar**.)

malt whisky Traditional kind of **Scotch whisky** made from malted barley only and distilled in a **pot still**.

mange-tout (*Fr.*) (masc.) [monje too] Thin green pea, eaten whole, pod and all. Also called snow pea and sugar pea. (Literally, 'eat everything'.)

maraschino [maras-keenoh] Italian **liqueur** based on distillation of sour (Maraska) cherries.

maraschino cherries Cherries, dyed bright red, preserved in a type of **maraschino** juice.

marbling The streams of fat contrasting with the lean in meat.

Margarita **Cocktail** made with **tequila**, **Cointreau**, and lemon juice.

margherita (*Ital.*) Simple style of **pizza** topping containing **tomato**, cheese, and herbs.

marinade (noun) Mixture of liquids (wine, lemon juice, **vinegar**, oil, **soy**) with herbs and seasonings, in which food is **marinated** to enhance its flavour.

marinara (*Ital.*) [marin-ahra] With **seafood**, e.g. **spaghetti** *marinara*. (*Il mare* means 'the sea'.)

marinate/marinade (verb) To soak food in a **marinade** (*See also* **macerate**.)

marinière, à la (*Fr.*) [ah lah marin-y-air] Method of preparing shellfish or fish in white wine with onions etc., e.g. **moules** *marinières*.

marjoram Compact shrub with small grey leaves and white flowers both of which are aromatic and are used as a seasoning herb. Similar to, but more subtle than **oregano**, it is one of the ingredients of a traditional **bouquet garni**.

Marmite [mah-mite] **Proprietary** name for a yeast extract.

marmite (*Fr.*) (fem.) [mar-meet] Cooking vessel, esp. one with two handles in which soup is cooked.

marmite petite (*Fr.*) [mar-meet pu-teet] (1) **Clear soup** or **broth**. (*See also* **consommé**.)
(2) Small cooking pot. (*See also* **marmite** *above*.)

marron (*Fr.*) (masc.) [ma-rro(n)] Chestnut (as in *marrons glacés*, 'candied chestnuts').

marsala [mar-sah-lah] Style of fortified red (almost brown) sweet **dessert** wine. Not to be confused with the Indian **masala** (spice).

Martini (1) Brand of **vermouth**.
(2) **Dry Martini** (cocktail).

Maryland, chicken (*USA*) Chicken **suprême** coated in breadcrumbs, deep-fried, often garnished with corn fritters, bacon, banana and tomato. (Maryland is a State in E. USA.)

Maryland cookies Chocolate-chip biscuits. (Maryland is a State in E. USA.)

marzipan Thick paste of ground almonds and egg white, used in confectionery, esp. **petits fours**, and to hold decorative icing on fruit cake.

masala (*Ind.*) [ma-sah-lah] Aromatic spice, e.g. **garam masala** ('hot spice'). Not to be confused with **marsala** (wine).

mascarpone (*Ital.*) [mass-kur-pony] Fresh, unripened dessert cheese used in place of **cream** in some sweet dishes. (*See also* **crème fraîche** *and* **ricotta**.)

mask To coat food thoroughly in a sauce before serving (*See* **nappé**.)

matsutake mushroom *See* **pine mushroom**.

mayonnaise Dressing or sauce of egg yolks and oil, flavoured with **vinegar**, salt, **pepper**, and **mustard**.

medallion [med-al-ee-on] Small round piece of meat shaped like a medallion and usually skinned and boned. (In French, *médaillon* [may-dye-yee-o(n)].)

mélange (*Fr.*) (masc.) [may-lahnzj] Mixture; medley.

melanzane alla parmigiana (*Ital.*) [melan-zahnay alla parmy-yahna] Classic baked dish of layered **eggplant**, tomato sauce, **mozzarella**, and **parmigiano**. (*Melanzanna* is Italian for 'eggplant'.)

Melba toast (1) Very thin toast made by splitting toasted bread and grilling the untoasted sides.
(2) Small thick squares of toast available commercially for use in **canapés**.
(Named after Dame Nellie Melba, 1861–1931, the famous Australian opera singer.) (*See also* **peach Melba**.)

menu (1) The range of food items served in an **establishment**
(2) The arrangement by which the items are offered (**set menu, à la carte** menu, etc.)
(3) Written list of the food items served (also called the **bill of fare**).
(*See also* **classic menu, menu d'agrément, menu dégustation, prix fixe**, *and* **table d'hôte**.

menu d'agrément (*Fr.*) (masc.) [menu dag-ray-mo(n)] Fixed price menu. (*See also* **prix fixe** *and* **table d'hôte**.)

menu dégustation Small portions of a range of the specialities of the **establishment**.

meringue [me-rang] Egg white whipped with sugar and baked. (*See also* **pavlova**.)

merlot (mairloh) Black grape variety noted for its **bouquet** and popular in blends, especially **cabernet-merlot**.

mesclun Mixed salad greens (especially curly **endive**) of varying colours and flavours, served with a **vinaigrette**.

méthode champenoise [may-toad sham-pen-warz] Method by which French champagne is made.

methuselah (meth-ooz-uh-lah) Large bottle of **champagne** containing the equivalent of 8 standard (75cl) bottles. (Methuselah is the oldest man in the Bible, said to have lived to be 969.) (*See also* **champagne bottle sizes**.)

meunière, à la (*Fr.*) [ah lah mur-nee-air] Served with a sauce of browned butter, lemon juice, parsley and seasoning. (*Meunière* means 'miller's wife' or 'female miller'.)

mezcal Mexican spirit distilled from the *mezcal azul*

cactus. **Tequila** is a superior type of mezcal.

meze/mezze (*pl.* **mezedes**) (*Grk. & Turk.*) [mez-zay/meze-thes] Substantial assortment of cold **hors d'oeuvres** including such items as **taramasalata** and **dolmades**, often almost a meal in itself. (Literally, 'half' – a half meal, the **hors d'oeuvre**). (*See also* **antipasto**.)

mignon (*Fr.*) [mee-neeyon] Small and dainty, as in **filet mignon**.

mignonette (*Fr.*) (fem.) [mee-neeyon-ett] (1) Coarsely-ground white **pepper**.
(2) Small cuts of meat elaborately prepared (e.g. **mignonettes d'agneau**).
(3) Potatoes sliced into thin sticks.
(4) Variety of lettuce.

milanese (*Ital.*) [milan-ay-zay] In the style of Milan (N. Italian city) e.g. **risotto alla milanese**.

mille-feuille (*Fr.*) (fem.) [meel fuh-ee] Puff-pastry cake layered with whipped **cream** and jam. Some savoury *mille-feuilles* are layered with a meat or fish sauce. (Literally, 'thousand-leaf'.)

minced meat/mince Any meat ground or minced. Do not confuse with **mincemeat**, *below*.

mincemeat (*UK*) Fruit mince; sweet spicy mixture of currants, apple, etc. usually with **suet** and **brandy**, used in mince pies at Christmas. Do not confuse with **minced meat**, *above*.

mineral water Water flavoured with minerals, often thought to be health-promoting. Sparkling mineral water is aerated with carbon dioxide, either 'naturally' (at its source) or by injection. (*see also* **Appolinaris**, **Evian**, *and* **Perrier**.

minestra (*Ital.*) [min-ess-tra] **Soup**. (*See also* **brodo**, **minestrone**, *and* **zuppa**.)

minestrone (*Ital.*) [min-ess-troh-nay] Thick vegetable and **pasta** soup. (*See also* **minestra**.)

mint Herb, of which there are many varieties (genus *Mentha*), used as a flavouring or **garnish** in sweet or savoury dishes. (*See* **crème de menthe** *and below*.)

mint sauce Thin sauce, served cold, of finely chopped garden **mint**, **vinegar** and sugar, served traditionally as an **accompaniment** to roast lamb.

mints, after-dinner Chocolates with **mint**-flavoured centres served with **coffee** after the meal.

minute steak [minit] Tender steak cooked for one minute only. (It is therefore not necessary to ask how the guest prefers the steak cooked.) (*See also* **entrecôte**, **filet mignon**, **porterhouse**, **rump**, **sirloin**, *and* **T-bone**.)

mirepoix (*Fr.*) [meer-pwah] **Diced** carrot, onion, and celery **sautéed** and used to flavour soups and stews. *Mirepoix au* **gras** is this mixture cooked with ham or bacon. (Created by chef to the Duc de Mirepoix,

1699–1757, French general.)

mirin (*Jap.*) Sweet rice wine, low in alcohol, used only for cooking in Japan. (*See also* **sake**.)

miroir (*Fr.*) (masc.) [meer-wah] Shiny fruit **glaze** completely covering a dessert. (Literally 'mirror'.)

mise-en-place (*Fr.*) (fem.) [meez-on-plass] The setting out of equipment, garnishes, etc. in preparation for service or cooking. (Literally, 'set in place'.)

miso (*Jap.*) [meessoh] Paste made from fermented **tofu** and used to make **miso shiru**.

miso shiru (*Jap.*) Soup made from **miso** and **stock** often eaten at breakfast time.

misto/mista (*Ital.*) (adj.) Mixed, e.g. **fritto misto**, **insalata mista**.

ml Millilitres (thousandths of a litre).

mocha/mocca [mokkah] (1) Strong variety of **coffee** bean.
(2) A combination of **coffee** and chocolate flavouring (as in mocha **coupe**).
(From Mocha, or Al Mukha, port in Yemen, from which the coffee beans were shipped.)

mocktail Non-alcoholic, or **virgin**, **cocktail**.

môde, à la (*Fr.*) [ah lah mode] In the manner of, e.g. *boeuf à la môde*.

mollusc(s) Type of shellfish having a soft unsegmented body (unlike **crustaceans**) and usually a shell. Molluscs include gastropods (snails, winkles, whelks etc), bivalves (scallops, clams, mussels, cockles etc.) and cephalopods (octopus, cuttlefish, squid etc.).

monosodium glutamate *See* **MSG**.

morel [morrell] Variety of mushroom (*Morchella esculenta*) with a crinkled and brownish pointed cap resembling the pitted bark of a tree. (*See also* **cep**, **oyster mushroom**, **pine mushroom**, *and* **truffle**.) (Do not confuse with **morello**.)

morello [mur-elloh] Dark, bitter cherry commonly used in jams and cooked **puddings**. (Not to be confused with **morel**.)

mornay Cheese sauce made with milk or cream to which dried **mustard** has been added. (Philippe de Mornay, 1549–1623, colleague of Henri IV of France.) (*See* **gratin**, **gratinée**.)

mortadella (*Ital.*) [mort-a-dell-ah] Lightly **smoked** large Italian sausage, pale in colour with spots of pork fat. It is sometimes flavoured with **parsley**, **pistachios**, **peppercorns**, **coriander** seeds, or green **olives** and served with the **antipasto**. (Mortadella is not a place; the origin of the name is disputed.)

moselle Rather sweet white wine from the **Mösel** river region of Germany.

moule (*Fr.*) (fem.) [mool] Mussel, e.g. *moules marinières*.

moussaka (*Grk.*) [moose-ah-kah] Minced meat and eggplant baked with a topping of cheese sauce.

mousse (*Fr.*) (fem.) [moose]   (1) Light and frothy dish, usually set with **gelatine**, in which the basic ingredient is folded with whipped **cream**. It can be sweet or savoury (*mousse de saumon* 'salmon mousse'; *mousse au chocolat* 'chocolate mousse').

(2) The bubbles in **sparkling wine**.

(*Mousse* means 'foam', 'lather', or 'effervesence'.)

mousseline (*Fr.*) (fem.) [moose-leen]   (1) **Puréed** fish or meat blended with **cream**.

(2) Sauce to which **cream** has been added, e.g. **hollandaise** *mousseline*.

moutarde (*Fr.*) (masc.) [moo-tard]   *See* **mustard**.

mozzarella (*Ital.*) [motsa-rella]   Italian cheese, waxy in texture which when cooked becomes stringy; the classic topping for pizza. (*See also* **brocconcini**, **cheddar**, **parmesan**, *and* **ricotta**.)

MSG   Monosodium glutamate. Salt used to enhance the flavour of meat, much used in Chinese cooking as an additive in processed foods. Some object to MSG being included in their food since it is thought it may cause an allergic reaction.

muddle   **Cocktail**-mixing term. To crush in the bottom of the glass with a special 'muddler' (miniature pestle) or the base of a bar spoon. (*See* **Old Fashioned**.)

muffin   (1) (*UK*) Round, flat yeast bun split and toasted and served buttered.

(2) (*USA*) Large cup cake usually containing fruit, e.g. blueberry muffin.

mulled wine   Red wine heated gently with sugar, spices, raisins, and **citrus** fruits and served hot. (*See also* **glühwein**.)

mulligatawny (*Anglo-Ind.*) [mully-guh-tawny]   Highly seasoned chicken soup with vegetables. (Literally, Tamil for 'pepper water'.)

muscat   (1) One of a number of varieties of grape, also known as **frontignac**.

(2) Another name for **muscatel**.

muscatel/muscadel [muss-kuh-tel]   Raisin; dried fruit of **muscat** grape.

muselet (*Fr.*) [moo-sell-ay]   Wire muzzle used to hold in the corks of sparkling wines.

mushroom   One of various kinds of edible fungus but usually the cultivated mushroom (*Agaricus bisporus*). (French *champignon*.) (*See also* **cep**, **morel**, **oyster mushroom**, **pine mushroom**, *and* **truffle**.)

mustard   Yellow or brown **condiment** made from seeds of the mustard plant (genus *Brassica*). There are many different kinds of mustard seeds and mustard styles, including everyday hot English mustard, sweet American mustard, and various French mustards which are commonly used in cooking. (French *moutarde*.) (*See also* **cress** *and* **Dijon**.)

naan/nan (*Ind.*) [nahn]   Flat puffy leavened bread best cooked in a **tandoor**.

nacho (*Mex.*) [nah-choh]   **Corn chips** served with spicy sauce of beans, tomatoes, and/or meat topped with grated cheese, soured **cream** or **guacamole**. (*See also* **enchilada**, **taco** *and* **tortilla**.)

nam pla (*Thai.*) [nam plah]   Salty, pungent fish sauce used in cooking. (*See also* **nuoc mam**.)

nam prik (*Thai.*) [nam prik]   Spicy shrimp sauce served as a **condiment**.

napkin   *See* **table-napkin**.

Napoléon (**brandy**)   Marketing term without technical or legal meaning used on labels of brandy, particularly **cognac**. (Napoléon Bonaparte, 1769–1821, was Emperor of the French.)

napolitana (*Ital.*) [napol-it-ahna]   From Naples, town in N. Italy. **Pizza** *napolitana* contains **tomato**, cheese, herbs, **garlic**, **olives**, and **anchovies**.

nappé(e) [nap-pay]   Covered evenly with sauce or jelly. (*See* **mask**.)

nasi (*Malay*) [nahsee]   Cooked rice.

nasi goreng (*Malay*) [nahsee gore-eng]   Fried rice with chicken meat or prawns, shredded **omelette**, onions and spices. (*Goreng* means 'fried'.)

nasturtium   Plant (*Tropaeolum majus*) whose leaves, flowers and seeds are all edible. The leaves have a pungent, peppery taste reminiscent of **watercress**. The flowers are vivid orange and may be torn up in salads. The seeds are **pickled** and used like **capers**.

native peach   *See* **quandong**.

natural   Uncooked, as in oysters natural. (*See also* **naturel**, **au**.)

nature (*Fr.*) (adj.) [natoor]   Plain, unadulterated or without **garnish**, cooked with no sauce. (*See also* **naturel**, **au**.)

naturel, au (*Fr.*) [oh na-toor-el]   In a state of nature; food cooked plainly and simply, or not at all, e.g. **huîtres** *au naturel* (oysters **natural**).

navarin (*Fr.*) (masc.) [nav-a-ri(n)]   Mutton (lamb) stew with vegetables, originally turnips. (*Navet* means 'turnip'.)

neat   **Liquor**-mixing term; undiluted (e.g. neat **whisky**).

nebuchadnezzar   Largest recognized size of bottle for **sparkling wine**, the equivalent of 20 standard 75cl bottles. (Nebuchadnezzar was the King of Babylon who conquered Judah and carried the Jews off into exile in 586BC.) (*See also* **champagne bottle sizes**.)

nem nuong (*Viet*) [nem nung]   Grilled minced-pork balls wrapped in **rice pepper** with lettuce, cucumber, and **mint**. (*Nem* means 'ham', *nuong* 'grilled'.)

newburg   Methods of cooking and serving shellfish, esp. **lobster** or **crayfish**, with a sauce of sherry, cream, and egg yolk. (Originally created by a New York chef called Wenburg, the first three letters of his name being transposed in the name of the dish.)

niçois(e) (*Fr.*) (fem. adj.) [neece-swaz] Literally from Nice (city in SE France). Typically **provençal** dishes, including **garlic**, **anchovies**, **olives**, green beans and **tomatoes**. The most famous dishes of this type are **salade niçoise** and **poulet sauté** *à la niçoise*.

nip (1) Small measure (of **spirits**).

(2) (*UK*) Quarter bottle.

noble rot *See* **botrytis**.

noisette (*Fr.*) (fem.) [nwah-zet] (1) Hazel-nut, or coloured or shaped thus. (*See* **beurre noisette** *and* **pommes noisettes**.)

(2) Small round tender piece of meat, usually lamb, cut from the **loin** or rib.

noodle(s) Food paste similar to **pasta** usually cut into thin strands or rolled into thin sheets (used as wrappers in Chinese cooking). Most European noodles are made from wheat flour and eggs though some are made of rice and a few of potatoes. Asian noodles are made from rice or wheat and seldom contain eggs. (From the German *nudel*, meaning 'dumpling'.) (*See also* **udon noodle**.)

nori (*Jap.*) [no-ree] Kind of seaweed, dried and pressed into thin sheets, used as an edible wrapping or casing for **sushi**.

normande, à la (*Fr.*) [ah lah nor-mahnd] In the Normandy (province in N. France) style; with apples and possibly **calvados** as well as **cream**, e.g. **pommes de terre** *à la normande*. (*See also* **normande sauce** *below*.)

normande sauce Rich sauce made with **cream** and fish **stock**. (French, **sauce** *normande*.) (*See also* **normande (à la)**, *above*.)

nose Wine-tasting term; the combination of the **aroma** and **bouquet** of a wine.

nouvelle cuisine (*Fr.*) (fem.) [noo-vell kwiz-een] Style of French cooking introduced in the early 1970s when healthier food was promoted and lighter sauces replaced the old heavy, creamy ones and alcohol was used relatively sparingly. (*See also* **cuisine minceur**.)

nuoc cham (*Vict.*) [nuok chum] **Nuoc mam** with **chilli**, **garlic**, sugar, and lime juice added and used as a dipping sauce. (*Nuoc* means 'water' or 'juice', *cham* 'dip'.)

nuoc mam (*Viet.*) [nuok mum] Salty, pungent fish sauce used in cooking. (*Nuoc* means 'water' or 'juice', *mam* 'sauce'.) (*See also* **nam pla**.)

nutrient Providing nourishment; a nourishing ingredient.

oeuf (*Fr.*) (masc.) [erf] Egg.

oeuf en cocotte [erf ahn ko-kot] Baked egg. (*See* **cocotte**.)

oeuf mollet [erf moll-ay] Soft-boiled egg.

oeufs à la neige (*Fr.*) [erf ah lah nayzj] **Floating islands**. (Literally, 'eggs like snow'.)

oie (*Fr.*) (fem.) [wah] Goose, e.g. **confit** *d'oie*.

okra Seedpod of *Hibiscus esculentis*, also called **lady's fingers** or **gumbo**. Popular vegetable in Middle Eastern and **creole** cooking.

Old Fashioned Cocktail of **rye whiskey** and soda poured over sugar flavoured with **Angostura Bitters**. The sugar is often **muddled** in the glass, so an Old Fashioned glass has a specially thick base.

olive (1) Small stoned fruit, often stuffed and served as an **appetizer** or used as a **garnish** in **cocktails**. They may be green (immature) or black (mature). (*See also* **Kalamata**, **Ligurian**, *and* **Spanish** olive.)

(2) **Paupiette** (beef olive).

olive oil Oil extracted from **olives**. 'Pure' olive oil is pressed under heat from the pulp and kernels of lower-grade olives. **Virgin** and extra-virgin oil are finer and simply crushed from the first pressing of the highest grade fruit.

oloroso Golden and sweet style of Spanish **sherry**.

omelette Eggs, beaten with seasonings and fried in hot butter until just set; fillings, e.g. mushrooms or cheese, are sometimes added before the omelette is turned from the pan.

on-the-rocks Cocktail-mixing term: poured over a large quantity of cubed ice (e.g. **Scotch** on-the-rocks).

oregano Leaves of plant similar to **marjoram** used as robust seasoning herb esp. in Mediterranean cooking.

oseille (*Fr.*) (fem.) [oz-ayuh] **Sorrel**.

osso buco (*Ital.*) [oss-oh boo-koh] Rich **casserole** of knuckle of **veal** in a **tomato**, wine, and vegetable sauce, traditionally served with rice garnished with **parsley** and lemon **zest**. (*Osso* is Italian for 'bone' and *buco* means 'hole' – 'bone with a hole' in it.)

ouzo/oyzo (*Grk.*) Aniseed-flavoured **spirit**, similar to **pastis**.

oyster Bivalve **mollusc** (shellfish) usually eaten raw. Colchester and Whitstable oysters are thought to be the best. *See also* **huître**, **Kilpatrick** *and* **natural**.

oyster cruet Accompaniments for raw oysters: pepper mill, chilli vinegar, Tabasco sauce, cayenne pepper.

oyster mushroom Large white mushroom (*Pleurotus ostreatus*) with a slight taste of **oysters**. Also known as abalone mushroom. (*See also* **cep**, **morel**, **pine mushroom**, *and* **truffle**.)

oyzo *See* **ouzo**.

paella (*Span.*) [pie-yella] Rice dish flavoured with **saffron** and containing chicken, **shellfish**, **chorizo**, peas and other vegetables.

paillard (*Ital.* from *Fr.*) [pie-yar] **Escalope** of **veal**. (Paillard was a 19th-century Parisian restaurateur.)

pain (*Fr.*) (masc.) [pa(n)] Bread. (*See* **pané**.)

pain au chocolat (*Fr.*) [pa(n)] oh shokohlah] **Croissant**

containing chocolate. (Literally 'chocolate bread'.)

pakora/pakhora/pakorha (*Ind.*) [pack-or-ah] Savoury **fritter** made of **chick-pea** flour containing spicy **diced** vegetables.

palate Upper part of the mouth; sense of taste.

pancake Thin flat **batter** cake, usually fried. (*See* **crêpe**.)

pancetta (*Ital.*) [panchetta] Pork belly rolled and eaten hot or cold; bacon.

pané(e) (*Fr.*) [pan-ay] Fried in breadcrumbs (*See also* **pain**.)

panettone (*Ital.*) [panuh-ton-ay] N. Italian Christmas cake made from yeast and containing dried fruit, spices and nuts.

panforte (*Ital.*) [panfortay] **Sweetmeat** containing **glacé** fruit and nuts.

papillote (*Fr.*) [pap-ee-yot] (1) Buttered paper; **en papillote**, cooked in buttered paper. (Fish is often served in this way.)
(2) Small frill of paper used to garnish **cutlet** bones.

pappadam/poppadum (*Ind.*) [poppa-dum] Very light and thin crisp wafer made from **lentil** flour cooked in oil, often served with **curry**.

paprika [pap-reeka] Red spice (*Capsicum annuum*) bought powdered and used both as a **garnish**, and for its colour and flavour in cooked dishes, esp. Hungarian **goulash**.

parfait (*Fr.*) (masc.) [par-fay] (1) Creamy iced **pudding**.
(2) Layered fruit and ice-cream dessert served in tall glasses.
(3) Smooth, savoury **paté**, usually of meat, blended with cream.

Parma ham Fine, raw smoked Italian ham (Italian **prosciutto** *di Parma*) from Parma, city in N. Italy.

Parmesan (*Ital.*) [parm-i-zan] Very hard dry cheese much used in Italian cooking. (Originally from Parma, city in N. Italy.) (*See* **Parmigiano**.)

Parmigiano (reggiano) (*Ital.*) [parmi-zjahnoh rezj-ee-ahnoh] **Parmesan** cheese produced in Parma, N. Italy. (It can only carry this label if produced in the region.)

pasta (*Ital.*) Staple food of Italy made of durum wheat flour (**semolina**) or potato, mixed with water, and, usually, egg and often sold dried. There are many varieties of pasta. (*See* **cannelloni, fettuccine, gnocchi, lasagne, linguini, penne, ravioli, rigatoni, spaghetti, tagliatelle, tortellini,** *and* **vermicelli**; *see also* **al dente** *and* **noodles**.)

pastis (*Fr.*) (masc.) [pas-teece] (1) Strong alcoholic drink flavoured with aniseed, similar to **ouzo**, e.g. **Pernod**.
(2) Any of several pastries made in SW France, e.g. *pastis Béarnais*. (Béarn is a province in SW France.)

pasto (*Ital.*) A meal. (*See also* **antipasto**.)

pastrami (*USA/Yid.*) [pass-trahmee] **Cured**, spiced roast beef **silverside** rubbed in spices and thick **pepper-corns**. It is usually sliced and served in **rye** bread

sandwiches with **dill pickles**.

pâte (*Fr.*) [paht] Dough, pastry or **batter**. (Not to be confused with **pâté** below.)

pâté (*Fr.*) (masc.) [paht-ay] Paste of **blended** meats or fish, flavoured with seasoniong, herbs and, sometimes, alcohol. (Not to be confused with **pâte** above.) (*See also* **parfait, rillettes,** *and* **terrine**.)

pâte à choux (*Fr.*) (fem.) [paht ah shoo] **Choux** pastry.

pâte brisée (*Fr.*) (fem.) [paht breez-ay] **Short-crust pastry**.

pâté de foie gras (*Fr.*) (masc.) [pat-ay duh fwa gra] **Pâté** of force-fed goose or duck liver made by **blending** the fattened livers with minced pork and **truffles**. (*Gras* is French for 'fat'.)

pâté en croûte (*Fr.*) (masc.) [pat-ay ahn croot] **Pâté** baked in a pastry case. (*See* **croûte**.)

pâte feuilletée (*Fr.*) (fem.) [paht fur-yet-ay] **Puff pastry**. (Also called pâté à feuilletage.)

pâté maison (*Fr.*) (masc.) [pat-ay mayzo(n)] Home-made **pâté**, made according to the chef's own recipe. (*See* **maison**.)

pâte sablée (*Fr.*) (fem.) [paht sab-lay] Sweetened **short-crust pastry**. (*Un sablé* means 'a shortbread'.)

pâte sucrée (*Fr.*) (fem.) [paht soo-cray] Rich, sweetened **shortcrust pastry**. (*Sucré* means 'sugared'.)

patisserie (*Fr.*) (fem.) [pat-ees-er-ee] (1) Pastry.
(2) Cake-shop; tea-room.

patty Small flat cake of meat (like the filling of a hamburger); a little pie.

pauchouse *See* **pochouse**.

paupiette (*Fr.*) (fem.) [paw-pee-ett] Thin slice of meat rolled with a stuffing (*paupiettes de* **veau**), sometimes referred to as an **olive** (beef olives).

pavé (*Fr.*) [pavay] (masc.) (1) Sponge cake or dessert of biscuits sandwiched in layers with creamy filling.
(2) Savoury **mousse** set in **aspic** and garnished with **truffles**.
(*Pavé* means 'paving stone'.)

pavlova Soft **meringue** cake filled with **cream** and topped with fruit. (Named for Anna Pavlova, Russian ballerina, 1882–1931.)

paysanne, à la (*Fr.*) (masc.) [ah lah pay-ee-zan] **Diced** vegetables used as **garnish**, e.g. **potage** *à la paysanne*; **braised** dishes cooked with vegetables, e.g. *côtes de* **veau** *à la paysanne*. (*Paysanne* means 'peasant woman'.)

peach Melba Poached peach halves enclosing **vanilla** ice-cream coated with raspberry **coulis** (French, **pêches** *Melba*). The original peach Melba was devised by the famous chef Auguste Escoffier (1846–1935) in honour of the Australian opera-singer Dame Nellie Melba. (*See also* **Melba toast**.)

pecan [pekahn/peecan] Smooth brown nut from the Mississippi region, USA; hickory nut.

pêche (*Fr.*) (fem.) [paysh]   Peach. (*See also* **peach Melba**.)

Peking   One of the five main styles of Chinese cuisine; Peking cuisine is light and delicate. (Peking, now called Beijing, is a city in N. China.) (*See also* **Cantonese, Fukien, Honan,** *and* **Szechwan**.)

Peking duck (*Chin.*)   The crisp, crackling skin of mandarin duck eaten in a **pancake** with **spring onion**, cucumber, and **hoi sin sauce**. The flesh of the duck is served separately.

penne (*Ital.*) [penay]   Short tubes of **pasta** cut at an acute angle. (Literally 'quills'.)

peperoni (*Ital.*) (pl.) [pepper-ohny]   Preserved **sweet peppers**. (*Peperoni* is Italian for 'capsicums'.) (Do not confuse with **pepperoni**.)

pepper   **Condiment** made from the dried berry-like fruit (**peppercorn**) of the pepper plant (*Piper nigrum*). (*See* **peppercorn**; *see also* **capsicum, cayenne,** *and* **sweet pepper**.)

peppercorn   Seed of the **pepper** plant picked and processed at one of three distinct stages:
(1) *Green* peppercorns picked while the seed is still soft and green; usually bottled in **brine** but occasionally available fresh. (*See* **poivre vert**.)
(2) *Black* peppercorns picked when the skin has turned yellow and the kernel has hardened. The berry is dried once the skin has been removed.
(3) Once the berry turns red, the outer coating is washed off and the kernel dried for *white* **pepper**. This has more bite but less **aroma** than the black peppercorn.
Black peppercorns are usually freshly ground from a pepper mill at table. Ground white pepper used to be served in a **cruet** and used at table but freshly-ground black pepper is now preferred by most people. (*See also* **poivre, au**.)

pepperoni (*Ital.*) [pepper-ohny]   Hard, spicy beef-and-pork **salami**. (Do not confuse with **peperoni**.)

peppers   *See* **capsicum, peperoni,** *and* **sweet pepper**.

Pernod [pair-no]   **Proprietary** brand of **pastis**.

Perrier   Brand of French **mineral water**.

persillade (*Fr.*) (fem.) [pear-sill-ahd]   Mixture of **garlic** and chopped **parsley**.

persillé (*Fr.*) [pear-sill-ay]   Dishes seasoned with a **persillade**, e.g. **boeuf** *persillade*.

pesto (*Ital.*) [pest-oh]   Paste made by blending **basil**, **Parmesan** cheese, **pine nuts**, garlic and olive oil. (*See also* **pistou**.)

petit déjeuner (*Fr.*)   Breakfast.

petit four (*Fr.*) (masc.) [put-ee-foor]   Small fancy cake or biscuit. There are different varieties: plain petits fours are dry and undercoated; fresh petits fours include miniature cakes, iced **marzipan** sweets, and sugar-coated fruits. (*Petit* means 'little' and *four* (usually) 'oven', so *petits fours* 'little baked things', 'little cakes'.)

petits pois   *See* **pois**.

pho (*Vict.*) [fo] (short 'o' as in hot)   Soup.

phosphorus [fos-fore-uss]   Non-metallic element found in all foods. Very high intakes can inhibit the absorption of **calcium**.

phyllo   *See* **filo**.

pickle   (1) (noun) **Condiment** of fruit or vegetables preserved in **vinegar** with sugar and spices, e.g. **dill pickle**, Branston pickle.
(2) (verb) To **preserve** vegetables or fruit in a **pickle** solution, e.g. pickled onions. (*See also* **brine, cure,** *and* **smoke**.)

pièce de résistance (*Fr.*) (fem.) [pee-yayss duh ray-zees-tahns]   The main dish of a meal, substantial and usually rather grand. (Literally, 'item of strength'.)

pilaff (*Turk.*) [peelaf]   Middle Eastern dish of spiced rice with meat, chicken, or fish, usually cooked together. (*See also* **pilau**.)

pilau (*Ind.*) [pee-low]   Indian version of **pilaff**, typically including chicken and/or mutton or goat's meat and spiced. (*See also* **biryani**.)

pilsner/pilsener   (1) Pale hop-flavoured **lager** originally made in Pilsen, Bohemia (now Plzen, Czechoslovakia). (2) Style of beer glass.

Pimm's   Properly 'Pimm's No. 1 Cup', an English **proprietary** gin-based flavoured liquor, usually served in summer mixed with lemonade or **ginger ale** and ice, and garnished with cucumber and **mint**.

pine mushroom   Large, golden mushroom (*Armiltaria edodes*) which grows under red pine trees. Also known as **matsutake mushroom**. (*See also* **cep, morel, oyster mushroom,** *and* **truffle**.)

pine nut   The seed of the Mediterranean stone pine. Pine nuts are an essential ingredient of **pesto**.

Pink Gin   **Cocktail** of gin served with a dash of **Angostura Bitters**.

pinot noir [pee-no nwaar]   Grape variety used in the famous French red **burgundy** wine. Pinot noir wines are usually soft and light; they are also part of the blend used to make French **champagne**.

pipe   To squeeze **cream**, icing, etc. in decorative patterns on a cake or other food item.

piperade (*Fr.*) (fem.) [peep-ay-rahd]   Stewed **tomato**, **capsicum**, onion, and **garlic** mixed with beaten eggs and cooked slowly over gentle heat.

piquant [pee-kant]   Spicy, appetizing.

piroshki (*Russ.*) [pi-rohsh-kee]   Savoury pasty.

pistachio [piss-tashee-oh]   Fruit of the *Pistacia* tree, native to the Middle East. Pistachio nuts are used in savoury and sweet dishes, esp. cream desserts and sliced meats where their bright green colour enhances their appearance.

pistou (*Fr.*) (masc.) [pees-too]   **Provençal** paste **condiment** made of sweet **basil**, and olive oil with **garlic** and

Parmesan cheese, similar to Italian **pesto**. Pistou soup (**soupe** *au pistou*) is popular.

pita/pitta (*Grk.*)   Flat round double-layered bread which can be cut open and filled; pocket bread.

pithiviers (*Fr.*) [peeteev-ee-ay]   **Puff-pastry** tart traditionally sandwiched with almond cream but often filled with a savoury mixture. The pastry top is usually **scalloped** around the edges and **scored** with curves radiating from the centre. (Pithiviers is near Orléans in Central France.)

pizza (*Ital.*) [peetsa]   Plate-like base of dough covered with topping which usually includes cheese, tomato and herbs. (*See* **capricciosa**, **margherita**, **marinara**, *and* **napolitana**; *see also* **calzone** *and* **focaccia**.)

platter   Large serving dish; a 'sizzling platter' is presented direct from the stove and so is usually made of cast iron. (*See also* **skillet**.)

ploughman's lunch (*UK*)   Cheese and **pickle** served with a hunk of bread and **beer**, esp. in local pubs.

plum pudding   *See* **Christmas pudding**.

poché(e) (*Fr.*) (adj.) [poshay]   Poached.

pochouse/pauchouse (*Fr.*) [poh-shooz]   Fish stew from Burgundy cooked with white wine. (Dialect version of **pêcheuse**, 'fisherwoman'.) (*See also* **bouillabaisse**.)

point, à (*Fr.*) [ah pwa(n)]   Medium, steak cooked so that it shows a tinge of pink blood. (*See also* **bien cuit**, **bleu**, *and* **saignant**.)

poire (*Fr.*) (fem.) [pwaar]   Pear.

poireau(x) (*Fr.*) (masc.) [pwah-roe]   Leek(s).

pois (*Fr.*) (fem.) [pwah]   Pea, usually eaten young as *petits pois*. (Literally 'little peas'.)

poisson (*Fr.*) (masc.) [pwah-so(n)]   Fish.

poivrade, sauce (*Fr.*) [sohs pwahv-rwahd]   Sauce consisting of a **mirepoix** mixed with **vinegar**, wine, and crushed green **peppercorns**, traditionally served with **game**. (*See also* **chevreuil**, **salmis**, *and* **venaison**.)

poivre (*Fr.*) (masc.) [pwahv-ruh]   Pepper.

poivre, au (*Fr.*) [oh pwahv-ruh]   With **pepper** or crushed **peppercorns** e.g. **biftek** *aux poivres*.

poivre vert (*Fr.*) [pwahv-ruh vair]   Green **peppercorn**, e.g. **poulet** *aux poivres verts*.

polenta (*Ital.*) [puh-len-ta]   Dough of thick porridge-like consistency made with cornmeal (maize flour). Cooked polenta can be fried or baked and served with meat dishes.

pollo (*Ital. & Span.*)   Chicken.

pomme (*Fr.*) (fem.) [pom]   Apple.

pomme de terre (*Fr.*) (fem.) [pom duh tair]   Potato. (*De terre* means 'of the earth'.) Note that in compounds such as those below, the words '*de terre*' are omitted.

pommes Anna (*Fr.*) (fem.) [pom anna]   Sliced potatoes cooked with butter in a pan to form a solid cake. It is served in slices. (Dish dedicated to Anna Deslions,

socialite in the Second Empire, *c.* 1860.)

pommes duchesse (*Fr.*) (fem.) [pom doo-shess]   Potatoes **puréed** with egg yolk and butter, **piped** around the edge of a dish, or into small shapes, and baked in the oven.

pommes frites (*Fr.*) (fem.) [pom freet]   Chipped potatoes deep-fried; French fries. (*See* **frite**.)

pommes noisettes (*Fr.*) (fem.) [pom nwa-zet]   Small potato balls **sautéed** in butter. (*See* **noisette**.)

pommes sautées (*Fr.*) (fem.) [pom soh-tay]   Cooked potatoes fried quickly, often with **shallots** or bacon to flavour. (*See* **sauté**.)

porridge (*Scot.*) [porij]   Breakfast dish of oatmeal cooked with milk or water and served hot.

port   Kind of **fortified wine**, originally developed in Portugal, often served after dinner.

porterhouse   Large, thick beef steak, similar to a T-bone steak, cut from the sirloin. (*See also* **entrecôte**, **filet mignon**, **minute steak**, **rump**, *and* **T-bone**.)

portion   Amount of food served to guests in any particular menu item.

potage (*Fr.*) (masc.) [pot-ahzj]   Soup, particularly thick (cream) soup. (*See also* **bisque**, **garbure**, **soupe** *and* **vichyssoise**.)

pot-au-feu (*Fr.*) (masc.) [pot oh fur]   Classic dish of beef cooked slowly with vegetables in liquid to form a **broth** which is eaten before the meat. (Literally, 'pot for the fire', so 'stewpot' or 'casserole'.)

pot roast   Joint of meat baked with vegetables and **stock** in a covered pan.

pot still   Traditional **still** used to distil **malt whisky**, **cognacs** and **armagnacs** whereby the spirit is distilled in batches, unlike the 'continuous still' used to distil most modern **spirits**.

poulet (*Fr.*) (masc.) [poo-lay]   Chicken, fowl.

poussin (*Fr.*) (masc.) [poo-sa(n)]   Baby chicken.

praline [pray-leen]   Confection of **caramelized** almonds or hazelnuts baked hard. It is added to some sweet dishes in the form of a fine, crushed powder. (Devised by Lassagne, chef to Marshal Duplessis-Praslin, *c.* 1630.)

preserve   (1) (noun) Preserved fruit; jam, jelly.
(2) (verb) To prepare food for storage; to **pickle**.

pretzel   Salted stick-like biscuit, shaped into knobs and curls, served as an apéritif, especially with beer.

princesse, à la (*Fr.*) [ah lah pra(n)-sess]   Garnished with asparagus tips.

Pritikin   Style of cooking food named after Nathan Pritikin (1915–85) who maintained that by reducing **cholesterol** levels many diseases caused by modern lifestyle could be prevented. The diet is low in fats and animal **protein**, has no added salt or sugar, and is high in fibre. (*See also* **cuisine minceur**.)

prix-fixe (*Fr.*) [pree fiks]   Fixed-price meal; **table d'hôte** menu. (*Prix* means 'price'.)

profiterole (*Fr.*) (fem.) [prof-ee-tay-rol] Small **choux-pastry** bun with a sweet creamy filling served in chocolate sauce. Those filled with a cheese mixture or savoury purée are often used to garnish soup.

proof Old measure of alcohol in **liquor** obsolete in UK, but still used in the USA (US 100° proof = 50% alc/vol).

proprietary The property of some person or body. A proprietary **liqueur**, **Grand Marnier** for example, can only be made by the company which owns the right to make it. (*See also* **generic**.)

prosciutto (*Ital.*) [prosh-choot-oh] Raw **smoked** ham sliced very thinly. (*See also* **Parma ham**.)

protein Constituent of food needed for growth and repair, found particularly in meat and dairy products, but also in **soya beans**, **lentils** and peas.

provençale, à la (*Fr.*) [ah lah prov-ah(n)-saal] In the manner of Provence (province in S. France); cooked with tomatoes and **garlic**.

pudding (1) Soft food item of ingredients mixed with or enclosed in flour or suet and usually steamed or baked, e.g. **bread and butter pudding**, **Christmas pudding** and **Yorkshire pudding**. (*See also* **black pudding** *and* **summer pudding**.)

(2) The **sweet** or **dessert** course of a meal.

puff pastry Delicate airy pastry rolled so that it forms thin layers when cooked. (*see* **pâte feuilletée**.)

pumpernickel (*Ger.*) [poom-purr-nickel] Solid, dark brown or black **rye** bread, often packaged for use as a base for **canapés**, cut into small circles or squares and sliced thinly.

punch Drink of wine or **spirits** with fruit juices or water flavoured with spices and often served hot. (*See also* **glühwein** *and* **mulled wine**.)

pungent With a strong taste or smell.

punt The hollow at the base of some wine bottles. It retains the deposit (if any) thrown by the wine and, especially in the case of **champagne** bottles, may be used to hold the bottle while pouring.

purée [pew-ray] (1) (*Fr.*) (fem. noun) Any food **blended** to a smooth, thick paste, e.g. *purée de* **volaille**, 'purée of chicken'.

(2) (*Eng.*) (verb) To **blend** into a purée (e.g. puréed potatoes).

quail Small **game** bird, nowadays farmed, usually served two birds to a guest.

quail egg Egg about one-third the size of standard hen's egg, often served hard-boiled as an **appetizer** (*See also* **Scotch egg**.)

quenelle (*Fr.*) (fem.) [ken-nell] Poached **dumpling** of **puréed** fish, egg white and **cream**. **Veal** or chicken is sometimes used instead of fish.

quiche (*Fr.*) (fem.) [keesh] Open pie or **flan**, filled with savoury custard holding other ingredients.

quiche Lorraine [keesh lor-aine] **Quiche** filled with savoury custard and bacon and topped with cheese. (Lorraine is a province in NE France.)

quince Hard yellow apple-like fruit delicately scented which when cooked turns pink. Often used in pies and **puddings** and makes excellent **preserves**.

quinine Bitter alkaloid obtained from cinchona bark, once the principal treatment for malaria and used as flavouring, e.g. in Indian **tonic**.

rack (of lamb) Joint of lamb cutlets cut from the rib **loin**. There are usually between four and six chops in the rack. (French **carré** *d'*agneau.)

raclette (*Swiss*) (fem.) [rack-let] Cheese **fondue** made by melting a whole Swiss cheese and scraping off pieces as they soften. It is usually eaten with plain potatoes, gherkins, **pickled** onions, and black **pepper**. (*Raclette* is French for a 'scraping'.)

radicchio (*Ital.*) [rad-eek-ee-oh] **Endive** with dark reddish-green leaves and distinctive white veins. Has pungent taste and mixes well with other salad greens.

ragoût (*Fr.*) (masc.) [rag-oo] Stew or **casserole** (e.g. *ragoût* d'**agneau**).

raita (*Ind.*) [rye-eeta] Yoghurt blended with **garlic** and cucumber and served as a cooling **condiment** with spicy dishes.

ramekin [ram-uh-kin] Small baking dish for one serving; miniature **soufflé** dish.

rang (*Fr.*) (masc.) [rung] Rank, brigade, team (of waiters). (*See* **chef de rang**.)

rare Meat cooked for only a short time so that the blood runs; underdone. (*See also* **bleu, à point**.)

ratatouille (*Fr.*) (fem.) [rata-too-wee] **Provençal** vegetable stew containing tomatoes, onions, egg plant, **capsicums** and **courgettes**, flavoured with **garlic** and ground **pepper**.

ravière (*Fr.*) (fem.) [ravee-ayr] Oval or rectangular-shaped serving dish.

ravioli (*Ital.*) (pl.) [rav-ee-oh-lee] Squares of **pasta** filled with meat, **ricotta** cheese, or a vegetable.

réchaud (*Fr.*) (masc.) [ray-show] Small stove or spirit-lamp used for table-side cooking or to keep food warm. (*Chaud* means 'hot'.) (*See* **chafing dish, chaud,** *and* **flambé**.)

réchauffé (*Fr.*) [ray-show-fay] (1) (masc. noun) Re-heated dish; a dish made up of left-overs. (*See also* **émincés**.)

(2) **réchauffé(e)** (adj.) Re-heated. (*Chauffé* means 'heated'.)

red pepper (1) **Cayenne pepper**.

(2) Variety of **sweet pepper** or **capsicum**.

reduce To thicken **stock**, or liquids such as white wine or

vinegar, by boiling rapidly without a lid thus reducing the quantity through evaporation.

rehoboam [re-huh-boh-um] Large bottle of **sparkling wine** containing the equivalent of 6 standard (75cl) bottles. (Rehoboam was King of Judah 10th century BC.) (*See* **champagne bottle sizes**.)

relevé (*Fr.*) [ruh-lev-ay] (1) (masc. noun) Meat course in the **classic menu** following the **entrée**, usually a dish carved from a joint.
(2) (adj.) Cooking term meaning 'highly seasoned'.

relish Condiment, **sauce**, or **pickle**, usually eaten with plain food. (*See also* **Gentleman's Relish**.)

rémoulade (*Fr.*) (fem.) [ray-moo-laad] **Mayonnaise** sauce seasoned with gherkins, **capers**, **anchovies**, and **herbs**.

rendang daging (*Indon.*) [rendan(g) dahging] Dry-fried beef **curry** cooked in **coconut milk** and spices.

reservation The booking of a table for a meal or bed for the night; the place thus booked.

restaurateur (*Fr.*) (masc.) [res-tara-tur] Manager or owner of a restaurant; the licensee. (Note *not* restauranteur.)

Rhine riesling Popular white wine grape variety, usually known internationally simply as **riesling**. It is used to make **hock**. (*See also* **riesling**.)

rice-paper Edible paper made from the pith of an oriental tree and used in Asian cooking. (*See also* **goi cuon** *and* **nem nuong**.)

rice vinegar Mild **vinegar** used in Asian cooking as a **pickling** agent, or to give an acidic or 'sour' taste to dishes. (*See also* **balsamic vinegar**, **malt vinegar**, **vinaigrette**, *and* **wine vinegar**.)

ricotta (*Ital.*) White, moist, light cheese made mostly from the **whey** of milk. (*See also* **mascarpone**.)

riesling (*Ger.*) [reece-ling] Dry white wine made from the **Rhine riesling** grape, from the Rhine region of Germany. (*See also* **hock, auslese** *and* **spätlese**.)

rigatoni (*Ital.*) (pl.) [rigga-toh-nee] **Pasta** made in the shape of short ridged tubes.

rillettes (*Fr.*) (fem. pl.) [ree-yettuh] **Minced meat**, usually pork, cooked in its own fat and made into a **pâté**. Served as cold **hors d'oeuvre**.

risotto (*Ital.*) (riz-ott-oh) Rice, preferably **arborio**, and vegetables (and sometimes meat or fish) cooked in **stock** until the liquid is absorbed by the rice.

risotto alla milanese [riz-ott-oh ala mil-an-ayz-ay] Rice cooked in **stock** with onions, flavoured with **saffron** and **Parmesan** cheese. (*Milanese* means 'in the style of Milan', city in N. Italy.)

rocket Pungent **cress** rather like spinach (*Eruca sativa*) used raw in **mesclun** mix for salad.

roe Fish eggs. (*See also* **caviare** *and* **lumpfish roe**.)

roesti/rösti [rur-stee] Swiss potato cake; grated potatoes formed into a cake and fried in butter.

rognon (*Fr.*) (masc.) [roh-nyo(n)] Kidney.

Romanov/Romanoff (*Fr.*) [roam-anoff] (1) **Garnish** of cucumber stuffed with **duxelles**.
(2) Creamed-potato cases filled with mushrooms in a **velouté** sauce, seasoned with **horseradish**.
(3) Strawberries **macerated** in **curaçao** served with **crème chantilly**.
(Romanov was the name of the dynasty which ruled Russia 1613–1917. Many French chefs dedicated dishes to the Imperial family.)

roquefort (*Fr.*) [rok-fore] Smooth and creamy **blue-veined** ewes' milk cheese. (Roquefort is a district in S. France.) (*See also* **dolcelatta, gorgonzola,** *and* **stilton**.)

rosé (*Fr.*) [rose-ay] Pink wine made by removing the skins of black (red) grapes early in the **fermentation** process resulting in a lighter colour and flavour than in an ordinary red wine.

Rossini *See* **tournedos Rossini**.

rosso Sweet, pink style of **vermouth**.

Rosso Antico Proprietary Italian **apéritif** infused with aromatic herbs. (Literally, 'Ancient Red'.)

roti (*Ind.*) [roh-tee] General term for bread, particularly flat unleavened bread like **chapati**; with **dahl** it is the staple food of northern India.

rôti (*Fr.*) (masc.) [roh-tee] Roast meat, e.g. *rôti de* **boeuf**. *Rôtis* (pl.) is a course in the **classic menu**.

rotisserie Device for roasting meat on a rotating spit so that it browns evenly.

rouille (*Fr.*) (fem.) [roo-ee] **Provençal** sauce of **garlic**, oil, and **stock** with red **chillies** and **saffron** served with fish dishes, esp. **bouillabaisse**. (Literally, 'rust' from its colour.)

roulade (*Fr.*) (fem.) [roo-lahd] Stuffed roll of food. A savoury roulade may be a thin piece of meat stuffed and rolled; a sweet one a chocolate sponge filled with **cream** before rolling.

roux (*Fr.*) (masc.) [roo] Blend of fat and flour which is used to thicken sauces. (*See* **béchamel**.)

rum Spirit distilled from sugar-cane or molasses. Rum comes in various styles and colours ranging from colourless (like **Bacardi**) to dark brown Jamaica rum.

rum baba *See* **baba**.

rump steak Tender cut of beef taken from behind the loin. (*See also* **entrecôte, filet mignon, porterhouse sirloin,** *and* **T-bone**.)

russe, à la (*Fr.*) [ah lah rooss] In the Russian style; often shellfish in an **aspic** jelly with **mayonnaise** or a **chaudfroid** sauce served with a **Russian salad**. (*See also* **charlotte russe**.)

Russian salad Salad of **diced** cooked vegetables mixed in **mayonnaise** and flavoured with either caraway or **pickles**.

Russian tea   Tea served without milk in a silver holder with a lemon slice.

rye   (1) **Cereal** used for making bread; rye bread is rather dark in colour and slightly bitter in taste.
(2) Rye **whiskey**; American whiskey distilled (mainly) from fermented rye.

sabayon (*Fr.*) [sab-eye-on]   Mixture of egg yolks, white wine, and sugar whipped together to form a rich foamy dessert usually served just warm. Similar to Italian **zabaglione**.

sabayon sauce   Sauce made from egg yolks blended with alcohol (particularly **champagne**) and usually served with fish.

sablé (*Fr.*) (masc.) [sab-lay]   Kind of **shortbread**.

saddle   Large cut of meat from the top of the back of the animal. (*See also* **loin**.)

saffron   Dried stigma of a kind of crocus flower used as a spice for flavouring. It colours food bright yellow, and is also used as a dye.

saignant(e) (*Fr.*) [say-nyo(n)(tuh)]   **Rare** and rather bloody (steak, etc.) but not 'blue'. (*See also* **bien cuit, bleu** *and* **point (à)**.) (Literally, 'bleeding'.)

sake (*Jap.*) [sah-kay]   Fermented, colourless rice wine, usually served warm. (*See also* **mirin**.)

salad dressing   *See* **French dressing, mayonnaise,** *and* **vinaigrette**.

salade (*Fr.*) (fem.) [sall-ahd]   Salad. (*See also* **insalata, niçoise, Caesar, Russian,** *and* **Waldorf**.)

salamander   Grill which heats from above, used for browning, etc.

salami (*Ital.*) [salaamee]   Highly-seasoned sausage served cold. (*See also* **kabana, mortadella,** *and* **pepperoni**.)

salmanazar   Large bottle size for **sparkling wine**, equivalent of 12 standard (75cl) bottles. (Salmanazar was the Assyrian King who conquered Israel in 721 BC. (*See also* **champagne bottle sizes**.)

salmis (*Fr.*) (masc.) [salmee]   **Ragout** of **game** bird of duck, often finished at table. (*See also* **salmis, sauce**.)

salmis, sauce (*Fr.*) [sohs salmee]   Sauce served with a **salmis** made with the cooking juices diluted with wine mixed with an **espagnole** sauce.

salmonella   Group of **bacteria** which can cause food poisoning.

salpicon (*Fr.*) (masc.) [sal-pee-ko(n)]   **Diced** pieces of meat, etc., held in a sauce and used to fill **canapés, vols-au-vent,** etc.)

salsa (*Ital., Span., & Mex.*) [sals-a]   (1) **Sauce**. (*See below*.)
(2) Combination of chopped and usually raw vegetables, served as a fresh **chutney**.

salsa di pomodoro (*Ital.*) [sals-a dee pom-uh-dorr-oh]   Tomato sauce. (Literally, 'sauce of tomato'.)

salsa verde (*Ital.*) [sals-a vairduh]   **Vinaigrette** with anchovies and **capers** or finely-chopped parsley added. (Literally 'green sauce'.)

salsa verde cruda (*Mex.*) [salsa vairduh crooda]   Uncooked green-tomato sauce served with **tacos, nachos, tortillas,** and **enchiladas**. (Literally 'raw' or 'unripe' 'green sauce'.)

saltimbocca (*Ital.*) [saul-teem-bow-kah]   Thin slices of **veal** and **smoked** ham rolled with sage leaves, **sautéed** and simmered in wine. (Literally, 'jump into mouth'.)

sambal/sambol (*Indon.*) [sam-bahl]   **Condiment** usually containing **chillies** and onion.

samosa (*Ind.*) [samohsa]   Small pastry with spicy filling deep fried and served as a **savoury**.

samovar (*Russ.*)   Metal urn, originating from Russia, for making tea at the table.

sashimi (*Jap.*) [sash-eeme]   Raw fish arranged in thin bite-sized pieces and served with **daikon radish** and **wasabi**. (Literally, 'pierced flesh'.)

satay (*Malay.*) [sah-tay]   Cubes of meat or fish on bamboo skewers, grilled on a charcoal grill, and served with **satay sauce**. (*See* **kebab**.)

satay sauce (*Malay.*)   Thick sauce made from crushed peanuts and lemon juice, often served with **satay**.

sauce   *See* **béarnaise, béchamel, beurre blanc, beurre noisette, beurre meurière, black bean, bolognaise, bordelaise, capricciosa, carbonara, charcutière, chasseur, chaudfroid, crème anglaise, Cumberland, demi-glace, devilled, diable, espagnole, florentine, French dressing, guacamole, hoi sin, hollandaise, horseradish, ketchup, lyonnaise, madère, maître d'hôtel, mayonnaise, meunière, mint, mornay, mousseline, nam pla, nam prik, newburg, normande, nuoc cham, nuoc mam, poivrade, relish, rémoulade, rouille, sabayon, salmis, satay, shoyu, soubise, soya, suprême, sweet-and-sour, Tabasco, tartare, teriyaki, thermidor, Thousand Island, velouté, venaison, vinaigrette, Worcestershire,** *and* **zingara**. (*See also below and* **crème (à la), mask, nappé, roux**.) (*French sauce* (fem.) [sohs] as in *sauce bérnaise*, Italian and Spanish **salsa** [sals-a].

saucière (*Fr.*) (fem.) [soh-see-ayr]   Sauce- or gravy-boat.

sauerkraut (*Ger.*) [sour krout]   **Pickled** white cabbage. (Literally, 'sour cabbage').

saumon (*Fr.*) (masc.) [sow-mo(n)]   Salmon.

sauté (*Fr.*) [soh-tay]   (1) masc. noun) Dish of quickly fried food.
(2) (adj.) (*sauté(e)*) Lightly fried (e.g. **pommes** *sautées*).
(3) (*Eng.*) (verb) Lightly fried – a 'sautéed' mixture, 'sautéed in butter', etc.

sauternes [so-tairn]   Lusciously-rich, sweet white **dessert wine** from Sauternes, district near Bordeaux, SW France.

sauvignon   *See* **cabernet sauvignon** *and* **sauvignon**

blanc.

sauvignon blanc [so-veenee-o(n) blo(n)] Grape variety used to make dry white wines including **fumé** blanc.

savarin (*Fr.*) (masc.) [sav-a-ra(n)] Large ring-shaped cake made with yeast dough served soaked in **rum** and filled with **cream** or custard. (Named after Jean-Anthelme Brillat-Savarin, 1755–1826, gastronome and writer.)

savoury (1) (adj.) Salty, piquant, tasty.
(2) (noun) Small savoury item; **canapé** (*See also* **classic menu**.)

scald (1) To dip fruit or vegetables in boiling water to remove impurities or prepare them for skinning or freezing.
(2) To heat (particularly milk) until just at the point of boiling.

scallion Green (immature) onion; spring onion.

scallop (skol-op) (1) (noun) Mollusc or shellfish (genus *Pecten*) contained in a big fan-like shell on which it is often served. The 'meat', which is opaque and browny-white when raw, with a 'coral' attached, turns white when cooked. (*French* **coquille**.)
(2) (verb) To decorate with semi-circular shapes; to **score** with such a pattern.

scalloped potatoes (*USA*) [skol-lopt] Sliced potatoes baked with milk. (*See* **pommes Anna**.)

scallopina (*Ital.*) (*pl.* **scallopini**) [ska-lop-een-ee] **Escalope** or thin slice of meat lightly crumbed and **sautéed**; traditionally a sauce of **marsala**, tomato, and **cream** is served with it.

scampi Variety of large prawn. (Plural of the Italian *scampo*; in French **langoustine**.)

schnapps (*Ger.*) [schnaps] N. European flavoured distilled **spirit** made from grain or potatoes, similar to **hollands gin**.

schnitzel (*Ger.*) [schnit-sell] Thin slice of meat, usually chicken or **veal**. (*See* **Wiener schnitzel**.) (*Schnitzeln* means 'to cut', so schnitzel means 'a slice'.)

scone [skon] Bread-like cake served in individual portions with jam and butter or thick **cream** (*See also* **Devonshire tea**.)

score To cut lines or marks into a surface, esp. in skin or rind.

Scotch Scotch **whisky**.

Scotch egg (*UK*) Hard-boiled egg encased in sausage meat, covered with beaten egg and breadcrumbs, deep-fried and served cold.

seafood Collective term for edible fish, shellfish in particular. (*See* **fruits de mer**, **marinara**, **pesce**, *and* **poisson**.)

seal To sear the surface of meat by intense heat to seal in the juices.

sec (*Fr.*) (fem. **sèche**) (sek/sesh] Dry (when referred to wine). But note that the word **sec** sometimes is confusingly applied to drinks that are not really dry, e.g. **triple sec** and **champagne**.

sekt (*Ger.*) [sekt] German **sparkling wine**.

sémillon [say-me-yo(n)] Grape variety used to make crisp dry white wines.

semolina (*Ital.*) Coarsely-ground grains of hard wheat or rice, used to make many **pasta** products, and **couscous**.

service cloth A (white) cloth or **table-napkin** used by the waiter in foodservice.

service plate Large plate covered with a **service cloth**, used, for example, to carry cutlery to tables once customers are seated.

serviette *See* **table-napkin**.

sesame seed Small seed from sesame plant, oily and nourishing, widely used in cooking, e.g. to make **halva** or sprinkled on loaves of bread. (*See also* **hummus** *and* **tahini**.)

set menu Menu allowing no choice to the guests, all items having been pre-selected by the **host**, typically used at **functions**.

sformato (*Ital.*) [s-form-ahtoe] Kind of **soufflé**, either sweet or savoury served with accompanying sauce of meat or flavoured **cream**.

shake and strain Cocktail-mixing term. The ingredients are shaken together with ice in a cocktail-shaker and strained through a **Hawthorn strainer** into the glass.

shallot Small brown onion (*Allium ascalonicum*) much used in French cookery to flavour sauces (e.g. **béarnaise**.) and also in E. Asian cuisine. The word is sometimes incorrectly used as if it meant **spring onion**. (In French **èschalot**.)

shank Cut of meat, esp. veal or lamb, from the leg. (*See also* **carré**.)

sherbet (1) Sweet flavoured effervescent drink.
(2) (*USA*) Water-ice or **sorbet**.

sherry **Fortified wine** made from white grapes, originally developed in Jerez in Spain. There are various styles, among them **fino** (dry and pale), **amontillado** (medium, dry, rather darker), and **oloroso** (sweet and golden). Cream sherry is very sweet and creamy.

shiraz [shi-raz] Grape variety, also called hermitage, suiting warm conditions. It produces robust red wines which benefit from long maturing.

shirred egg Baked egg.

shish kebab (*Turk.*) [shish kuh-baab] Small pieces of meat, usually lamb, cooked on a skewer. (*See* **kebab**.)

shooter Layered **cocktail** without ice served in a small glass or test-tube.

shortbread Crumbly sweet biscuit of flour (originally oatmeal) and butter.

shortcake Dessert of sweet pastry or cake sandwiched with fruit, esp. strawberries, and **cream**.

shortcrust pastry Basic pastry mix made by combining flour, fat, and water. It may be sweetened in which case sugar is added. Egg or lemon juice may replace the water. (*See* **pâte brisée**, **pâte sablée**, *and* **pâte sucrée**.)

shoyu (*Jap.*) [show-yu] Popular style of Japanese **soya sauce**; it is less salty and lighter than the most common Chinese varieties.

shuck (*USA*) To remove from shell or cob.

shwarma/chawarma (*Leb.*) [sha-warma] *See* **döner kebab**.

sideboard Table or chest for holding plates and glass, and from which food is served; a waiter's **station**.

silver service Formal style of food service whereby food items are transferred by the waiter to the guests' plates from service dishes at the table.

silverside Boneless hindquarter of beef usually salted and **pot roasted**.

sirloin Choice joint of beef taken from the upper **loin** which includes the **fillet**. It is often boned and rolled with the fillet removed. It can be cut into steaks. (*See also* **entrecôte**, **filet mignon**, **porterhouse**, **rump**, *and* **T-bone**.)

skillet Frying pan; cast-iron pot.

slivovitz Plum **brandy** from the Balkans. (*Sljiva* means 'plum' in Serbo-Croatian.)

sloe gin **Liqueur** of sloe berries soaked in **gin**.

smallgoods Cooked meats and meat products, sausages, salamis, **pâtés**, etc. (*See also* **charcuterie**.)

smoke To **preserve** or **cure** food, e.g. ham, salmon, or turkey, by drying it above smoking wood or peat with mixtures of sugar, spices, and **liquors** added to impart special flavours.

smorgasbord (*Swed.*) Self-service buffet (Literally, 'lump of butter' (*smörgås*) + 'table' (**bord**). In Scandinavia a *smörgåsbord* is a very substantial meal of several courses, including especially dishes of herrings.)

smørrebrød (*Dan.*) [shmuruh-brur(t)] Open sandwich.

snow pea *See* **mange-tout**.

snow pea shoots Small shoots from the **snow pea** plant, usually served mixed in green salads.

soda-(water) Water aerated with carbon dioxide.

sodium chloride Salt.

sommelier (*Fr.*) (masc.) [som-ell-ee-ay] Expert wine-waiter.

sorbet (*Fr.*) (masc.) [sor-bay] Light soft frozen mixture of **puréed** fruit or fruit juice with some **liquor** and **sugar syrup**; **water ice**. Sorbets are often served between courses to freshen the **palate**. (*See also* **classic menu**.)

sorrel (sorrul] Green-leaf vegetable with a slightly bitter taste. It is used to make soup and, when young, mixed in green salad. (French *oseille*.)

soubise (*Fr.*) (fem.) [soo-beez] An onion sauce or **purée** of onion and rice.

soufflé (*Fr.*) (masc.) [soo-flay] Sweet or savoury sauce mixture to which beaten egg whites have been added which cause it to rise once baked. It is almost always served hot, but a cold sweet soufflé is made from fruit **purée** to which egg white is added, e.g. *soufflé aux fruits* (fruit soufflé), *soufflé au* **fromage** (cheese soufflé), *soufflé au chocolat* (chocolate soufflé).

soupe (*Fr.*) (fem.) [soop] Soup, esp. those containing bread. (*See also* **bisque**, **consommé**, **garbure**, **julienne**, **marmite petite**, **pistou**, **potage**, *and* **vichyssoise**.)

sour cream *See* **cream**, **soured**.

sourdough Piece of dough left over from a previous batch and used as a 'starter' to leaven a new batch. Sourdough bread has a crisp crust and soft inner crumb, a slightly sour taste, and is usually baked by traditional methods.

sous chef (*Fr.*) [soo shef] Deputy chef. (*Sous* means 'under'.)

Southern Comfort US **proprietary liqueur**, based on **bourbon whiskey** with peach flavourings.

souvlaki (*Grk.*) [soov-lahkee] Grilled or barbecued meat, esp. lamb, wrapped in **pita** bread with **humus** and salad; meat cooked on a skewer. (*See also* **kebab**.)

soya/soy bean Round bean, the same size as a pea, rich in protein, used to make **tofu**, etc.

soya/soy sauce Vital ingredient and popular **condiment** of E. Asian **cuisine**, made from **soya beans** and water with other ingredients such as wheat, **vinegar**, salt, etc. There are many different kinds of soya sauce, including the Japanese **shoyu** and **teriyaki sauce**.

spaetzle/späzle (*Ger. & Alsace*) [spaytz-luh] Small poached **dumplings** of flour, eggs, and cream, usually used to **garnish** meat dishes or served as an **entrée**, *au gratin*.

spaghetti (*Ital.*) (pl.) [spag-ay-tee] **Pasta** cut into long strings.

spanakopita (*Grk.*) [spana-kohpeeta] Pasty made of **filo pastry** containing spinach and cheese.

Spanish olive Particularly mild-tasting green **olive** suitable for use in **cocktails**.

spare-ribs The rib bones of pork or beef, usually **marinated** and baked.

sparkling wine Wines made effervescent (bubbly) by the natural action of the carbon dioxide gas produced by **fermentation**. **Champagne** is the most famous kind of sparkling wine.

spatchcock Dressed young chicken or **game** bird that is split open and grilled or fried without being allowed to hang and mature.

spätlese (*Ger.*) [shpayt-layz-uh] Sweet dessert wine made from late-picked **riesling** grapes. (*See also* **auslese** *and* **riesling**.) (*Spätlese* means 'late-picked'.)

späzle *See* **spaetzle**.

spice Aromatic or pungent vegetable substance used to flavour food, e.g. **coriander**, **turmeric** or **pepper**.

spirits General term for **distilled** alcoholic liquors, including **brandy**, **gin**, **rum**, **tequila**, **whisky** and **vodka**.

split Small or half-bottle (285ml) of an effervescent drink like **soda** or **tonic**.

spoom **Sorbet** stirred with **meringue** so that it foams. (In Italian *spuma* [spoo-mah].)

spring roll Deep-fried Chinese-style **pancake** parcel containing minced meat and vegetables. (*See also* **cha gio** *and* **goi cuon**.)

spumante (*Ital.*) [spoo-man-tay] Sparkling; Italian **sparkling wine**.

squab [skwob] Young pigeon.

staphylococcus Bacterium causing food poisoning found in human throats and noses, and septic cuts.

starch Carbohydrate found in cereals and potatoes.

station (1) Section of the dining-room for which a waiter or team of service staff is responsible.

(2) Table or **sideboard** where a waiter keeps the equipment necessary for service; a waiter's work station.

steak tartare *See* **tartare** *and* **tartare steak**.

steamboat Style of Chinese cooking where a pan of **broth** is placed on a heat source in the centre of the table into which diners dip raw food until it is cooked. At the end of the meal this **broth**, which has become quite rich, is eaten as soup.

still Apparatus used to distil **spirits**. (*See* **distillation** and **pot still**.)

stillroom Store or pantry for small items of food and beverage needed for service but not provided by the kitchen or larder.

stilton (*UK*) Rich, creamy **blue-veined** cheese, now usually served on cheeseboards. Traditionally a whole stilton was presented and scooped out with a spoon, with **port** filling the hollow so created. (Stilton is a village in central England.) (*See also* **dolcelatta**, **gorgonzola**, *and* **roquefort**.)

stir and strain Cocktail-mixing term. Ice is placed in a mixing glass, the **liquors** are added and stirred until cold, then strained into the serving glass using a **Hawthorn strainer**.

stir fry (1) (verb) E. Asian method of preparing food whereby the ingredients are chopped into small pieces and cooked over a fast heat often in a **wok** while continually being stirred.

(2) (noun) A stir-fried dish.

stock Broth made by simmering bones and vegetables used as the basis for **sauces**, gravies, soups, and stews.

stout Strong dark **beer** brewed with roasted **malt**.

Stroganov *See* **boeuf Stroganov**.

strudel [stroo-del] Dessert with case of **filo pastry**, e.g.

apple strudel. (German *Apfel Strüdel*. *Strüdel* means 'whirlpool'.)

sucré(e) (*Fr.*) [sookray] Sugared. (*Sucre* means 'sugar'.)

suet [sooet] Solid fat from around the kidney of beef or mutton, fresh or dried, used in traditional English **Christmas** (plum) **pudding** and in steamed pastry dishes, e.g. steak and kidney **pudding**.

sugar syrup Sweet **liquor** made of sugar and water, boiled and used when making desserts or poaching fruit and in some **cocktails**; **gomme syrup**.

sukiyaki (*Jap.*) [sooky-yahkee] Small lumps of meat cooked in oil at table with diners helping themselves from the common pot, **fondue**-style. (*Suki* means 'scoop' and *yaki*, 'grilled'.)

summer pudding (UK) Dessert of white bread soaked with fresh red and/or black berries and currants and turned out to serve.

sundae [sunday] Ice cream dessert with topping of fruit, nuts, or syrup.

sun-dried tomato *See* **tomato**.

supper (1) Insubstantial late evening snack or very light meal taken after dinner or tea.

(2) (UK) Informal evening meal replacing a more formal dinner.

suprême (*Fr.*) (masc.) [soo-praym] (1) Breast and wing of poultry or **game**, e.g. *suprêmes de volaille* (chicken breasts in sauce).

(2) **Fillet** of large fish. (*See also* **suprême, sauce**.)

suprême, sauce (*Fr.*) [sohs soo-praym] Rich sauce containing **cream** and butter.

sushi (*Jap.*) [soo-shee] Bite-sized rice balls or sandwiches flavoured with **vinegar** and topped with **marinaded** raw fish or some other delicacy, often wrapped in **nori**.

Suzette *See* **crêpes Suzette**.

sweet (1) (adj.) Tasting of sugar; opposite of sour.

(2) (noun) Small item of confectionery usually mainly of sugar or chocolate.

(3) (noun) The sweet or **dessert course** of a meal. (*See* **entremets** *and* **pudding**.)

sweet-and-sour In Chinese cuisine, dishes cooked with a sauce made from sugar, **soy sauce**, and **vinegar** or lemon, usually thickened with cornflour.

sweetbreads Pancreas or thymus of an animal (usually **veal** or lamb) when used in cooking. (*See* **abats**.)

sweet corn/maize *See* **corn**.

sweetmeat Sugar-coated confection; small fancy cake. (*See also* **fondant** *and* **petit four**.)

sweet pepper Capsicum or bell pepper; green, red, yellow, or purple pepper. Soft, well-fleshed vegetable (*Capsicum annuum*) related to the hot **chilli**, but not the pepper spice. (*See* **pepper**.)

syllabub (UK) [silla-bub] **Dessert** of sweetened cream with lemon juice and wine or **brandy**.

Szechwan [sitch-wahn] One of the major styles of Chinese cuisine, and typically hot and spicy. (*See also* **Cantonese, Fukien, Honan,** *and* **Peking**.) (Szechwan, now spelt Sichuan, is a province in NW China.)

Tabasco [tab-ass-coh] Spicy **proprietary** sauce made from the pungent tabasco **chilli** pepper. Sold in small bottles, it is used to season meat and egg dishes and **cocktails**. (Tabasco is a state in Mexico.)

tabbouleh/tabouli (*arab.*) [taboo-lee] Salad of **cracked wheat**, onion, **mint**, tomato, *and* **parsley**.

table d'hôte (*Fr.*) [tahbl doht] Type of menu offering limited choice at a fixed price for the whole meal. (*See* **prix fixe**.)

table-linen Tablecloth and **napkins**; napery (not necessarily made from linen cloth).

table-napkin Serviette; a cloth placed on diners' laps and used to protect their clothes and to wipe their fingers and mouths.

table wine Wine that is drunk with a meal; unfortified still wine. (*See* **fortified wine, sparkling wine,** *and* **wine**.)

taco (*Mex.*) [tahkoh] Sandwich in a crisp **corn pancake**; small **tortilla** wrapped around a filling usually of meat and/or beans and cheese. Ready-made taco shells are available commercially.

tagliatelle (*Ital.*) (pl.) [tie-ya-telluh] Long ribbons of **pasta** curled around one another.

tahini/tahina (*Arab.*) [tuheen-ee] **Sesame seed** paste, an ingredient of **hummus**. (*Tahina* means 'ground' or 'crushed'.)

tamarind (*Arab.*) Fruit of the tamarind tree (*Tamarindus indica*) the black pulp of which is used in Indian cuisine. It is rarely available fresh in the UK but is compressed in a block or bottled as a paste.

tandoor (*Ind.*) (noun) [tun-door] Open-topped clay oven.

tandoori (*Ind.*) (adj.) [tun-door-ee] Food that has been cooked in a **tandoor** (e.g. tandoori chicken).

tannin Ingredient of wine, esp. full-bodied red wine, derived from pips and stalks which gives a drying, furry sensation to tongue and gums.

tapas (*Span.*) [tap-ass] Substantial cocktail snacks or **appetizers**, often served in bowls from which guests select the food. (*See also* **hors d'oeuvres**.)

tapas bar **Brasserie** or wine-bar at which **tapas** is served.

tapénade (*Fr.*) [tapay-nahd] **Provençal** thick paste of crushed **olives, anchovies, capers, garlic,** and oil.

taramasalata (*Grk.*) [tarra-mah-sall-ah-tah] Soft pink creamy paste of fish **roe** with olive oil and **garlic**, usually served as part of the **hors d'oeuvres** or **meze**.

tarragon Plant with long narrow green leaves used as a flavouring herb. The French variety is much finer, but

difficult to grow. Russian tarragon is sturdier, but coarser. Tarragon is one of the ingredients of **fines herbes**.

tartare, à la (*Fr.*) [ah lah tar-tar] Literally, 'in the manner of the Tartars', the once-terrifying nomadic hordes of Central Asia. (*See below*.)

tartare sauce [tar-tahr] **Mayonnaise** sauce made from hard-boiled egg yolks, onion, **chives**, and **capers** served with fish.

tartare steak/steak tartare [tar-tahr] Minced raw beef garnished with **capers**, minced onion, parsley and served with a raw egg-yolk. (In French **biftek** *à la* **tartare**.)

tarte (*Fr.*) (fem.) [tart] Tart, e.g. **tarte tatin**.

tarte tatin (*Fr.*) [tart tata(n)] Upside-down apple tart. (The Tatin sisters, restaurateurs, popularized the dish in the early 1900s.)

T-bone Beef steak on a T-shaped bone cut from the **fillet** end of the **sirloin**. (*See also* **entrecôte, filet mignon, porterhouse, rump,** *and* **sirloin**.)

tea (1) Mildly stimulating beverage made by infusing the dried leaves of the tea-bush in boiling water. The two main styles are green (or **China**) tea and black (or Indian) tea. There are many varieties, e.g. Assam, **Darjeeling, Earl Grey, English Breakfast,** jasmine, etc. Some drinks are called 'tea' although they are not made with tea-leaves, e.g. **herbal teas**. (*See also* **iced tea**.)
(2) Meal at which tea is served, e.g. afternoon tea; the main (informal) evening meal.

tempura (*Jap.*) [tem-poor-ah] Strips of fish, shelled prawns, or vegetables fried in a light **batter** and served very hot, usually with grated **daikon radish**.

teppanyaki (*Jap.*) [tep-an-yak-ee] Meat, fish and vegetables fried at the table. (Literally, 'table-grilled'.)

tequila Mexican **spirit**, of which there are two varieties, white and gold, distilled from the cactus-like **mezcal** azul plant. Tequila is an ingredient of many **cocktails**, e.g. **Margarita**. (*See also* **mezcal**.)

teriyaki (*Jap.*) [terri-yah-kee] Meat or fish **marinated** in **teriyaki sauce** and grilled. (Literally, 'sunshine-grilled' – glazed and grilled.)

teriyaki sauce **Soya sauce** brewed with sweet rice wine, **vinegar**, sugar, and spices.

terrine (*Fr.*) (fem.) [teh-reen] (1) Oblong straight-sided cooking dish with a tight-fitting lid. (Not to be confused with a **tureen**.)
(2) Chopped and minced meat of different varieties (or occasionally fish) mixed with vegetables and seasoning and cooked in a **terrine** until they form a 'loaf' which is sliced and served cold.

thermidor Recipe for **lobster** or **crayfish** served baked in their shells with a creamy sauce and hot **mustard**, often **au gratin**. (Thermidor was the name of the hottest month in the new calendar introduced at the French

Revolution.)

Thousand Island dressing (*Canada & USA*) Sauce of **mayonnaise** flavoured with **tomato sauce**, onion, and **chilli**. (The Thousand Islands are in the north-east of Lake Ontario.)

thyme [time] Shrub with small powerfully pungent leaves used as seasoning herb, especially in soups and stews, and stuffings. A component of the traditional **bouquet garni**, thyme is also a vital element in **Cajun** cooking.

Tia Maria Rum-based, coffee-flavoured **liqueur** from Jamaica.

timbale (*Fr.*) (fem.) [tam-bahl] (1) Cup-shaped mould. (2) Food pressed into a timbale, served turned out in the shape of an inverted cup. (3) Pie-crust baked in a timbale and filled with a creamy savoury mixture (**croûte** *à timbale*). (4) **Dessert** of fruit or a **cream** presented in a cup-shaped basket made from biscuit or pastry dough.

tiri-mi-su (*Ital.*) [teera mee soo] Cake of **maccrated** biscuits (**ladyfingers**) sandwiched with a **cream** made of sweetened **mascarpone** and separated eggs. (Literally 'pick-me-up'.)

tisane [tizann] *See* **herbal tea**.

tofu (*Jap.*) [toe-foo] Highly nutritious **curd** made from **soya beans** and which looks like a lump of soft cheese or firm custard. It is a versatile ingredient which tastes of little but absorbs the flavour of accompanying food or sauce.

tokay Classic sweet white unfortified **dessert wine** of Hungary.

tomato Versatile vegetable used in many cooked dishes and **chutneys**, and eaten raw in salads. Roma, also known as Italian plum, tomatoes are used fresh and for canning. Other tomato products include tomato **purée** (also known as 'tomato paste') and tomato **ketchup**. Cherry tomatoes are a miniature variety. Sun-dried tomatoes are preserved in oil. (*See* **salsa di pomodoro**.)

Tom Collins **Cocktail** containing equal measures of **gin** and lemon juice with a dash of **Angostura Bitters**, and **soda**.

tom ka gai (*Thai*) [tum kah gye] Spicy chicken soup with **coconut milk**. (*See also* **tom yam** *below*.)

tom yam (*Thai*) [tum yum] Spicy **clear soup** made with **lemon grass**. (*See also* **kom ka gai** *above*.)

tom yam kung (*Thai*) [tum yum koong] **Tom yam** with prawns added.

tonic Short for '**Indian tonic** water', a non-alcoholic aerated water flavoured with **quinine**, used as a mixer in various **cocktails** and mixed drinks, e.g. **gin**-and-tonic. (It is called 'Indian' because the beverage was developed in India where quinine was used as a protection against malaria.)

torte (*Ger.*) [tor-tuh] Rich cake made in layers, sandwiched together with **cream** and covered with chocolates, fruit, or nuts. (*Compare* **tourte**.)

tortellini (*Ital.*) (pl.) [tor-tell-een-ee] **Pasta** filled with meat or cheese, rolled into small packages and served in a sauce.

tortilla (*Mex.*) [tor-tee-ya] Flat, round **pancake** made of maize (cornmeal) served hot and usually filled with meat or beans and a sauce. (*See also* **enchilada**, **nacho**, *and* **taco**.)

tounedos (*Fr.*) (masc.) [toor-nay-doh] Small round slice of beef **fillet** from the centre of the 'eye'. (Literally, 'turn (the) back'.) (*See* **bifteck**, **filet mignon**, **médallions**, **mignonnettes**, *and* **noisettes**.)

tournedos Rossini **Tournedos** served on fried bread, originally garnished with **foie gras** and **truffles**. (Devised by Gioacchino Rossini, 1792–1868, composer of operas and famous gastronome.)

tourné(e) (*Fr.*) [toor-nay] Turned, shaped.

tourte (*Fr.*) (fem.) [toort] Round pie or tart. Savoury *tourtes* have a pastry lid, sweet ones usually do not. (Do not confuse with **torte**.)

toxin Poison.

traminer One of a group of grape varieties used to make white wine, the most popular of which is **gewürztraminer**.

tranche (*Fr.*) (fem.) [trahnsh] A slice (of fish, meat, etc.). (*See also* **trançon** *and* **darne**.)

trancheur (*Fr.*) [tron-sher] One of the restaurant staff who carves in the dining room.

trançon (*Fr.*) (masc.) [tro(n)so(n)] Slice, usually of large flat fish cut through the bone. (*See also* **darne**.)

trattoria (*Ital.*) Italian restaurant, usually quite small.

trifle **Dessert** dish of sponge cake (often soaked in sherry) topped with fruit, custard, and cream.

tripe Lining of cow's stomach. (French *tripe* [treep].)

triple sec Very sweet white **curaçao**, e.g. **Cointreau**.

tronc (*Fr.*) [tronk] A box for tips received by restaurant staff. The money is usually shared out weekly.

trotters Feet of hoofed animal, esp. pig's feet.

truffle (1) Edible fungus (**tuber**) found underground, especially near the roots of oak trees, highly prized as a savoury delicacy. (In French *truffe* (fem.) [troof]). (2) Rich, creamy chocolate **sweet**, shaped into a ball; a chocolate truffle. (So called because it resembles the truffle tuber.)

truite (*Fr.*) (fem.) [trweet] Trout.

truite au bleu (*Fr.*) [trweet oh bluh] Freshly-caught trout, cleaned and plunged into a **court-bouillon**. (*See also* **bleu**.)

tuber Vegetable which swells underground, e.g. potato, **Jerusalem artichoke**, or **truffle**.

tuile (*Fr.*) (fem) [tweel] Almond wafer curved like a tile and served as a **petit four**. (*Tuile* means 'tile'.)

tumbler Simple, straight-sided glass for serving water and soft drinks.

tureen [ture-reen] Deep covered dish from which soup is served at the table. (Do not confuse with **terrine**.)

Turkish coffee Strong, dark, sweet **coffee** served in small cups; **Greek coffee**.

turmeric Mildly peppery spice, bright yellow when ground to powder, used in most **curry** mixtures, usually called *haldi* in India.

tutti frutti Ice-cream mixed with **diced glacé** fruit which has been **macerated** in alcohol. (Literally, 'all the fruits' in Italian.)

tzatziki (*Grk. & Turk.*) [tsat-seekee] Yoghurt mixed with **garlic** and cucumber and served as an **appetizer** or dip with the **meze**.

un/une (*Fr.*) (masc./fem.) [u(n)/oon] A. (The indefinite pronoun – e.g. *un* **goujon** *de* **poisson**, *une* **quiche**.)

Underberg **Proprietary** brand of German **bitters**, taken both as a tonic and a **digestif**; it is drunk straight from the bottle in one mouthful.

underliner Plate, usually with a **doily** on it, placed under another dish, such as a soup bowl; an underplate.

vacherin (*Fr.*) (masc.([vasheri(n)] (1) Round cows' milk cheese. (*Vache* means 'cow'.)
(2) Dessert consisting of layers of crisp **meringue** sandwiched with **cream**, similar to **pavlova**.

vacuum infused coffee *See* **Cona coffee**.

vanilla Sweet and fragrant flavouring obtained from the bean of the vanilla orchid (*Vanilla planifolia*). (*See also below*.)

vanilla bean Long pod of the **vanilla** containing the seeds producing the distinctive flavour. When the pod is boiled with liquid, dishes so flavoured have a slightly speckled appearance.

vanilla essence Concentrated extract of the **vanilla bean** used to flavour sweet dishes in place of the bean.

vanilla sugar Sugar stored in a container with a **vanilla bean** which imparts the vanilla flavour to the sugar.

varietal Adjective used to describe wine made from a particular variety of grape, e.g. **chardonnay**. (*See also* **generic**.)

veal Calf's meat. The finest is fed exclusively on milk.

veau (*Fr.*) (masc.) [voh] **Veal**.

vegan [vee-gan] Strict **vegetarian**; person who eats no animal products at all, not even milk or eggs.

vegetarian Person who does not eat animal (or fish) products, especially the flesh of slaughtered animals. Many vegetarians do eat eggs and consume dairy products (milk, cheese, etc.). *Compare* **vegan**.

velouté (*Fr.*) (masc.) [vuh-loot-ay] Thick velvety sauce made from white chicken, veal or fish **stock**, rather than milk, and a white **roux** to which **cream** is often added.

venaison (*Fr.*) (fem.) [venay-so(n)] **Venison**; the meat of any large **game** animal. (*See also* **chevreuil**, **poivrade**, *and* **salmis**.)

venaison, sauce (*Fr.*) [sohs venay-son] **Sauce poivrade** to which fresh cream and red currant jelly have been added, traditionally served with **game** and dishes '*en chevreuil*'. (*See also* **venaison**.)

venison [ven-sun] Meat of deer. (*See also* **venaison**.)

verde (*Ital.*) [vairduh] Green.

vermicelli (*Ital.*) (pl.) [vairmi-chelly] Long thin threads of **pasta** sometimes coiled into rings; **noodles**. (Also known as **capellini**.)

vermouth [ver-muth] Flavoured **fortified wine** available in three principal styles: dry (or **French**), sweet (**rosso** or Italian), and **bianco** which is golden and medium sweet. (*Rosso* literally means 'red' and **bianco** 'white'.)

viande (*Fr.*) (fem.) [vee-ond] Meat.

vichyssoise (*Fr.*) (masc.) [vee-shee-swaz] Creamy soup made of **puréed** leeks and potatoes, served chilled and garnished with **chives**. (*See also* **garbure** *and* **potage**.)

Vichy water (*Fr.*) [veeshee] Mineral water from Vichy (spa town in central France).

Vienna coffee **Coffee** topped with thick, rich **cream**. (Vienna is the capital of Austria.)

vin (*Fr.*) (masc.) [vi(n)] Wine.

vinaigrette (*Fr.*) (fem.) [vin-uh-gret] Mixture of oil and **vinegar** or lemon juice used to dress salads. Other ingredients, especially **mustard** or herbs, may be added. (*See* **French dressing** *and* **wine vinegar**.)

vindaloo (*Ind.*) [vin-daloo] Very hot S. Indian **curry**, spiced and flavoured with **vinegar**.

vinegar Fermented acidic **liquor** made from wine, cider, **malt**, **spirits**, or rice. (French *vinaigre*; literally, 'sour wine'.) (*See* **balsamic**, **malt**, **rice**, *and* **wine vinegar**; *see also* **vinaigrette**.)

vin ordinaire (*Fr.*) vi(n) or-din-air] Moderately priced everyday wine; **house wine** bought in bulk by an **establishment** and often served from **carafes**.

vintage [vin-tij] (1) (noun) Season when grapes are harvested (as in *the vintage was late this year*).
(2) (noun) Wine made from the season's produce; the year the wine is made (as in *the 1992 vintage*).
(3) (noun) Wine from a single year (as in *1992 was a good vintage*).
(4) (adj.) Wine or **port** of special quality (*vintage wine*); of high quality (as in *a vintage year*).

virgin Without alcohol. (*See* **cocktail**.)

virgin olive oil Finest olive oil; oil extracted from the first pressing of the olives, and which contains no additives.

vitamin Any of a group of substances found in food which help regulate body processes essential to health and growth. Vitamins are classified by letters and numbers (vitamin, A, B₂, C, D, E, etc.).

vitello (*Ital.*) **Veal.**

vodka **Spirit** made from grain; in the West usually colourless and flavourless but in Russia and Poland often flavoured. It is most popular as an ingredient in **cocktails**, e.g. a **Bloody Mary**.

voiture (*Fr.*) [vwat-yoor] Trolley used in the dining room for various purposes such as carving or carrying hors d'oeuvres, sweets, cheeses or liqueurs.

volaille (*Fr.*) (fem.) [voll-eye-yuh] Poultry.

vol-au-vent (*Fr.*) (masc.) (*pl.* **vols-au-vent**) [voll oh vahn] Round case of **puff pastry** filled with a savoury mixture held in a creamy sauce and capped with a lid. Tiny ones are served as cocktail **savouries** and larger ones as an **entrée**. (Literally, 'flight in the wind'.) (*See also* **croustade**.)

VSOP Very Superior Old Pale, a technically meaningless termed used on labels to market **cognac**.

waffle [wofful] Small crisp cake made of **batter**, baked in a utensil with hinged halves (a waffle-iron). (From Dutch *wafel* meaning 'wafer'.)

waiter's friend Tool that is a combination of bottle-opener and corkscrew.

Waldorf salad Salad made with lettuce, **diced** apples, walnuts, celery and **mayonnaise**. (From the Waldorf Hotel, New York, where it was invented.)

wasabi (*Jap.*) [woss-ah-bee] Extremely hot Japanese **horseradish**, served in the form of a green paste as a **condiment** to accompany **sashimi** and **sushi**.

water-chestnut The crunchy **tuber** of an Asian sedge (*Eleocharis tuberosa*) commonly used in Chinese cookery. Usually bought canned.

watercress Green leaf vegetable (*Nasturtium officinale*) with small, round leaves and a pungent flavour. (*See also* **cress** *and* **nasturtium**.)

water ice Iced dessert made of **puréed** fruit, **sugar syrup** and egg white. (*See* **sorbet**).

Wellington *See* **beef Wellington**.

Welsh rabbit/Welsh rarebit (*UK*) Savoury made of melted cheese mixed with milk, seasonings etc. on hot toast.

whey Watery unfattening part of milk, separated from the **curd**, used to make some kinds of light cheese, e.g. **ricotta**.

whisky/whiskey **Spirit distilled** from **fermented** corn (barley, rye, wheat or maize). There are many styles. **Scotch** whiskies are by far the most popular. Most Scotch whiskies are blends of **malt whiskies** (made from barley) and grain whiskies (distilled in bulk from fermented wheat and maize). American and Irish whiskey are spelt with an 'e'. Other varieties drop the 'e'. (*See also* **bourbon** *and* **rye**.)

whitebait Sprats; small young fish, usually fried and eaten whole.

white pepper *See* **pepper** *and* **peppercorn**.

Wiener schnitzel [veener shnit-sell] **Veal escalope** coated in breadcrumbs and egg, and **sautéed**. (From Wien – Vienna – capital of Austria.)

wild rice Not a variety of common white rice which the dark brown grains resemble in shape, but *Zizania aquatica*, a grass native to North America. Turns slightly purple when cooked.

wine (1) Alcoholic drink made from fermented grape juice, e.g. **burgundy**, **claret**, **champagne**, etc. (2) Any fermented vegetable juice which is **distilled** to make spirits.

wine vinegar **Vinegar** distilled from (grape) **wine** and used in **béarnaise sauce**, **vinaigrette**, etc. Some are infused with herbs, spice, or fruit, e.g. **tarragon**, **chilli**, or **raspberry**. (*See* **balsamic vinegar**, **French dressing**, *and* **malt vinegar**.)

wok (*Chin.*) Large basin-shaped (hemispherical) frying-pan with a lid and two handles, much used in E. Asian cookery, esp. for **stir-fried** dishes.

won ton (*Chin.*) Small noodle-dough **dumpling**, either boiled in soup or deep fried.

Worcestershire/Worcester sauce Spicy sauce made of **vinegar**, molasses, sugar, spices, etc.

wurst (*Ger.*) [voorst] Sausage.

yam nang mu (*Thai.*) [yum nang moo] Pork skin salad.

Yorkshire pudding (*UK*) Savoury **batter pudding** traditionally served with roast beef.

yum cha (*Chin.*) Banquet usually served mid-morning and lasting over three hours. Many small dishes are served on a central turn-table from which guests help themselves. (*Yum* means 'drink', *cha* 'tea'.)

zabaglione (*Ital.*) [zab-ay-on-nay] Light foamy dessert made by whipping egg yolk, sugar, and alcohol (traditionally **marsala**) over a low heat. Served just warm. (*See* **sabayon**.)

zakouski (*Russ.*) [za-koo-skee] Appetizers – tiny open sandwiches spread with caviar, smoked sausage, usually served with vodka.

zest (of **citrus** fruit) Outer rind of citrus peel without the pith, and the scented oil it produces. It is used to enhance the citrus flavour.

zingara (*Fr.*) (adj.) [zjan-gahra] Containing **paprika** and tomato. (*Zingaro* means 'gypsy'.)

zucchini Courgette

zuppa (*Ital.*) [zuppah] Thick soup. (*See also* **brodo** *and* **minestra**.)

zuppa inglese (*Ital.*) [zuppa inglay-say] **Dessert** or **pudding** made from sponge cake, chocolate and custard; **trifle**. (Literally, 'English soup'.)

Index